The Future of Private Retirement Plans

Edited by
Dallas L. Salisbury

EBRI
Employee Benefit Research Institute®
Education & Research Fund

Education and Research Fund
2121 K Street, NW, Suite 600
Washington, DC 20037-1897
(202) 659-0670
Web sites www.ebri.org www.asec.org www.healthchec.org www.choosetosave.org

Papers based on the Employee Benefit Research Institute-Education and Research Fund policy forum, "The Next 25 Years of ERISA: The Future of Private Retirement Plans," held in Washington, DC, December 1, 1999.

Library of Congress Cataloging-in-Publication Data

The future of private retirement plans : an EBRI-ERF policy forum / edited by Dallas L. Salisbury.
p. cm.
Includes bibliographical references (p.).
ISBN 0-86643-095-4
1. Pension trusts--United States--Congresses. 2. Defined benefit pension plans--United States--Congresses. 3. Retirement income--United States--Congresses. 4. Retirement--Economic aspects--United States--Congresses. 5. Pensions trusts--Government policy--United States--Congresses. I. Salisbury, Dallas L. II. Employee Benefit Research Institute (Washington, D.C.). Education and Research Fund.

HD7105.45.U6 N49 2000
331.25'2'0973--dc21 00-029409

The premier organization for employee benefits research

EBRI
EMPLOYEE BENEFIT RESEARCH INSTITUTE®
EDUCATION & RESEARCH FUND

Established in 1978, the Employee Benefit Research Institute (EBRI) is the only nonprofit, nonpartisan organization in the United States totally committed to original public policy research and education on economic security and employee benefits.

EBRI's overall mission is to encourage, to contribute to, and to enhance the development of sound employee benefit programs and sound public policy through objective research and education.

EBRI does not lobby or endorse specific approaches. Rather, it provides balanced and unbiased analysis of alternatives based on the facts. Through its activities, EBRI advances knowledge and understanding among the public, the news media, and government policymakers of how employee benefits function and why they are critically important to our nation's economy.

Since its inception two decades ago, EBRI has grown to include a cross section of the public and private sectors with an interest in economic security programs. EBRI is funded by membership dues, grants, and contributions from foundations; businesses; labor unions; trade associations; health care providers and insurers; government organizations; and service firms, including actuarial firms, employee benefit consulting firms, law firms, accounting firms, and investment management firms. International members look to EBRI's work to gain understanding of the U.S. economic and employee benefit systems.

Today, EBRI is recognized as one of the nation's most authoritative, objective, and reliable resources on the rapidly changing employee benefits sector—health, savings, investment, retirement, work/family issues, demographics, and economic security.

Table of Contents

Policy and What Lies Ahead

List of Tables and Charts

Tables

Charts

About EBRI-ERF Policy Forums

The Employee Benefit Research Institute-Education and Research Fund (EBRI-ERF) holds two policy forums per year. The goal of the policy forums is to bring together a cross section of EBRI sponsors, congressional and executive branch staff, benefit experts, and representatives from academia, interest groups, and labor to examine public policy issues. It is a roundtable discussion featuring verbal and written exchange among speakers and participants. The roundtable format is designed to encourage discussion.

Past EBRI-ERF policy forums include:

5/5/99 "Severing the Link Between Health Insurance and Employment"

12/2/98 "Beyond Ideology: Are Individual Social Security Accounts Feasible?"

5/6/98 "The Future of Medical Benefits"

12/3/97 "Do Employers/Employees Still Need Employee Benefits?"

4/30/97 "Retirement Prospects in a Defined Contribution World"

12/4/96 "Assessing Social Security Reform Alternatives"

4/30/96 "Comprehensive Tax Reform: Implications for Economic Security and Employee Benefits"

12/7/95 "The Changing World of Work and Employee Benefits"

5/11/95 "When Workers Call the Shots: Can They Achieve Retirement Security?"

10/26/94 "The Future of Employment-Based Health Benefits"

5/4/94 "Retirement in the 21st Century: Ready or Not?"

10/6/93 "The Changing Health Care Delivery System"

5/5/93 "Pension Funding and Taxation: Achieving Benefit Security"

12/1/92 "Rationing: Making Choices and Allocating Resources in the Health Care Delivery System—Implications for Access, Quality, and Costs"

4/29/92 "Paternalism vs. Empowerment: What Benefits Should/Will Employers Provide?"

9/25/91 "Retirement Security in a Post-FASB Environment"

5/2/91 "Pension Portability and Preservation: Assuring Adequate Retirement Income in the 21st Century"

Preface

The Employee Retirement Income Security Act of 1974 (ERISA) marked incorporation into the law of policy recommendations developed by the Pension Committee appointed by President Kennedy. Its focus was on minimum standards for fiduciary conduct, participation, vesting and coverage, and participant security in the event of a defined benefit plan termination.

ERISA made major changes. ERISA quickly led to the termination of thousands of pension plans that could not, or would not, change to accommodate the law. Federal officials viewed this as an accomplishment, as benefits were secured.

In hindsight, the most significant aspect of ERISA (as amended over the years) was the fact that its standards changed pension plans from programs that primarily paid a benefit at retirement age to those who had long service, to programs that paid benefits whenever an employee of even short service (at least five years) left an employer. As a result, the financial dynamics of plans changed. Also, ERISA effectively expanded the traditional definition of a pension plan to include defined contribution plans, not just defined benefit plans. And with amendments in 1978 to the Internal Revenue Code, the die was unintentionally cast for "reinvention" of the retirement capital accumulation system in the United States.

EBRI and EBRI-ERF conducted their first policy forum in June of 1979. This book is based upon our 47th policy forum. All have been designed to further understanding of economic security programs and to help fulfill our core mission: to contribute to, to encourage, and to enhance the development of sound employee benefit programs and sound public policy through objective research and education.

EBRI was founded in 1978 by leaders in the employee benefits field with a vision of building an objective research and education organization. This volume carries forward the mission of providing a basis for sound decision making and program design. It is dedicated to those in the nation who have worked for decades to provide the nation with retirement income security.

The Executive Summary of the book provides a tight overview of the session, so I will not do that here. I will simply note that the book provides a picture of pensions and the motivations for them decades before ERISA was enacted; provides a data-based picture of where the system is today; and then provides substantial insight as to where the system might go in the future—and with it, the prospects for retirement economic security.

I want to thank Jack VanDerhei, Paul Yakoboski, Pamela Ostuw, and Alicia Willis for organizing and conducting the policy forum; Cindy O'Connor for production of forum materials and the book; and Stephen Blakely and Deborah Holmes for copyediting.

Any views expressed are of the authors and should not be attributed to the officers, trustees, members, or staff of EBRI or its Education and Research Fund. In publishing this work, EBRI-ERF is making no effort to influence any specific legislation; rather, it is seeking to provide decision makers with information that might help them to evaluate proposals.

Dallas L. Salisbury
President & CEO, EBRI-ERF

April 2000

About the Authors

William Arnone is a Partner and National Director of Employee Financial Education and Counseling for Ernst & Young LLP in New York. He is responsible for the strategic positioning, design, managemen,t and marketing of financial education and counseling services to employees in employer-sponsored programs. He has extensive experience assisting large companies in the realignment of their defined benefit, defined contribution, and hybrid plans with their business and human resources objectives. Prior to joining Ernst & Young, Arnone was a Principal, Benefit Consultant and National Director of Financial and Retirement Planning Services for Buck Consultants, Inc. During his 13 years at Buck, he developed and conducted custom-tailored seminars covering all aspects of financial and retirement planning. Arnone is a member of the Board of Trustees of the Employee Benefit Research Institute. He is also a Founding Member of the National Academy of Social Insurance. He served on the Academy's Board of Directors from 1986 to 1994. He graduated from Fordham College with a B.A. in political science in 1970. He received a J.D. from New York University Law School in 1973. Arnone was selected as one of the first Charles H. Revson Fellows on the Future of New York City by the Columbia University School of Business for 1979–1980.

Robert Birnbaum, Managing Director at Credit Suisse Asset Management, is responsible for the development of defined contribution plan business. He joined in 1998 from J.P. Morgan Investment Management, where he was a Managing Director and, during his tenure, headed the defined contribution area; marketing strategy and communications; and North American Personal Financial Services. Previously, Birnbaum was in charge of mutual funds at Fred Alger Management; a senior product manager in charge of tax-advantaged products at Vanguard Group; and the director of marketing at American Future Systems. He was named an Impact Player of the Year by *Defined Contribution News* (an Institutional Investor publication) in June 1999. Birnbaum is a member of the board of directors of the National Defined Contribution Council and a trustee of the Employee Benefit Research Institute. He also is the author of "Understanding Participant Behavior: A Research-Based Approach" in the Employee Benefit Research Institute's *Retirement in The 21st Century*... Ready Or Not, and has spoken at numerous industry conferences. Birnbaum holds an A.B. in anthropology from Columbia University and an M.B.A. in finance from the University of Pennsylvania's Wharton School.

Stephen Blakely is managing editor and director of communications and for the Employee Benefit Research Institute, with responsibility for production of EBRI publications and EBRI communications initiatives. Prior to joining EBRI in June 1998, Blakely was senior associate editor at *Nation's Business* magazine, covering pension and insurance issues. His previous editorial experience includes news coverage of Congress as a reporter for the *Congressional Quarterly Weekly Report*, and daily newspaper coverage of national, state and local issues for Ottaway Newspapers, a division of Dow Jones.

David S. Blitzstein has been the Director of the United Food and Commercial Workers International Union (UFCW) Office of Negotiated Benefits since 1990. The office advises UFCW local unions in collective bargaining on pension and health insurance issues and consults with the Union's 150 jointly trusteed health and welfare and pension plans nationwide. Blitzstein also serves as a trustee of the $3.5 billion UFCW Industry Pension Fund and the UFCW National Health and Welfare Fund. Blitzstein represents the UFCW as a member of the working committee of the National Coordinating Committee for Multiemployer Plans (NCCMP is a lobbying group for multiemployer plans), a member of the Employee Benefit Research

Institute (EBRI), a Director of the Pension Research Council of the Wharton School - University of Pennsylvania, and a Director of the National Commission for Quality Assurance (NCQA). Previously, Blitzstein served as the Director of Corporate Strategies for the United Mine Workers of America. Currently, Blitzstein still serves as a trustee of two UMWA Funds in the construction industry. He is a graduate of the University of Pennsylvania and holds a master of science degree in labor studies from the University of Massachusetts in Amherst.

William J. Dennis, Jr. is currently a Senior Research Fellow at the NFIB Education Foundation in Washington, D.C., and directs its research activities. He has been employed since 1976 in various research capacities by the National Federation of Independent Business, the nation's largest small business trade association. Dennis's research activities focus on small business and public policy. Recent publications include: "Research Mimicking Policy: Entrepreneurial/Small Business Policy Research in the United States," in *Handbook of Entrepreneurship*, (Blackwell, in press); "Business Regulation as an Impediment to People Moving From Welfare to Self-Employment" (*Journal of Labor Research*): *Business Starts and Stops* (Wells Fargo/NFIB Education Foundation), *The Public Reviews Small Business* (NFIB Education Foundation), *Small Business Problems and Priorities* (NFIB Education Foundation); "More Than You Think: An Inclusive Estimate of Business Entries" (*Journal of Business_Venturing*); "Measuring Business Formations and Dissolutions: A New Time Series" (Babson Entrepreneurship Research Conference); *Motivating Safety in the Workplace* (Insurance Research Council); "Small Business Job Creation: The Findings and Their Critics" (*Business Economics*); *A Small Business Primer* (NFIB Education Foundation); and "Is the New Entrepreneurial Era Over?" (*Journal of Creative Behavior*). Dennis speaks frequently on small business topics. He received a Special Advocacy Award for research from the U. S. Small Business Administration in 1998.

John DeStefano is Vice President of the Participant Services Group for Fidelity Institutional Retirement Services Company (FIRSCo). He has responsibility for leadership of the 350-employee call center in Covington, KY, serving Fidelity's retirement participants. During his 12 years with Fidelity Investments, DeStefano has held many positions in both the Retail and Institutional organizations, including VP of Operations and Transfer of Assets. He holds an undergraduate degree in accounting and finance from Bridgewater State and an MBA from SMU.

Howard Fluhr is president and chief executive officer of The Segal Company. He joined the company in 1969. He is a Fellow of the Society of Actuaries, a Fellow of the Conference of Consulting Actuaries, a Fellow of the Canadian Institute of Actuaries, a Member of the American Academy of Actuaries and the International Actuaries Association, as well as an Enrolled Actuary. He has served as a board member and vice president of both the Conference of Consulting Actuaries and the American Academy of Actuaries. He consults on both benefits and human resources issues and strategy. He is a graduate of New York University, with degrees in math and philosophy.

Brian H. Graff, Esq., began serving as the American Society of Pension Actuaries executive director on November 8, 1996. ASPA is an organization of more than 3,700 members who provide actuarial, consulting, and administrative services to approximately one-third of the qualified plans in the United States. ASPA's purpose is to educate pension actuaries, consultants, administrators, and other benefits professionals and to preserve and enhance the private pension system as part of the development of a cohesive and coherent national retirement income policy. An attorney and certified public accountant, Graff was formerly legislation counsel to the U.S. Congress Joint Committee on Taxation, where he provided policy and technical analysis relating to pensions and employee benefits, health care, Social Security, and worker classification to members of Congress and their staffs. Graff also drafted statutory language for Congress, including substantial portions of the recently enacted Small Business Job Protection Act of 1996 and the Health Insurance Portability and Accountability Act of 1996. Prior to working on Capitol Hill, Graff was associated with the Washington, DC law firm of Groom and Nordberg, Chtd., which specializes in employee benefits. Graff served as a delegate to the recently held White House/ Congressional National Summit on Retirement Savings. He is also a member of the U.S. Chamber of Commerce Employee Benefits Committee and serves on the Board of the Small Business Council of America. Graff received his doctoral degree in law cum laude from the University of Pennsylvania Law School in Philadelphia in May of 1992. He holds a bachelor of science in accounting with distinction from Cornell University in Ithaca, NY.

Kathleen E. Havey currently serves as manager of pension policy at the United States Chamber of Commerce. In that role, she represents the Chamber before Congress and the Administration on issues pertaining to retirement and employee benefits law. Prior to working for the Chamber, Havey was employed by the American Society of Pension Actuaries, where she handled their government affairs responsibilities. From 1991 to 1998, Havey worked for Congresswoman Nancy Johnson, a senior member of the Ways and Means Committee, where she handled tax and trade policy, including retirement benefits issues. Havey is a graduate of the University of Notre Dame in South Bend, IN.

Richard A. Ippolito is a professor on the faculty of George Mason University School of Law. He was chief economist at the Pension Benefit Guaranty Corporation from 1986 to 1999. He has published many articles and several books on applied price theory including those involving the regulatory, tax, financial, and productivity aspects of pensions. His latest book, *Pension Plans and Employee Performance*, was published by the University of Chicago Press in 1998. He received his Ph.D. in economics from Chicago in 1974.

Peter McCauley is manager, corporate pension and savings plans, for Pharmacia & Upjohn Company, with responsibility for the design, implementation, administration, and compliance of all corporate pension and savings plans located in the United States and Puerto Rico. McCauley received his degree from St. Joseph's College and took graduate studies at Michigan State University. He is past president of the International Society of Certified Employee Benefits Specialists. McCauley is currently a member of the Society's long-range planning committees and a member of the International Foundation's CEBS Committee.

Ken McDonnell joined EBRI in June 1991 as a research assistant. Since then, his job functions have changed with the changing needs of EBRI's membership. Ken's current title is Information and Member Relations Associate. The duties that come with the position are: primary contact for information inquiries from member firms, academics, nonprofits, and state government officials; writing the monthly EBRI Fact Sheet; and lead author on EBRI's Databook on Employee Benefits. In addition, Ken has authored several Notes articles, chapters in the 5th edition of EBRI's Fundamentals of Employee Benefits Programs, and two Issue Briefs. Prior to joining EBRI Ken worked as a staff assistant at the National Council of State Housing Agencies. Ken has a B.A. in International Relations and Russian History and M.A. in German History from Northern Illinois University.

Byron Oliver has been president of CIGNA Retirement & Investment Services—the retirement benefits business of CIGNA Corporation—a leading provider of employee benefits across the United States and throughout the world, since 1988. CIGNA Retirement & Investment Services, based in Hartford, CT, provides a full range of integrated retirement benefits designed to be fully linked with health care, life, and disability benefits. The business manages more than $55 billion in assets for more than five million retirement investors at more than 7,000 companies or organizations. Shortly after earning a Ph.D. from Cornell University, Oliver joined CIGNA in 1972, developing management experience in systems insurance underwriting, product management, and sales. Byron also is a strong advocate of an improved national retirement policy, recently participating in the White House National Summit on Retirement.

Scott Peterson is a principal with Hewitt Associates and the national practice leader of the firm's services for defined contribution plans. His role is to set the overall direction of the firm's services in this area, guide and assure appropriate systems development, facilitate "best practices" information sharing among associates in North America, and do whatever it takes to assure highest quality services to clients in this service area. Previously, Peterson was manager of Hewitt Associates' Defined Contribution Plan Services for the Eastern United States. He joined Hewitt Associates in 1978. He holds Bachelor of Science and Master of Business Administration degrees from Indiana University.

Bill Pierron works on health policy for the Department of Labor's Pension and Welfare Benefits Administration, which he joined in December 1999. Among the issues that he follows are health plan liability and ERISA preemption, small group purchasing and pooling arrangements, and retiree medical coverage. Prior to joining DOL, Pierron was public affairs associate at EBRI, a position he held for four years. Before joining EBRI, he handled health and senior citizens' issues for Congresswoman Jolene Unsoeld, and, before going to work on Capitol Hill, he spent eight years doing public relations work for SAFECO Insurance Companies in Seattle, WA. He has a BA and JD from Washington University in St. Louis, MO, and a Masters Degree in Journalism from Columbia University in New York, NY.

John C. Rother is the Director of Legislation and Public Policy for the AARP. He is responsible for the federal and state legislative advocacy activities of the Association, based on in-depth policy research and public information programs. He is an authority on Medicare, managed care, long-term care, Social Security, pensions and the boomer generation's retirement situation. Prior to coming to AARP, Rother served eight years in the U.S. Senate as Special Counsel for Labor and Health to former Senator Jacob Javits (R-NY), and as Staff Director and Chief Counsel for the Special Committee on Aging under its Chairman, former Senator. John Heinz (R-PA). He serves on several Boards and Commissions, including Generations United, the Health Care Quality Forum, the National Committee for Quality Assurance, the Foundation for Accountability in Health Care, the National Academy on Aging, and Citizens for Long Term Care. He has served as a member of the Board of the Corporation for National Service, the Institute of Medicine, the ERISA Advisory Council for the Secretary of Labor; as a member of the Secretary's Blue-Ribbon Advisory Commission on the FDA (Edwards Commission); and as a member of the Commonwealth Fund's Commission on Elderly People Living Alone. In 1996, Rother was on special sabbatical assignment to study the consumer implications of the managed care revolution and the economic challenges facing the boomer generation. Rother is an honors graduate of Oberlin College and the University of Pennsylvania Law School.

Dallas Salisbury is president and CEO of the Employee Benefit Research Institute (EBRI), Washington, DC. EBRI was founded in 1978 to provide objective, unbiased information regarding the employee benefit system and related economic security issues. The objective: that decisions be made based on verifiable facts. Salisbury joined EBRI at its founding in 1978. EBRI has earned widespread regard as an organization that "tells it like it is." The Institute does not lobby and does not advocate or oppose any policy position. Its mission: "to contribute to, to encourage, and to enhance the development of sound employee benefit programs and sound public policy through objective research and education." The Institute provides information that is central to financial and human resources planning and to public policy analysis. Salisbury is also chairman and CEO of the American Savings Education Council (ASEC), and the Consumer Health Education Council (CHEC). Both are partnerships of public- and private-sector institutions that undertake initiatives to raise public awareness about what is needed to ensure long-term economic and health security. ASEC and CHEC are part of the EBRI Education and Research Fund. Salisbury is currently a member of a number of commissions and study panels, and he serves on many editorial advisory boards. He is a Fellow of the National Academy of Human Resources, the recipient of the 1997 Award for Professional Excellence from the Society for Human Resources Management, and the 1998 Keystone Award of the American Compensation Association. He has served on the Secretary of Labor's ERISA Advisory Council and the Presidential PBGC Advisory Committee, has been an advisor to numerous government agencies and private organizations, and is on the committees of many professional organizations. He has written and lectured extensively on economic security topics. Salisbury was one of 39 statutory delegates to the 1998 National Summit on Retirement Savings, hosted by the President and congressional leaders, and he moderated one of two general session panels. The EBRI/ASEC Choose to Save education campaign was featured in the other general session panel. Prior to joining EBRI, he held full-time positions with the Washington State Legislature, the U.S. Department of Justice, the Pension Benefit Guaranty Corporation (PBGC), and the Pension and Welfare Benefits Administration of the U.S. Department of Labor. He holds a B.A. degree in finance from the University of Washington and an M.A. in public policy and administration from the Maxwell School at Syracuse University.

Donald H. Sauvigné is Director, US Capital Accumulation Programs, for the IBM Corporation. Sauvigné has held numerous staff and leadership positions at several locations and one international unit. Currently, he manages the design and administration of IBM's retirement and capital accumulation programs, insurance offerings, and financial planning. This includes a 401(k) plan with over 220,000 accounts and assets in excess of $20 billion and defined benefit retirement plans covering over 140,000 active participants with a 42 billion trust. An HR professional, his specialty skills focus on employee benefits. He is a Trustee of Employee Benefit Research Institute (EBRI), a member of the ERISA Industry Committee (ERIC) Board of Directors, a prior member of the Board of Trustees for the Council on Employee Benefits (CEB), and a founding member of the American Savings Education Council (ASEC). He is a frequent contributor to articles on Human Resources and Capital Accumulation and is recognized for his strategic thinking on Benefits and Human Resources Management. Sauvigné holds a B.A. from Providence College and a M.B.A. from Syracuse University.

Kenneth D. Simonson is Senior Economic Advisor to the Chief Counsel for Advocacy, U.S. Small Business Administration. He works with the Chief Counsel for Advocacy, Jere W. Glover, and his staff of attorneys, economists, regional advocates, communications people, and entrepreneur-in-residence to advocate and produce research on small business issues in both the public and private sectors. Simonson has over 25 years of public policy experience, including 13 as vice president and chief economist for the American Trucking Associations. There he was in charge of all federal tax policy and a wide range of other economic and regulatory issues. He also worked with President Reagan's Commission on Industrial Competitiveness, the U.S. Chamber of Commerce, the Federal Home Loan Bank Board, and Norman B. Ture, Inc., an economic consulting firm. Simonson is a contributing editor of *Fleet Owner* magazine, for which he writes a monthly column, "The Bottom Line." He has written eight booklets explaining tax provisions in plain English, contributes frequently to a variety of business and professional publications and conferences, serves as vice president for programs of the National Economists Club, and co-chairs the Tax Economists Forum.

Jack Stewart is Assistant Director-Pension at the Princiapl Financial Group. The Principal has long been a national leader in providing record-keeping, administrative, and investment services to thousands of retirement plan sponsors. Stewart is currently Director of Pension Market Research Efforts at Principal. He manages all pension legislative and regulatory compliance activities at the Principal and closely tracks major pension issues being discussed in Washington, D.C. A business graduate of Iowa State University, Stewart entered the pension field in 1976. He has taught in-house training classes for sales representatives, industry groups, customers, and Hill staff.. He is a past member of the IRS Assistant Commissioner's Exempt Plan Advisory Group and has testified before Congress, the Internal Revenue Service (IRS) and U.S. Department of Labor on key pension issues. Stewart received his APA designation in 1993 and is a Fellow of the Life Management Institute.

Jack VanDerhei is a faculty member at Temple University's School of Business and Management (Department of Risk, Insurance, and Healthcare Management) and the Research Director of the EBRI Fellow's Program. In the last 15 years Dr. VanDerhei has more than 80 publications devoted to employee benefits and insurance but his major areas of research include (1) the financial and fiduciary aspects of private defined benefit and defined contribution retirement plans and (2) Social Security reform. He is currently the project director of both the Social Security Reform Analysis Program and the Defined Contribution and Participant Behavior Research Program. His most recent publications include "Potential Consequences for Employers of Social Security Privatization: Public Policy Research Implications" (with Kelly A. Olsen) and "Risk Aversion and Pension Investment Choices" (with Vickie L. Bajtelsmit). He is the editor of Benefits Quarterly and Search for a National Retirement Income Policy (University of Pennsylvania Press), a co-author of Pension Planning: Pension, Profit-Sharing, and Other Deferred Compensation Plans (Irwin/McGraw-Hill) and a member of the Advisory Board of the Pension Research Council at the Wharton School. Dr. VanDerhei has served as a consultant for the Pension Benefit Guaranty Corporation, the U.S. Department of Labor, the International Foundation of Employee Benefit Plans and the International Society of Certified Employee Benefit Specialists program. He has also served as an expert witness in litigation focussing on plan sponsor liability issues for participant directed 401(k) plans as well as asset reversion issues.

Paul Yakoboski is a Research Associate with the Employee Benefit Research Institute (EBRI), specializing in pension and retirement income security issues. His current research focuses on retirement plan sponsorship and participation trends, 401(k) plans and worker decisionmaking, lump-sum distributions and benefit preservation, the future retirement income security of today's workers and the education of workers in participant directed plans. Yakoboski is also Chair of the Research Committee for the American Savings Education Council and he is a member of the National Academy of Social Insurance. He has a B.S. in economics from Virginia Polytechnic Institute and State University and a M.A. and Ph.D. in economics from the University of Rochester. Dr. Yakoboski worked in the Human Resources Division of the U.S. General Accounting Office before joining EBRI in 1991.

Executive Summary

by Stephen Blakely, EBRI

More than a quarter-century ago, Congress enacted the landmark law that still governs employment-based retirement plans in the United States. The Employee Retirement Income Security Act of 1974 (ERISA), after more than two decades of amendments and regulatory embellishments, remains the basis of the federal government's approach to retirement plan regulation.

But in 1999, its 25th anniversary year, ERISA drew a mixed review: Widely praised for achieving its goal of greater retirement security for those American workers who have pensions, it is simultaneously criticized for contributing to the demise of the traditional defined benefit corporate pensions that it was created to secure and encourage. The number of these traditional pension plans paying life annuities at retirement has sharply declined, while new forms of defined benefit plan (with "individual accounts" and "lump-sum distributions") and defined contribution plans (typified by the 401(k)) have increased their position of dominance.

Whatever the reasons for this change (and views differ as to whether it is good or bad), the fact remains that the technological and global forces transforming the American economy are also affecting the retirement asset accumulation and income security of American workers. These sweeping changes, coupled with the looming retirement of the post-World War II "baby boom" generation, raise difficult policy challenges for the nation, not to mention labor and management. As demonstrated by the current controversy over "cash balance" pension plans, basic issues are involved: the employer-employee relationship, the ability of companies to attract and retain workers, the benefit provided to short-service relative to long-service workers, and the future economic security of an aging American labor force.

What are the developments and trends that are likely to affect retirement plans in the *next* 25 years? How will they be likely to affect employers, workers, the government, and society in general? What is the future of private retirement plans in the United States?

Policymakers, reporters, leading thinkers on benefits, employers, and labor representatives examined these questions during the Dec. 1, 1999, policy forum on "The Future of Private Retirement Plans," sponsored by the Employee Benefit Research Institute Education and Research Fund (EBRI-ERF). Attended by more than 100 invited experts, the policy forum examined the history and objectives of retirement plans, current trends in both defined benefit and defined contribution plans, how technology is affecting retirement plans, and how the politics of change are likely to affect the future of retirement plans in the United States.

The answers to those questions have national implications that go far beyond just retirement, according to David Blitzstein, an executive of the United Food and Commercial Workers Union: "There is reason to believe that the survival of the $3 trillion defined benefit pension system is at risk," he warned. "The decline in defined benefit plans is symptomatic of greater social change, and possibly a portent of future social and economic conflict in America."

Retirement Plan Objectives

The perceived reasons for having retirement benefits have changed dramatically in recent decades for both plan sponsors (employers and unions) and workers, according to Dallas Salisbury, president and CEO of EBRI. For employers, past motivators for having a traditional defined benefit plan (essentially an annuity, paid for entirely by the company) were "morale, keeping channels for promotion open, and facilitating work force reductions"—in other words, using retirement program design to manage the labor force. By contrast, defined contribution plans (individual accounts), and profit-sharing plans in particular, were seen as helping workers identify with the profitability and productivity of the enterprise and thereby helping to motivate the work force.

For instance, Salisbury noted a 1966 study by the American Enterprise Institute that concluded employee benefits were the primary job-change motivator for workers. By contrast, a 1998 survey by the Society for Human Resources Management and Commerce Clearing House found that only 11 percent of the population cited employee benefits as a job-change motivator (the major factors were economic).

The lesson for employers? "The mere presence of a more generous benefits package will not attract and retain employees," Salisbury said. This is "a fundamentally different conclusion" than employers would have reached 30 years earlier, and reflects the growing consensus that "long-term security can best be achieved through personal development and professional growth." Indeed, the high cost of 1950s-style, one-size-fits-all defined benefit plans may even be a precursor to long-term economic insecurity of workers, because that type of plan is an obvious target for cost-cutting during economic downturns, studies suggest.

These changes coincided with significant changes in the tax treatment of individual account retirement plans in the Revenue Act of 1978, as well as the creation of new pre-tax individual account options (such as individual retirement accounts (IRAs) and 401(k) plans) that did not exist in the 1960s. Other factors included the creation of the Pension Benefit Guaranty Corporation (PBGC) and other legislative and regulatory changes (such as shortened vesting rules) that resulted in significant new costs and disincentives for traditional defined benefit retirement plans. Compounding the shift were demographic changes (longer life expectancy and higher risks for plan sponsors), an increasingly fast and competitive global economy, falling unemployment rates, and a rapidly evolving technology sector for which traditional defined benefit retirement plans have held little appeal, Salisbury said.

He noted that as the new century begins, there is a growing emphasis on individual accounts and the use of lump-sum distributions, regardless of retirement plan design (including lump sums in final-average pay defined benefit plans), and the prospect of broader coverage and more individual retirement capital being accumulated. On the other hand, individuals are also being required to make far more retirement planning decisions themselves, such as contribution rates and asset investments, and longevity calculations that can affect their lifetime retirement economic security. Clearly, the trend is away from a paternalistic, one-size-fits all retirement plan, and toward individual responsibility for retirement security, Salisbury said, for better or for worse.

"Like it or not, many individuals increasingly want responsibility," he said. "And whether they want it or not, increasingly they are being given that responsibility."

Defined Benefit Plans

The decline in traditional defined benefit plans is well-documented and continuing, according to Richard Ippolito, a professor at George Mason University, former chief economist at the PBGC, and a widely published author on defined benefit and defined contribution plans. Comparing the past several years of data and the steady decline in both number of defined benefit plans and covered lives, Ippolito said: "All of the negative trends that I had known about during the late 1980s and the early 1990s were still in full play by the end of the 1990s. There is almost no good news for the defined benefit industry."

For instance, he noted, only about 40 percent of all pension-covered workers in the private sector currently have a defined benefit plan—compared with 85 percent in the early 1980s—and the trend is still negative. Compounding the bad news is the fact that funding ratios have deteriorated: 10 or 15 years ago, the average funding ratio for defined benefit plans was about 140 percent of liabilities, compared with perhaps 110 percent today, he added.

Among the key reasons for this decline in defined benefit plans, according to Ippolito:

- The change in the industrial patterns of employment in America, in which employment has favored the small service industry and been unfavorable to large industrial firms that have favored on defined benefit plans.

- Administrative costs for operating defined benefit plans, which have been especially burdensome on small and medium-size plans.
- Competition from 401(k) salary deferral plans, which are easier for employees to understand, and which came along just as the cost and complexity of defined benefit plans began to skyrocket.
- Tax policy that has restricted funding of defined benefit plans.

To Ippolito, federal tax policy is clearly to blame for the declining funding levels of defined benefit plans. "I have put the reversion tax squarely at the top of the list as the main culprit for a firm's inclination not to fund their plans as they used to," Ippolito said. "Tax policy has just been catastrophic for the [defined benefit] industry."

Ippolito also predicted that the trend-lines for defined benefit plans will get worse, because of the emergence of cash balance plans. Even though cash balance plans are technically classified as defined benefit plans, "they are in reality defined contribution plans," he said. He also predicted that 1999 Department of Labor data will show that, for salary plans with at least $25 million in assets, cash balance plans will account for more than 10 percent of all defined benefit retirement plans in the nation.

One of his more surprising research findings, Ippolito said, is that defined contribution plans have proven to be effective at attracting workers who are savers—and who bring with them the good working habits and skills that employers want. While pensions in general have this effect, he said, even defined basic contribution plans—and especially 401(k) plans—are surprisingly effective at attracting good workers. He predicted more research will be done on this aspect of pension plans and on how employers can use them to improve worker quality.

"The data are just indisputable that the people who do not save have all sorts of bad worker traits: They are less likely to be promoted, they are more likely to be fired, they earn less, they are more likely to take sick leave, and so on," Ippolito said. "401(k) savers are not the same workers as the nonsavers."

Cash Balance Plans

Concerning the controversy over cash balance plans, Larry Sher of the consulting firm PricewaterhouseCoopers noted that typical worker satisfaction surveys show that defined benefit plans typically rank close to last among all employee benefits, even though many employers spend more on their defined benefit plan than on many other benefits—notably the 401(k) plan, which usually ranks high with workers.

Converting to a cash balance plan allows companies to "marry the two together and communicate a retirement program—employer-provided retirement benefits—in the same language," Sher said.

Other popular factors for employers, he added, were the portability of cash balance benefits, accruing benefits "more evenly and rationally," flattening costs, removing the disincentive for long-term workers to stay just for the pension, and attracting new employees who are likely to appreciate the benefit.

Noting the strong interest in cash balance conversions by the news media, older workers, and, as a result, by lawmakers, Sher predicted that Congress is likely to pass legislation mandating greater disclosure to workers of the individual effects from a conversion, and possibly legislation that would restrict "wear-away" in conversions, along with possible regulatory action by the Internal Revenue Service and other federal agencies.

But he warned that if new restrictions do pass, "any new mandates will turn employers away from the entire defined benefit system...many [employers] will just look for the quickest way to the exits."

But David Blitzstein, of the United Food and Commercial Workers Union, was less than sympathetic and sharply critical of claims that employers are converting to cash balance plans to better meet the needs of younger workers, citing instead "cost and competition" as the main motivation.

Labor Concerns

For labor unions, which successfully negotiated the earliest pensions in the nation in the coal, auto, and steel industries in the late 1940s and early

1950s, the decline of defined benefit plans is viewed as a tragedy.

Blitzstein said the labor movement espouses an institutional system of economics (supported by some legal rulings) in which "the human and social costs of work do not totally fall on the workers themselves," and that benefits like pensions are treated as a fixed social overhead cost that has equal status with the fixed costs of capital. These costs, he added, should not be shifted to others or subsidized by the government. He said union bargaining objectives in pension negotiations traditionally have focused on protecting workers from five retirement risks: replacement rate adequacy, Social Security adequacy, Social Security retrenchment, longevity, investment risk, and inflation.

Even though unions view defined benefit plans as "a natural outcome of our political and economic philosophy," Blitzstein acknowledged that "economic and social trends have turned against both organized labor and defined benefit pension plans." Underlying these changes is the emergence of the so-called "new economy," with its low unemployment, job growth, wage moderation and growing prosperity gap, which is changing the rules that govern the labor market.

Blitzstein said this new economy is leading to the displacement of "the social-contract model" by a model that promotes individual responsibility, employee empowerment, and corporate flexibility, but at the expense of risk-sharing and the breakdown of group insurance. While this has been greatly enhanced by the current record-setting stretch of economic and stock market growth, he strongly questioned "whether the individual responsibility model can survive the test of a prolonged market downturn or a recession."

He also noted evidence that most Americans are not saving sufficiently to prepare for their retirement, and that the model of individual responsibility—implemented through defined contribution plans—seems likely to fail when put to the test. The result will be a political and financial crisis if and when large numbers of Americans face poverty in old age, he suggested, and warned that if a collapse of the financial markets occurs, "the psychological pain of shrinking defined contribution accounts would be something akin to the bank failures of the Great Depression." Among the options if that happens, he suggested, is federal legislation mandating minimum employer-paid retirement contributions, similar to the federal minimum wage.

Small Business Concerns

Concerning the well-documented "pension gap" between small and big firms, Denny Dennis of the National Federation of Independent Business noted that various surveys have found small employers do not offer retirement plans because they cannot afford the cost and because they often have a lower paid, high-turnover work force that is not interested in retirement benefits. He also noted that small firms frequently face a tradeoff: If they offer any benefits at all, it is more likely to be health insurance than a retirement plan, because that is a higher priority for their workers.

The high rate of failure in small businesses also works against pension benefits, he added. The average life span of a small business is only five years, and only one small firm in 20 will live 20 years or more—meaning that the risks of operating a retirement plan for many small businesses are just too high, given the other commercial forces they must contend with, Dennis said.

Dennis cited the EBRI Small Employer Retirement Survey and other research that has shown the two key factors in getting more small businesses to offer a retirement plan are either greater profits or a government subsidy (such as the provision of tax credits). He added that the administrative burdens of complying with the highly complex, expensive, and difficult federal regulations that govern defined benefit plans present a "straightjacket" that many small business owners simply avoid.

"There are peculiarities of the work force, and that is one of the reasons a flexible system is very nice," Dennis said. "For the majority [of small business owners], there is no doubt: Defined benefit programs just aren't in the cards."

Ken Simonson, of the Office of Advocacy in the Small Business Administration (SBA), reviewed the recent laws and his office's efforts to help lessen the regulatory burden on small entities, nonprofit firms, and small local governments. For instance, the SBA also has an Office of Interagency Affairs, whose role is to enforce or encourage agencies to go along with the mandates of the Regulatory Flexibility Act of 1980 and the Small Business Regulatory Enforcement Fairness Act of 1996 (SBREFA), which require federal agencies rules to consider the economic impacts of a new rule or regulation on small entities.

Simonson noted that many small firms used contingent or temporary workers to control their labor costs, avoid benefit problems, and handle project-specific needs. This is frequently the case in the high-tech sector, which is characterized by high turnover, specialized skills, and often very young workers who are interested in stock options rather than traditional forms of compensation and benefits.

Simonson commented that the cumulative effect of various new pension laws and regulations has been to send the message to employers that "you absolutely can't trust Congress to leave the rules alone, and any time they are going to change them, they are going to make things worse." That is a major factor in employers' distrust of the current debate over cash balance plans, he added.

Kathy Havey of the U.S. Chamber of Commerce reported that Chamber business surveys have found that corporate spending on retirement benefits as a percentage of payroll increased by more than 25 percent between 1975 (the year after ERISA was enacted) and 1998. She said the Chamber is forming a partnership with the Labor Department and SBA to help educate and assist small businesses that want to set up a retirement plan, to help explain the options and operations of a plan.

For financial firms that sell and operate retirement plans for small businesses, these factors cumulatively mean that defined contribution plans are the only type that are of significant interest. Jack Stewart of The Principal Financial Group expressed little optimism for the success of proposed new simplified defined benefit-type retirement plans for small businesses, such as the Secure Assets for Employees (SAFE) and the Secure Money Annuity or Retirement Trust (SMART) proposals. These plans, in different ways, would establish individual accounts for each employee, allow more portability from job to job, provide a certain base benefit figured on a percentage of pay times years of service, and would have simplified filing requirements and no or lower PBGC premiums. But even if they become law, Stewart said, they are unlikely to make much difference.

Principal sells about 2,500 401(k) plans to employer-sponsors each year, and undertook an initiative about three years ago to expand its sales of defined benefit plans as well. The results, according to Stewart, "have been so-so at best"—the number of defined benefit plans sold by Principal went from about 50 to 100 per year, but less than two dozen were brand-new plans. "You can see there is not the demand out there from employers," he said.

Stewart said one possible way to expand small business retirement plan sponsorship would be to simplify the administrative and reporting retirements, by having firms file only one form with the federal government for both defined benefit and defined contribution plans. But he added to the drumbeat of pessimism about the future of defined benefit plans: "I think it is clear the demand by smaller employers for defined benefit plans will continue to decrease."

■ Defined Contribution Plans

With defined contribution plans, such as 401(k)s, the burdens of paying into a retirement plan and making investment decisions with the assets fall on the individual plan participant—not the employer, as is the case with traditional defined benefit plans—and there is no guaranteed payout (annuity). The ultimate size of the nest egg depends on decisions that participants make individually about how much to contribute to their account and how the account investments perform. While employers typically (but voluntarily) match a portion of a worker's contribution, responsibility for the retirement account ultimately is the employee's.

Nevertheless, defined contribution plans are far more popular with employees than traditional defined benefit plans. Scott Peterson of Hewitt Associates cited several of the well-documented reasons why workers participate in these plans:

- Obtaining the company match.
- Receiving frequent communications from the plan sponsor.
- Having the flexibility to change contribution levels and investment allocations. For many employees, being able to change allocations to

adapt to changing economic conditions is seen as an element of safety and security, Peterson said.

- Passive enrollment, which has been shown to significantly improve worker participation in a retirement plan.

Peterson noted that research has shown that the *presence* of a company match appears to be more important than the *level* of the match in getting employees to participate in a 401(k). "We know that the presence of a match itself does have a significant impact," Peterson said. "But an employee's decision to contribute appears not to be significantly impacted by the level of match."

He also noted there have been major changes the past 10 or 15 years in how plan sponsors communicate with participants. "Increasingly, there is a focus on giving people a good sense of how to be smart investors and savers, how to use the plans in a wise way, and how to plan for their own retirement and take responsibility for it."

Peterson cited several "best practices" that are common among successful 401(k) plans: a company match, automatic enrollment of participating workers 30 days after employment, innovative communications that allow participants to plan and invest for their own retirement, and periodic monitoring of investment results and adjustment of participant allocations, as needed.

401(k) Asset Allocation

How are 401(k) participants actually using their accounts and managing their assets? According to the latest analysis by EBRI and the Investment Company Institute (ICI), using the largest 401(k) participant database in the nation, almost three-quarters of all 401(k) balances were invested directly or indirectly in equity securities at year-end 1998. Specifically, 49.8 percent of total plan balances are invested in equity funds, 17.7 percent in company stock, 11.4 percent in guaranteed investment contracts (GICs), 8.4 percent in balanced funds, 6.1 percent in bond funds, 4.7 percent in money funds, and 0.3 percent in other stable value funds.

However, there is wide variation around the average: About 28 percent of all 401(k) participants have more than 80 percent of their account balances invested in equity funds, while an equal share (28 percent) hold no equity funds at all. Younger 401(k) participants tend to have more of their assets concentrated in equity funds, while older participants invest more heavily in fixed-income assets, the EBRI/ICI analysis found.

The average account balance for active 401(k) participants grew by 26 percent from 1996 to 1998, largely due to the continuing bull market in equities, the EBRI/ICI analysis found. However, it also shows wide variation around the $47,004 average balance at year-end 1998: Nearly three-quarters of the participants have account balances below the average, while 13 percent of participants have account balances greater than $100,000. There are several factors accounting for this variation, such as the age of 401(k) participants, how long they have been at their current job, and their contribution behavior. The median (mid-point) account balance among active 401(k) participants was $13,038 at year-end 1998.

The EBRI/ICI database provides 1998 information on 7.9 million active participants in 30,102 plans holding nearly $372 billion in assets. It contains accounts for 11 percent of all 401(k) plans, 22 percent of all 401(k) participants, and about 27 percent of the assets held in 401(k) plans. The data include demographic information, annual contributions, plan balances, asset allocation, and loans, and are broadly representative of the universe of 401(k) plans.

Rollovers and Distributions

One of the major concerns about defined contribution plans is whether workers will keep their defined contribution retirement savings in a tax-deferred account when they change jobs, or whether they will "cash out" the assets for some nonretirement use.

John DeStefano of Fidelity Investments noted that the impending retirement of the baby boom generation will soon create huge demands for retirement assets because Americans will be retiring in record numbers. In 1950, only 12 million people in the United States were over age 65, and projections are that there will be 35 million in 2000 and 68 million in 2015, or fully 20 percent of the national population, he noted.

DeStefano reported on research by his firm showing that changes in demographics and economic trends are increasing the number of terminated employees and those eligible to take distributions from their defined contribution plan. These employees fall into two categories: retirees and job changers. He noted the high turnover rate among American workers, citing statistics that the average worker changes jobs seven times during his or her career, and that more than 50 percent of the work force has been in their current job less than five years. For defined contribution savings plans, this means that most workers have (or will have) several smaller 401(k) or 403(b) accounts with different employers, each with different investment options. This raises the danger that "they may cash out when they leave and lose all of their tax benefits," he noted. "We are definitely seeing an increasing trend of employees who are terminated and who are struggling with their distribution decision."

For these workers, there are four options: leave the assets in the former employer's plan (if they have more than $5,000 in assets); roll the assets over into an IRA; move the assets into their new employer's retirement plan; or cash out the assets, pay the tax penalty, and use them for nonretirement purposes. Based on Fidelity's data, DeStefano said, about half are leaving their assets in the former employer's plan (mostly "due to inertia," he adds), while the majority of those who take distributions are rolling over their assets into an IRA.

While estimates vary on how many workers "cash out" their accounts and either spend or reinvest the assets in taxable accounts, DeStefano said Fidelity has found the majority of those who cash out do so largely out of ignorance. "We have found that the trend is in large part due to a lack of knowledge on the participant's part," he said. "Over one-third said they had not received any information from their former employer about their distribution options or the tax consequences associated with these options, and 15 percent didn't know that they had the option to remain in the plan." As a result, Fidelity has taken various steps to increase employee education and knowledge about their distribution options and the associated tax consequences.

Technology

Many speakers at the policy forum testified to the various ways technology—specifically the Internet and Web-based information systems—is forcing major changes in the expectations and behavior of retirement plan sponsors (employers) and participants (workers). Both are demanding a wider range of choices and options, fast and individualized response, and better control over their defined contribution plans and accounts.

Byron Oliver of Cigna Retirement Services, a major provider of retirement plan services, reported that his company has seen extremely rapid growth in the number of 401(k) participants who conduct their account activity electronically: Starting from scratch just two years ago, a third of all the company's 401(k) transactions are now conducted over the Internet, and by 2000 that is expected to reach 50 percent. Not only is electronic administration of 401(k) plans more efficient for plan sponsors, he said, it creates almost revolutionary ways to improve communications with participants.

"It [the Internet] provides us a phenomenal opportunity to do education in ways that we have never done before, provide the information in ways that we have never done before, do training and open different sites around the country," he said. "We are going to see phenomenal impacts."

He also observed that five or six years ago, the typical 401(k) plan had only three or four investment options, account statements were mailed once a quarter, and communication with participants was largely perceived to be the enrollment process. Today, by virtue of technological changes, Cigna's average 401(k) plan has a dozen investment choices; workers have the capability to make investment changes 24 hours a day, seven days a week through the Internet, call centers, and voice response systems; and enrollment is a very small part of the process.

Bill Arnone of the consulting firm Ernst & Young said Internet operation of 401(k) plans also helps promote a self-reliant mindset among workers, and that it is in the employer's interest for people to take more control and to engage employees as active partners in a unified enterprise. One result, he believes, is that the technology generates greater appreciation among workers for their employers' investment in total compensation and benefits.

Arnone described three different stages of Internet usage by plan sponsors. The lowest is where a company uses it only for providing on-line brochures and information to workers. Moderate usage is where a company utilizes it for participant enrollment, while back-office administrative functions are still done off-line. The advanced level is where transactions are integrated and all databases are linked so that there is a consistent and coherent approach to benefits for the end-user.

A more surprising result is that the technology is forcing a change in whether employers can provide merely "education" or "advice" to their employees, who are responsible for their own investment decisions in a defined contribution plan, and who are demanding greater support. Both employers and regulators are struggling to redefine how this affects a plan sponsor's fiduciary responsibility and potential liability for investment loses.

"It seems to me there is a very big distinction between an employee who says, 'The provider recommended a course of action for me and I then made the decision,' and one where the employee says, 'The provider made the decision for me.' To me, that is the key distinction," Arnone said.

He predicted that a larger issue of employer responsibility will arise when employers have the ability, through data linkage, data integration, and data mining, to take a "snapshot" of their entire employee population and analyze how people are positioned for retirement security, by age of employee, tenure with the company, level of pay, gender, ethnicity, and other diversity issues.

"Can you imagine the power of being able to look at your employee population at any point in time and slice and dice the data like that?" he asked. "It gives whole new meaning to the notion of fiduciary liability and fiduciary responsibility, but it seems to me this is the likely outcome of the Web-sourcing revolution."

Jason Scott of Financial Engines also raised the question of whether people will use Internet technology—and its capability for making fast asset allocation changes—for good purposes or bad. Scott said his firm has tracked its customers' 401(k) transfers during sharp drops in the stock market, and has found that "some people do, in fact, buy high and sell low." But he added that those who do "are still a very, very small percentage of the total population," and that so far his firm has not seen a net outflow from investment funds in 401(k) plans during market dips.

The Politics of Change

But to some critics, that way of thinking ignores the political repercussions for retirement plan sponsors if there is a deep-enough and long-enough drop in stock values to ravage the 401(k) accounts of millions of Americans. Among many speakers at the EBRI-ERF policy forum, there were bleak assessments of the ability of Congress to change federal retirement policy without unintentionally making matters worse for both employers and their workers.

"Today we have a situation where everyone is a winner because of the stock market," said John Rother of the AARP. "That is not going to continue. And when that is no longer the case, that is going to change the politics of this whole debate."

Rother argued that the dispute between defined benefit and defined contribution plans is irrelevant to the 50 percent or so of all Americans who do not have access to an employment-based retirement plan and who lack tax-favored mechanisms for accumulating retirement capital. He also said that shifting the risk of retirement adequacy from employers (through defined benefit plans) to individuals (through defined contribution plans) ignores the fact that "there is an alarming number of 'grasshoppers' in our society, people who are basically in a live-for-today mode."

While it may be tempting to let those people bear the consequences of their own irresponsibility, he warned, there are enough of them to potentially create an angry block of voters too big to ignore. "If we just let that go, then we are creating a very, very powerful constituency to expand Social Security in the future. We are creating a very powerful constituency to raise taxes on employers in the future," Rother said. And with the baby boom generation about to start retiring, he predicted there is little time left to head off a political and sociological battle between the relatively few Americans with retirement assets and the many without.

Don Sauvigné of IBM warned about the risk to both employers and workers if Congress legislates on retirement policy on a piecemeal basis. Acting in response to political pressure, while restricting the flexibility of employers to adapt to a rapidly changing economy, could have profoundly negative consequences for workers, he warned.

"We still do not have any substance of a national, formal retirement policy underlining the debate," he said. "The labor market and the employers have got to have the opportunity to be successful—because if we are not successful, we won't continue the commitment to the social contract. We won't be able to."

Sauvigné described the political response to IBM's cash balance conversion in 1999 as governance by anecdote, and warned of "the consequences of unintended actions" if the federal government imposes even more restrictions on employment-based retirement plans.

He predicted that the 2000 presidential and congressional elections will be crucial to what happens to retirement plans in the coming years. "I think the year 2000 really is the foundation year for the future and a lot of these decisions," he said.

Leon Piper of Delta Airlines commented that his company must deal with a diverse work force that demands different types of retirement benefits—either the annuity of a defined benefit plan or the individual account of a defined contribution plan. Delta meets those demands by providing both types of plans, he observed, and predicted that Congress will face its own political difficulties if it tries to promote one type of plan over the other.

Even though pension debates have focused on policy issues in the past, Brian Graff of the American Society of Pension Actuaries predicted that it is already too late to keep retirement plans from being politicized. He noted that Vice President Gore issued a campaign statement in 1999 critical of cash balance plans, and that congressional Democrats have actively targeted retirement as a "hot button" political issue in the 2000 election campaign. The controversy over cash balance plans reflects the aging of the baby boomers and the growing public unease about paying for retirement, he said.

"You have a likely presidential nominee talking about 'wear-away,'" Graff said. "Now, is that scary or what? These issues are becoming increasingly political."

Graff predicted that politicizing retirement policy will force a re-examination of core retirement security issues that haven't be subjected to major policy debate in the 25 years since ERISA was enacted—specifically, vesting and participation rules, coverage standards, and spousal protection and nondiscrimination rules. And because defined contribution plans have become the dominant type of retirement plan in the United States, he also predicted that Congress will move to impose on 401(k) plans many of the same types of restrictions that led so many employers to abandon traditional defined benefit plans.

Because the politics are changing, so too will the focus of retirement policy, he added. While the interests of employers and retirement plan sponsors historically have been the main policy focus, participant concerns are now more likely to receive attention, despite the fact that retirement benefits are voluntarily provided by plan sponsors and can be terminated. The next five to 10 years "are going to be very different than they have ever been before, because of the increasingly political nature of these issues," Graff said.

What Are the Objectives, Whose Objectives Are They, and How Well Are They Being Met?

1

The Development of Private Retirement Programs

by Dallas L. Salisbury, EBRI

Introduction

A review of the state of private pensions must begin with a clear understanding of what a "pension plan" is. While this sounds obvious, it is necessary because the "legal" meaning has clearly changed over the past 25 years. The Employee Retirement Income Security Act of 1974 (ERISA) states:

> Any plan, fund, or program which was heretofore or is hereafter established or maintained by an employer or by an employee organization, or by both, to the extent that by its express terms or as a result of surrounding circumstances, such plan, fund, or program—
> (A) provides retirement income to employees, or
> (B) results in a deferral of income by employees for periods extending to the termination of covered employment or beyond, *regardless of the method of calculating the contributions made to the plan, the method of calculating the benefits under the plan or the method of distributing benefits from the plan*.[1]
> (emphasis added)

This represented an expansion in concept from the first full version of the legislative proposal, H.R. 2, which limited plans to those which

> *for the purpose of providing for its participants or their beneficiaries, by the purchase of insurance or annuity contracts or otherwise, retirement benefits, and includes any deferred profit-sharing plan which provides benefits at or near retirement*.[2] (emphasis added)

H.R. 2 was closer to the traditional dictionary definition of a pension: "*a retirement or disability allowance*." (emphasis added)

ERISA also created requirements and standards for vesting, funding, participation, fiduciary behavior and a termination insurance program for private employer and union employee benefit plans. Public employee plans were exempted from the provisions of ERISA. The state of private employer pensions today is the result of these rules as they interact with economics, demographics, and competition.

ERISA expansion of the definition of "pension plan" to include capital accumulation plans with lump sum-distributions at "termination of covered employment," as opposed to "at or near retirement," actually serves to clearly highlight the "State of Private Pensions" in the United States. Both the public and private sector have moved in the direction of sponsoring fewer plans that only pay benefits "at or near retirement," and have created more and more plans that pay at "termination of covered employment." The result has been dramatic changes in defined benefit pension plans—those that promise a fixed accrual and benefit without reference to the funding method—and growth in the number of defined contribution plans—those that promise payment of funds contributed, adjusted for investment earnings, but promise no fixed benefit.

---

[1] *Employee Retirement Income Security Act of 1974, Public Law 93-406, Title I, Sec. 3 (2)*

[2] *Legislative history, April 1976, Vol. I, p. 7.*

Table 1.1
PUBLIC AND PRIVATE PLAN GROWTH, 1940–1996

	1940	1950	1960	1996
Covered Workers (millions)	5.5	12.4	25.7	59.9
Private	4.1	9.8	21.2	42.7
Public	1.4	2.6	4.5	17.2
Fund Assets ($billions)	$2.5	$12.3	$53.0	$5,751.0
Private	2.4	12.0	52.0	3,936.0
Public	0.1	3.0	1.0	1,815.0
Total Work Force (millions)	56.0	63.8	72.1	142.9
Percentage Covered	9.8 %	19.4%	35.6%	41.9%
Private Net Flows ($billions)	$0.3	$2.0	$5.4	$324.0
Private Net Contributions ($billions)	$0.2	$1.7	$3.7	$–30.0

Source: Daniel M. Holland, "Private Pension Funds: Projected Growth" (National Bureau of Economic Research, 1966); Employee Benefit Research Institute tabulations of the March 1997 Current Population Survey, and the *EBRI Pension Investment Report.*

Where Did We Start?

The first reported pension plan in the United States was established in 1636 as the Plymouth Colony settlers' military retirement program. In 1759, a pension plan was established to benefit widows and children of Presbyterian ministers. Gallatin Glassworks' established a profit-sharing plan in 1797. The U.S. government provided pensions to widows following the Civil War. In 1875, the American Express Company established a formal corporate pension plan.[3]

The statutory tax treatment of pensions was formally legislated through the Revenue Act of 1921, which exempted interest income of stock bonus and profit-sharing plans from current taxation and deferred the tax to employees until distribution. Statutes enacted since 1921 have permitted employers to deduct a reasonable amount in excess of the amount necessary to fund current pension liabilities (1928); made pension trusts irrevocable (1938); and established nondiscriminatory eligibility rules for pension coverage, contributions, and benefits (1942). These provisions were incorporated into the Internal Revenue Code (IRC) of 1954, amended substantially by the Employee Retirement Income Security Act of 1974 and several added statutes, including the Tax Reform Act of 1986 (TRA '86).[4]

The most rapid growth in plans occurred during the 1940s and 1950s in response to collective bargaining activity. During this period of wage and price controls, expenditures for employee benefits could still increase, providing a strong driver for plan establishment. Table 1.1 provides an early summary picture of public and private plan growth, as presented by Daniel M. Holland in 1966.[5] As it shows, early growth was dramatic. And, while it combined "private industrial pension and deferred profit-sharing plans," according to Holland's inference statements and by he did not view either to be "pensions." Today, that has changed. The 1996 data from the U.S. Bureau of the Census combine all plan types under the single heading of "pension," as do the data from the Federal Reserve.

---

[3] *Allen, Everett T., Joseph J. Melone, Jerry S. Rosenbloom, and Jack L. VanDerhei,* Pension Planning: Pensions, Profit-Sharing, and Other Deferred Compensation Plans. *Seventh edition (Homewood, IL: Richard D. Irwin, Inc., 1992)*

Employee Benefit Research Institute, EBRI Databook on Employee Benefits, *Third edition (Washington, DC: Employee Benefit Research Institute,-X995).*

Rosenbloom, Jerry S., The Handbook of Employee Benefits: Design, Funding and Administration *(Homewood, IL: Dow Jones-Irwin, 1996).*

[4] *For further information, see Employee Benefit Research Institute,* Fundamental of Employee Benefit Programs, *Fifth edition (Washington, DC: Employee Benefit Research Institute, 1997).*

[5] *Daniel M. Holland,* Private Pension Funds: Projected Growth *(Cambridge, MA: National Bureau of Economic Research, 1996).*

Types of "Pension" Plans

Defined Benefit Plans

In a defined benefit plan, the employer agrees to provide the employee a nominal benefit amount at retirement based on a specified formula, and increasingly in recent years to provide for lump-sum payment of the accrued present value at termination of employment. The formula is usually one of three general types: a flat-benefit formula, a career-average formula, or a final-pay formula.

Flat-Benefit Formulas

These formulas pay a flat dollar amount for each year of service recognized under the plan.

Career-Average Formulas

There are two types of career-average formulas. Under the first type, participants earn a percentage of the pay recognized for plan purposes in each year they are plan participants. The second type of career-average formula averages the participant's yearly earnings over the period of plan participation. At retirement, the benefit equals a percentage of the career-average pay, multiplied by the participant's number of years of service.

Final-Pay Formulas

These plans base benefits on average earnings during a specified number of years at the end of a participant's career; this is presumably the time when earnings are highest. The benefit equals a percentage of the participant's final average earnings, multiplied by the number of years of service. This formula provides preretirement inflation protection to the participant but can represent a higher cost to the employer.

Flat-benefit formulas are common in collectively bargained plans or plans covering hourly paid employees. Career-average and final-pay formulas are most common in plans covering nonunion employees. Under pay-related formulas, an employer has some discretion in defining pay for plan purposes provided the definition does not discriminate in favor of highly compensated employees, subject to the statutory and regulatory definition of compensation used in testing for nondiscrimination. Under ERISA's minimum standards, there is also some leeway in determining what employment period will be recognized in the benefit formula. The benefit may reflect only the plan participation period or may be based on the entire employment period.

Bank of America made a transition to the first "cash-balance defined benefit plan" in 1985. Now, approximately 14 percent of defined benefit plans are of this type. They generally function based on a career-average formula and communicate the benefit as an individual account present value.[6] These plans have become quite controversial.

Defined Contribution Plans

In a defined contribution plan, the employer makes provision for contributions to an account established for each participating employee. The final retirement benefit reflects the total of employer contributions, any employee contributions, and investment gains or losses. Sometimes the accumulated amount includes forfeitures resulting from employer contributions forfeited by employees who leave before becoming vested. As a result, the level of future retirement benefits cannot be calculated exactly in advance. Employer contributions to defined contribution plans are often based on a specific formula such as a percentage of participant salary or of company profits. The plans may be designed to include pretax or after-tax employee contributions, which may be voluntary or mandatory. There are several types of defined contribution plans. In a money purchase plan, employer contributions are mandatory and are usually stated as a percentage of employee salary. In a profit-sharing plan, total contributions to be distributed are often derived from a portion of company profits. Stock bonus plans are similar to profit-sharing plans but usually make contributions and benefit payments in the form of company stock. A target benefit plan is a cross between a defined benefit plan and a money purchase plan—with a targeted benefit used to determine the level of contributions but with contributions allocated to accounts as in a money purchase plan. A thrift, or savings, plan is essentially an employee savings account, often with

---

[6] *See Carol Quick, "An Overview of Cash Balance Plans,"* EBRI Notes, *no. 7 (Employee Benefit Research Institute, June 1999): 1–7.*

Table 1.2
PRIVATE EMPLOYER PENSION PLANS

Year	Single-Employer Defined Benefit	Single-Employer Defined Contribution	Multi-Employer Defined Benefit	Multi-Employer Defined Contribution
1975	101,214	207,437	2,132	311
1985	167,911	461,158	2,261	805
1995	67,682	622,584	1,810	1,328
1999[a]	40,000	700,000	1,800	1,500

Source: U.S. Department of Labor and author's estimate.
[a]Estimate.

employer matching contributions. In a 401(k) arrangement, an employee can elect to contribute, on a pretax basis, a portion of current compensation to an individual account, thus deferring current income tax on the contribution and the investment income earned. In an employee stock ownership plan (ESOP), employer contributions to employee accounts must be primarily in company stock.

What Is the Pension Landscape Today?

Congress acted in 1984 to change the pension system for federal civilian employees. Prior to 1987, the only retirement plan was a final pay defined benefit plan. For those hired after the 1984 act, a new reduced defined benefit plan was accompanied by a generous 401(k)-type plan. Those already working had the option of remaining in the old plan or shifting to the new plans. Congress had also acted in 1978 to add two new sections to the Internal Revenue Code, Sec. 125 and Sec. 401(k). Regulations in 1981 led to a massive transition of traditional profit-sharing plans into 401(k) plans, meaning that the employee could contribute pretax dollars. Sec. 457 and Sec. 403(b) gave state and local governments and nonprofit organizations this same opportunity. Legislation since 1986 has moved all these so-called "salary-reduction" plans closer together in design and rules, with nearly all employers now able to establish 401(k) plans. Current congressional legislative proposals would further this process. Moreover, in recent years a number of states have debated proposals either to introduce expanded supplemental "salary reduction" plans or to replace defined benefit plans with defined contribution plans. Demographic change and economic competition make it likely that these debates and trends will continue.

Table 1.2 presents data from the U.S. Department of Labor on private employer pension plans in terms of number of plans. The trend lines are clear: defined benefit plans are on the decline and salary reduction plans are becoming the primary "pension" plans in the nation. The numbers on multi-employer plans provide further evidence of the trend toward increasing use of supplemental and primary defined contribution programs.[7, 8]

Unions, participant advocates, and many others have not been happy with these trends. Traditional defined benefit plans, as noted, provide annuity income that assures some level of economic security for the remaining lifetime of the participant, and frequently of the beneficiary. This, in fact, represents the old English definition of a "pension." Unions have traditionally viewed pensions as seeking to provide security against the risk of economic losses resulting from factors over which the worker has no control (through employer commitment to provide a predetermined income stream under certain circumstances).[9] Such losses

---

[7] Private Pension Plan Bulletin, *"Abstract of 1995, Form 5500 Annual Reports," no. 8 (Spring 1999).*

[8] *See Kelly Olsen and Jack VanDerhei, "Defined Contribution Plan Dominance Grows Across Sectors and Employer Sizes, While Mega Defined Benefit Plans Remain Strong: Where Are We and Where Are We Going,"* EBRI Issue Brief *no. 190. (Employee Benefit Research Institute, October 1997).*

[9] *Thomas F. Duzak, "Defined Benefit and Defined Contribution Plans: A Labor Perspective," in Dallas L. Salisbury, ed.,* Economic Survival in Retirement: Which Pension is for You? *(Washington, DC: Employee Benefit Research Institute, 1982).*

could occur as a consequence of:

- Unanticipated expenses or income loss,
- Layoff or termination, or,
- Retirement with inadequate savings to maintain real income for the remainder of an individual's lifetime.

One union counselor noted in 1982:

Defined contribution plans which determine the amount of income to the employee is a function of the employer's profit, or the price of the company's stock, or the investment yield of a fixed pool of assets, are not compatible with the concept of a wage versus income security trade-off. It is virtually impossible to construct plans which provide desirable levels of income replacement and which also represent an equivalent value to all employees in the covered population...the collective bargaining process requires a pooling of economic strength in order to achieve an objective which is determined to by the group as a whole; but at the same time, the process dictates a sacrifice of individuality... secure protection against the consequences of management's actions.

While many unions have negotiated defined contribution plans since 1982, it is my sense that those who are concerned about pensions providing economic security in retirement continue to hold these views.

Employer preferences for pensions focus more on economic performance than on retirement income security. Pensions are viewed favorably if they serve to:

- Improve corporate efficiency.[10]
- Improve morale.
- Keep channels for promotion open.
- Facilitate work force reduction.
- Encourage employee identification with profit.
- Are most cost-effective and least administratively intense.
- Attract and hold capable employees.[11]

A 1998 survey conducted by the Society for Human Resource Management found that higher salaries elsewhere and dissatisfaction with potential career development at an organization are the most significant threats to employee retention, with only 11 percent of respondents citing benefits as a job change motivator.

A senior corporate executive noted in 1998 that "not having benefits at some threshold level will repulse employees, but the mere presence of a more generous benefits package will not attract and retain employees."[12] This view is explains employers' increasing flexibility in recent years and their effort to include environmental factors in program design by:

- Responding to favorable tax laws that provide an incentive to provide benefits.
- Responding to demands in labor negotiations.
- Responding to social and indirect government pressures.
- Responding to inherent advantages of group purchase/provision.
- Responding to shareholder desires and competition.

Considering the fact that the foregoing trends have occurred in spite of the relatively consistent philosophy by union leaders and those focused on retirement income delivery, and that the previously discussed factors driving employers and individuals seem to be accelerating, it seems unlikely that the movement toward individual accounts and individual control will end in the foreseeable future.

Borrowing While Still Employed

The availability of loans to participants is an exception to ERISA's general principle that transactions between a plan and parties in interest—such as participants—are prohibited because of potential abuse of funds earmarked for retirement. Plan

---

[10] *Jerry S. Rosenbloom and G. Victor Hallman,* Employee Benefit Planning, *Third edition (Englewood Cliffs, NJ: Prentice-Hall, 1991).*

[11] *For a summary of research, see Emily S. Andrews,* Pension Policy and Small Employers: At What Price Coverage? *(Washington, DC: Employee Benefit Research Institute, 1989); Richard A. Ippolito,* Pensions, Economics and Public Policy *(Philadelphia, PA: Pension Research Council, University of Pennssylvania; 1986); and Richard A. Ippolito,* Pension Plans and Employee Performance Evidence, Analysis, and Policy *(Chicago: The University of Chicago Press, 1997).*

[12] *See Charles G. Tharp, "Yes," in Dallas L. Salisbury, ed.,* Do Employers/Employees Still Need Employee Benefits? *(Washington, DC: Employee Benefit Research Institute, 1998).*

loans are generally not treated as taxable distributions and are restricted to limited circumstances defined under IRC Sec. 72 and ERISA Sec. 408(b)(1).

A plan loan must be described in writing. The amount of a new loan plus the outstanding balance of any other plan loans cannot exceed the lesser of $50,000 or the greater of one-half of the present value of the employee's nonforfeitable accrued benefit under the plan, or $10,000. The $50,000 limit is reduced by the excess of the highest outstanding loan balance during the one-year period ending on the day before the new loan is made, over the outstanding balance on the date of the loan. A plan is permitted to impose a minimum loan amount as high as $1,000.

Loans must be repaid within five years. A longer term is available only for loans used to acquire the participant's principal residence. The loan must require substantially level amortization payments, payable at least quarterly. The interest rate must reasonably reflect rates charged on comparable loans made on a commercial basis. Interest paid to the plan also does not increase the individual's basis in the plan or tax-deferred annuity. Loans to owner-employees from Keogh plans continue to be prohibited transactions. The loan must be adequately secured so that, in the event of a default, the participant's retirement income is preserved and loss to the plan is prevented. Up to 50 percent of a participant's vested accrued benefit may be loaned without additional security being required.

A 1999 report found that loans in today's plans are very common.[13] Over half of 401(k) plans now offer a loan option, 70 percent of participants are in plans offering loans, and 18 percent of participants borrowed in 1996. The average unpaid balance as a percentage of account balances was 16 percent. Loan ratios tend to decrease with age, dropping from 30.0 percent for participants in their 20s to 9.8 percent for those in their 60s.

Rollovers Upon Lump-Sum Distribution

In general, lump-sum distributions from a qualified pension plan may be rolled over tax free into an individual retirement account (IRA) or another retirement plan. The transfer must be made within 60 days of the participant's receipt of the distribution from the first plan. The most recent comprehensive data on lump-sum distributions and rollovers are from the 1993 Current Population Survey. Nearly half of those with recent distributions reported having rolled over all of the funds into a tax-qualified program, compared with 17 percent of those with such distributions prior to 1960. The mean amount of recent distributions was $11,237, and the median amount $3,496.[14]

A recent analysis by John Sabelhaus (Congressional Budget Office) looked at individual retirement accounts (IRAs) in terms of the proportion of account balances that had come from rollovers as opposed to contributions. By year-end 1997, IRAs held over $1.948 billion in assets. Of this amount, $182.9 billion was from direct contributions, compared to $747 billion from rollovers.[15] These numbers suggest that, as a vehicle for new savings, IRAs have not proven particularly popular, they are proving quite useful but as a vehicle for portability and preservation they are proving quite useful.

How Are Plan Assets Being Allocated Among Investments?

Traditionally, assets in most pension plans were invested on a pooled basis, with plan sponsors or trustees making allocation decisions across managers, equities, bonds, etc. With the combination of the growth of mutual funds, the prevalence of 401(k) plans, and computer advances, individual participants now make many of the allocation decisions. The *EBRI Pension Investment Report* provides summary data on allocation from 1950 to

---

13 *Jack VanDerhei, Russell Galer, Carol Quick, and John Rea, "401(k) Plan Asset Allocation, Account Balances, and Loan Activity,"* EBRI Issue Brief *no. 205 (Employee Benefit Research Institute, January 1999).*

14 *See Dallas L. Salisbury, ed.,* When Workers Call the Shots: Can They Achieve Retirement Security? *(Washington, DC: Employee Benefit Research Institute, 1995).*

15 *See John Sabelhaus, "Projecting IRA Balances & Withdrawals,"* EBRI Notes*, no. 5 (Employee Benefit Research Institute, May 1999): 1–3.*

Table 1.3
ASSET ALLOCATION

	Private Trusteed Defined Benefit			Private Trusteed Defined Contribution			Public Plans			401(k)		
	Equity	Bond	Other	Equity	Bond	Other	Equity	Bond	Other	Equity	Bond	Other
1985	41%	29%	30%	38%	17%	45%	30%	58%	11%			
1990	34	40	26	35	17	48	32	43	25			
1996	46	32	22	43	12	45	56	28	16	68%	10%	22%
1998	53	27	20	48	10	42	68	25	7	50	6	44

Source: Jack VanDerhei, Russell Galer, Carol Quick, and John Rea, "401(k) Plan Asset Allocation, Account Balances, and loan Activity," *EBRI Issue Brief* no. 205 (Employee Benefit Research Institute, January 1999); Jack VanDerhei, Sarah Holden, and Carol Quick, "401(k) Plan Asset Allocation Account Balances and Loan Activity in 1998" *EBRI Issue Brief* no. 218 (Employee Benefit Research Institute, January 2000).

1997 (public plans) and 1998 (private plans).[16] The January 1999 *EBRI Issue Brief* No. 205 provides data on asset allocation within 401(k) plans.[17] Table 1.3 summarizes aggregate allocation for several year-ends for private trusted defined benefit and defined contribution plans, and for public plans and individual allocation as of year-end 1996 (1997 and 1998 data on 401(k) plans will be published by EBRI in early 2000).

With both plans and participants these average allocations hide variation across plans and individuals. They suggest at least two things: first, asset allocation shifts a lot over time; second, that individuals invest more aggressively than the average plan board. For example, some public plans have had legal prohibitions against investment in equities, while others have been able to be very aggressive. Large trusteed private plans tend to be more heavily invested in equities than small plans, and there is substantial variation by individual 401(k) participants when the numbers are viewed by age, income, and tenure.

Plan Termination

Although pension plans must be established with the intent that they will be permanent, employers are permitted to terminate their plans. As table 1.2 shows, terminations have been heavy. If a defined benefit plan terminates with assets greater than the amount necessary to pay required benefits, the employer may recover the excess assets and use them for business or other purposes. A 50 percent excise tax is imposed on the amount recovered. ERISA established plan termination insurance to protect participants' defined benefits in the event a defined benefit plan terminates with insufficient assets to pay benefits. The program does not apply to defined contribution plans. There are separate programs for single employer and multi-employer plans.[18]

With a strong economy, strong markets, and many large employers remaining in the Pension Benefit Guaranty Corporation's (PBGC) premium pool by making a transition to cash-balance plans instead of moving all the way to defined contribution programs, PBGC has had several good financial years. As of September 30, 1998, PBGC's single employer program had $17.6 billion in assets, against 12.6 billion in current liabilities. However, PBGC notes exposure to likely future terminations of an added $20 billion. Should future government actions make it legal to shift to defined contribution plans but not to cash balance, and should this occur during a period of weak markets, PBGC could well see a flood of new terminations.

---

16 EBRI-ERF Pension Investment Report: 4th Quarter 1998 *(Washington, DC: Employee Benefit Research Institute, May 1999).*

17 *Jack VanDerhei, Russell Galer, Carol Quick, and John Rea, "401(k) Plan Asset Allocation, Account Balances, and Loan Activity,"* EBRI Issue Brief *no. 205 (Employee Benefit Research Institute, January 1999).*

18 *See Pension Benefit Corporation Annual Reports, online at www.pbgc.gov/ or in hard copy from PBGC. The most recent year is 1998.*

Meeting Changing Needs With Plan Design Changes

The sections above have highlighted, with numbers, the shift taking place in pension coverage, asset allocation, and relative levels of net contributions to plans. Further, the numbers show that the proportion of the work force covered by plans is not growing. They also show that IRAs are proving effective as portability devices. All of this is related to demographic changes in the American work force and in the general population that have influenced, and are likely to continue influencing, the provision and design of pension plans.

An Aging Population

One change in progress is the shift in the U.S. population's age distribution. Members of the large baby-boom cohort (individuals born between 1946 and 1964) currently constitute a disproportionately large part of the overall work force, especially in new and fast-growing industries. As this cohort ages, and the smaller baby-bust cohort (individuals born between 1964 and 1975) enters the labor force, the age distribution of the work force will shift toward older workers, whose needs and preferences may differ from those of younger workers. As the baby-boom cohort begins to retire, an increasing proportion of Americans will be elderly and living longer and will depend on sources other than employment for income and vital services. These forces will affect both income security and health care insurance programs.

Developments in the retirement plan market represent a response to work force changes. There is now a large body of literature that uses government data to show that the work force has always had high turnover and that few workers have spent 25 years or more with one employer. This is true not only for the private sector but for the public sector as well. Defined contribution plans provide a career average benefit, as noted above, which serves to deliver more to most workers (due to relatively short service) than defined benefit plans. For the employer, they provide a known cost that can be budgeted. The defined benefit cash balance plan does the same, while giving the participant less investment risk. Both plans provide lump-sum distributions, which are more popular with workers. They are portable, and they eliminate any risk related to a former employer going out of business or running off with the money.

What Income Do Plans Provide?

Worth Magazine ran a cover in 1996 with the words: Why Retire? The accompanying article gave all the reasons that a person might not want to retire, considering future prospects of longer life, better health, better medical care, and multiple careers. Many other publications have published stories with similar themes, such as: Will you be able to afford to retire? Will you retire in poverty? Why you aren't saving enough? The end of retirement! These articles often tend to cast a negative light on the future and to paint the past as a time when all achieved the great American Retirement Dream with little effort.

The American work force, viewed from an income perspective, is a pyramid: there is only one Bill Gates at the point, but there are more than 25 million individuals below the poverty level, creating a very wide pyramid base. The population, ranked by assets, shows a similar configuration: 3.5 million households have net worth of $1 million or more–3.5 percent of households, compared with a pyramid base of more than 60 percent who effectively have a net worth of zero at best, or negative. While savings would be desirable for those in this 60 percent of the pyramid, they have never been savers. This shows up with retirees today.

Contrary to the picture often painted by the popular media, most of today's retirees did not prepare for retirement. The 1999 Retirement Confidence Survey conducted by the Employee Benefit Research Institute found that just under one-third of current retirees had done any financial or life planning prior to retirement. Among workers, 32 percent report having done nothing to date, and less than one-half of these consider what they have done to be adequate.

Census data do tell us that today's retirees are well off financially compared with earlier retirees; however, the media picture of a generation of retirees on golf courses and cruise ships represents a telescope focused on the tip of the iceberg. Fully 80 percent of retiree households today have total income of less than $23,000 per year. For the top 25 percent, nearly one-quarter of income still comes from Social Security; 25 percent from working; 25 percent from savings; and a final 25 percent from employment-based pensions. These income data underscore a critical fact: current retirees who are in the top 20 percent income bracket depend on continued work after age 65, as well as personal savings and an employer plan. The contention by some that what will be "different" for the baby-boom and x generations is work after age 65 ignores the fact work is already essential for millions of retirees in order to have a "decent" income. What is true for current retirees will be true for future retirees. Social Security alone does not provide an adequate income by any standard other than a high replacement rate for some. Is 120 percent of $5,000, or a below poverty floor, an adequate income?

Retirement Planning Is Needed Throughout the Pyramid

A 1996 survey by the National Endowment for Financial Education found that the financial planner's average client has median net worth of $400,000, median annual gross income of $75,000, and median annual discretionary income of $10,000. In other words, these individuals are near the top of the pyramid. Yet many financial planners report that that these clients have difficulty saving enough to meet retirement income goals, for various reasons. The top two barriers to saving reported by planners were (1) procrastination and (2) confusion over how to begin planning for retirement. Behind these were (3) lack of information or awareness, (4) poor cash management, (5) paying off debt, and (6) college education funding. A 1999 report by Fidelity Investments found that, among 401(k) participants, fewer than 10 percent were very confident that they would be economically prepared for retirement. And these are the haves! For the population at large, the 1999 Retirement Confidence Survey found similar barriers, but one-third of respondents to this survey said they simply did not have any money they could save; one-third said that they did not have enough to save regularly, and one-third reported saving regularly.

The planners' survey found that clients generally expected to have the same standard of living during retirement as they had while working, not better or worse. The Retirement Confidence Survey found that 18 percent expected better, 20 percent expected less, and 62 percent expected about the same. Social Security was expected to be the primary source of income.

The public does not feel prepared financially for retirement, although most planners think that the average client is prepared. The fact that these clients already have high net worth probably makes this inevitable. Why doesn't the baby boomer save more today? A series of surveys have revealed with common findings on barriers: funding education costs, personal debt, the potential for job loss and downsizing, and meeting daily living expenses. Fully 25 percent of workers state simply that they will live for today, each day, will worry about retirement income should retirement ever happen. Retirees give the same reasons for not having saved more for retirement, according to the survey.

For retirees, relatively new concerns include meeting health care costs, the prospect of long-term care costs, and outliving their assets and income sources. These retiree concerns provide a partial list of items that should be more heavily stressed to workers today. Clearly, in the new millennium they will have to be emphasized, as the prospects for longer life make savings and retirement planning action all the more essential.

Retirement Planning in the New Millennium Will Be Easier

Several factors combine to promise better retirement planning, across the pyramid, in the new millennium:

- Savings education is now beginning in K through 12.
- Debt management is receiving regular attention.
- Medical miracles and life extension are around us every day as reminders.
- Technology makes it easier and easier to build the information needed for planning and to do it.
- The infrastructure of organizations, individuals, and technology to facilitate planning is growing rapidly.
- The Internet makes retirement planning possible for everyone.

Planners Can Help Bring Discipline to the Individual Process

Technology can make implementation easy. Many vendors are offering inexpensive bookkeeping programs that allow constant generation of income statements, balance sheets, and projections, making it easy for individuals to determine possible retirement budgets. Books and guides, in print and on-line, provide the reasons to plan and explain the major steps required to determine an individual's retirement standard of living in terms of income, medical and other insurance protection, and estate planning. These materials can also help individuals to plan a retirement budget, with full consideration of the consequences of inflation; the importance of timing throughout one's life, i.e., the value of starting to save and plan while young versus the burden of waiting; and the necessity for a bridge job and continued employment for those who have waited too long versus the possible pleasures of early retirement for those who have started early.

The ability to get detailed information on income sources is a button or phone call away. Social Security currently will send a report on accrued benefits on request, and soon will send annual statements to all workers. Participants in defined contribution plans now receive quarterly statements, but in the new millennium most participants will be able to get the information on-line anytime. The biggest planning job will be to determine all of an individual's retirement earnings as he or she moved from job to job. Even defined benefit plans are getting better at providing regular information as a result of both the legal requirements and employers' and unions' desire to have the plans appreciated.

■ Can We Return to "The Way We Were?"

Writing prior to the enactment of ERISA, one leading actuary noted:

> A defined benefit final pay pension plan may be selected precisely because it is the only type of plan which permits the employer to design a pension formula that takes both sources of retirement income—Social Security and company benefits—into account. By doing so, a firm can provide higher paid employees a proportionately greater company pension. This compensates for the fact that these individuals receive a lower percentage of final earnings from Social Security."[19] ... Such a plan may also be necessary to reward an employee whose salary has increased rapidly or whose service was relatively short. Additionally, only a pension can reward past as well as future service and base the total benefit on final average pay. Finally, some companies believe that they are better able to assume investment risk...... The corporate viewpoint on the defined benefit versus defined contribution issue is formed by various competing factors: (1) whether its financial position can sustain the economic uncertainties posed by a defined benefit plan; (2) the extent to which competitive factors determine benefit levels and types; and (3) the corporation's perception of its responsibility to provide for employees' retirement and other financial needs.

What this attorney highlighted in this pre-ERISA discussion remains accurate today. What has changed is the regulatory environment, the work force, world economics, technology, and feelings of security. Taken together, they suggest that we will not return to the design dominance of yesterday, regardless of the economic security consequences. Or, perhaps because of them.

■ How 25 Years Have Changed Demands/Motivations for Retirement Plans[20]

The government does influence action, and ERISA changed the drivers of design in a number of ways:

---

19 *Robert B. Peters, "Defined Benefit and Defined Contribution Plans: A Corporate Perspective," in Dallas L. Salisbury, ed.,* Economic Survival in Retirement: Which Pension Is for You? *(Washington, DC: Employee Benefit Research Institute, 1982).*

20 *See Daniel M. Holland,* Private Pension Funds: Projected Growth *(Cambridge, MA: National Bureau of Economic Research; 1996); Daniel M. Holland,* Private Pensions and the Public Interest *(Washington,*

- From a no vesting minimum standard to immediate vesting in some cases;
- From asset use in a plan for building the firm to arms-length transactions;
- From clear "capital accumulation" to "retirement plan" distinctions, to limited distinctions;
- From selective provision of lump sums allowed to an "all or none" requirement;
- From less government tax revenue from lump sums to greater government tax revenue from lump sums;
- From a retirement income focus to a cash portability focus;
- From regulatory and tax incentive bias toward defined benefit plans to a strong regulatory and tax incentive bias toward defined contribution plans;
- From a clear emphasis on employer/union provision advantages to an increased focus on individual self-determination and "retail delivery"; and
- From a paternalistic assessment basis of social obligation and corporate identification to one of maximum satisfaction of the largest number of workers.

As one expert has put it, the movement from "golden handcuffs" to an employee/employer contract of partnership, personal accountability, and self-reliance moved the nation away from traditional defined benefit, employer-pay-all plans focused on encouraging an employee to remain with a single employer until "normal retirement age" and toward greater financial and psychological independence and identification with the service firm versus the employer.[21]

Plan design and recruitment activity have moved:

- From broad based attraction to key employee attraction;
- From delivery of fast vested matches in short-term savings programs to vested matches for long-term savings programs;
- From delivery of final pay annuities to long-term workers to smaller accumulations for all workers and a focus on lump-sum distributions[22], and
- From employers, unions and plans bearing the burden of long-term risks (investment, inflation, mortality) to transferring these risks to individuals and families.

Major employers and unions have always provided pension coverage similar to the coverage that is available today. More than 95 percent of pension plan participants are in large employer settings. Most large employers with 401(k) plans now use employer stock in the plans; some of the largest unions have negotiated stock ownership or outright employee ownership. As one senior executive put it in 1998: "Employee ownership allows the corporation to build partnership and a high performance work culture."[23] As another executive notes:

> While income security is an issue, it is increasingly being recognized that long-term security can best be achieved through personal development and professional growth. Ironically, the presence of high-cost '1950s, one-size-fits-all benefits' may, in fact, be a precursor to job insecurity as cost-cutting measures may be necessary for an organization to carry this heavy burden. There is a general question of whose responsibility it is to provide retirement income. There is increasing emphasis today on the notion that it is up to individuals to

---

DC: American Enterprise Institute, 1970); Norman B. Ture with Barbara A. Fields, The Future of Private Pension Plans *(Washington, DC: American Enterprise Institute, 1994); Dallas L. Salisbury and Nora Super Jones, eds.,* Pension Funding and Taxation: Implications for Tomorrow *(Washington, DC: Employee Benefit Research Institute, 1994); and Dallas L. Salisbury, ed.,* When Workers Call the Shots: Can They Achieve Retirement Security? *(Washington, DC: Employee Benefit Research Institute, 1995).*

[21] *See Charles G. Tharp, "Yes," in Dallas L. Salisbury, ed.,* Do Employers/Employees Still Need Employee Benefits ? *(Washington, DC: Employee Benefit Research Institute, 1995).*

[22] *Steven G. Vernon,* Employee Benefits: Valuation, Analysis and Strategies *(New York: John Wiley & Sons, Inc., 1993).*

[23] *See Charles G. Tharp, "Yes," in Dallas L. Salisbury, ed.,* Do Employers/Employees Still Need Employee Benefits ? *(Washington, DC: Employee Benefit Research Institute, 1998).*

provide a greater portion of their own retirement security.

For at least the decade ahead, such views are likely to dominate pension decision-making. Many of these views are now entering the debate over the future of Social Security, and many of same pressures and attitudes reviewed in this article can be found in that debate. In short, whatever what one would like the pension world of the future to be from a normative perspective, this descriptive review suggests that it will look more like the pension world of the 1990s than that of the 1970s.

2

Society, Values, and Retirement Programs

by Robert Birnbaum, Credit Suisse Asset Management

Introduction

I am a baby-boomer—a typical member of that demographic bulge, sometimes described as the "pig in the python," which has, for better or worse, greatly influenced our country's economic and social fabric. Thinking about the next 25 years of ERISA, and implications for retirement security, brought me to the somewhat startling realization that in 25 years—the year 2025—*I* will be among the retired. In this discussion, rather than considering issues of income adequacy and actuarial soundness, important as these are, I'd like to focus on people: who am I—and who is my generation—going to be in 2025?

William Gibson wrote, "The future is available now, it is just not evenly distributed." What do we know *today* about the people that we are going to be in the year 2025? What is the psychological and physiological environment that we are going to be operating in? How does the very meaning of "retirement security" change? What cultural changes can we look forward to? How will financial institutions adapt?

It turns out that we actually know less about the aged than we think we do. There is a lack of good information about the developmental, psychological, and social needs of the old. We can empathize with children because we have been young, and we remember some of what happened to us when we were young and we even remember some of what we felt. But there is really not much in our experiences that help us understand the old.[1] That lack of understanding will grow to be a cultural divide.

The Future Is Today

The wave of change is upon us now. James Atlas wrote in *The New Yorker* that soon, for the first time in history, many middle-aged people (which today are roughly synonymous with the baby-boom generation) will have more living parents than they do children.

The Federal Highway Administration predicts that by the year 2020, the number of drivers age 65 and older will account for 20 percent of the drivers on the road. This was reported in The *New York Times* in an article explaining why new road signs are going to be popping up all over New York State with large letters so that people could see them.[2] It brings to mind the phrase, "a nation of Florida's," used by demographers. That proportion—20 percent of the population over age 65—is the *current* proportion of the population of Florida that is over age 65. One more element of the future that is available to us now.

The Environment of the Old

Mae Sartner wrote, "The trouble is that old age is not very interesting until one gets there." It is a foreign country with an unknown language to the young and even to the middle-aged.[3]

Old age is often viewed as a single stage of life, but nowhere else in life does a single stage provide so inadequate a description. People over age 65 can be divided into at least three life stages. The young old, which is 65 to 75 or so, the old old, which is 75 to 90 or so, and the very old. And to compare somebody who is 95 to somebody who is 65

---

[1] *Pipher (1999), p. 48.*

[2] New York Times, *Nov. 16, 1999, p. B 27.*

[3] *Pipher (1999), p. 15.*

is not unlike comparing somebody who is five years old to somebody who is 35 years old.[4]

Older people live in a world designed for young people, and that is true in the financial world as well. In the physical world, they can't drive and they can't walk through shopping malls or airports. They can't deal with rushed doctors in a managed care environment. The environment under which older people have to make decisions is one that does not suit them very well.

Their psychological environment can in part be described as making decisions under conditions of despair and stress. Eric Erickson described old age as a stage of life in which the individual must try to balance their sense of ego integrity with a sense of despair.[5] People are reviewing their lives. It is very hard to find a person who can look back and not feel some sense of despair or some sense of disappointment with what has happened in their lives. So despair is a key part of what older people go through.

Mary Pipher is more emphatic. She suggests that we should think of the more vulnerable elderly as victims of chronic post-traumatic stress disorder. That is, they have experienced so many losses that they are "ordinary healthy people for whom all hell has broken loose." The old don't suddenly develop bad personalities, they are overwhelmed by events.[6]

How Will Cultural Values Change?

As people get older, the balance between autonomy and dependency shifts. This has many cultural implications. In mainstream psychology, healthy development has been conceptualized as a process of basically increasing autonomy and independence. (Speaking as one who has done a lot of work in 401(k) plan participant communications, autonomy and independence are constant themes. This is one of the reasons that people like 401(k) plans and online trading—they appeal to these cultural values of autonomy and independence.) Dependency has become something that is perceived as weak and shameful.

Many of us can recognize this view of dependency from our own family situations. Closeness is frequently regarded with suspicion and enmeshment. Obligations become resentment and requests for care are labeled as attempts to control. Mary Pipher cites this change in the meaning of dependency to a shameful condition as the factor that turns "elders into the elderly." They don't want to be dependent, and the young don't want to be sucked in.[7]

It's important to realize that cultural values are more temporary than most of us recognize. This is not to idealize our time or any other particular time. But over the course of this century, the relative values of dependence and autonomy have been completely reversed.

Richard Lowe cited a study that was done in Muncie, Indiana, in 1924. Parents were asked what quality they most desired in their children. At the top of the list were obedience and conformity. In 1974, the same question was asked and the list was exactly reversed. What modern parents most desired for their children were autonomy and independence.[8]

Anthropologists suggest that very deep economic and demographic forces drive some cultural values. I think we can speculate that, as the baby boomers have shown a powerful ability to shape cultural values to fit the needs of our generation, we can look forward to a time when dependence or perhaps interdependence acquires higher cultural value.

Loneliness is also a factor in dependency. And in the financial world, loneliness has implications on the negative side for potential for fraud and exploitation, and perhaps on the positive side regarding potential good institutional responses.

Loneliness is a dependency issue because obviously older people like to talk, like anybody else. People depend on their own family—that is who they can talk to. For older people, their choice is often limited to their adult children. But because they don't want to be a burden, they will frequently retreat into silence and loneliness, and so loneliness becomes a dependency issue as well. [9] And, for

[4] *Schaie and Willis (1996), p. 81.*

[5] *Schaie and Willis, (1996) p. 82.*

[6] *Pipher (1999), p. 182.*

[7] *Pipher (1999), p. 78.*

[8] *Pipher (1999), p. 79.*

[9] *Schaie and Willis (1996), p. 91.*

some, this form of dependency will cause them to seek new communities.

Mary Pipher writes:

> One of the cruel ironies of old-old age is that often when people suffer losses they must search for new friends and new homes. It's a horrible time to try to solve problems with a geographical. Yet moves cannot be avoided. . .the search for a home is made more frightening by our deep cultural mistrust of institutions for the aged. [10]

In fact, if we look again to see how the present can tell us about the future, consider the new long-term care communities and institutions—the places where sometimes people are driven during this search for a new home. Some of us are familiar with those because we have parents living in them, or considering them. In financial terms, these are actually quite extraordinary. To enter a facility, you "buy-in." You might buy in for several hundred thousand dollars and then you are guaranteed a place for life. Remarkably, what you have done is made an unsecured loan to a developer. And sometimes these places do go bankrupt and the people who bought-in are left with nothing. Is this the course of action that many of us would take, were we not operating under conditions of stress and despair?

Basically, financial institutions know how to solve the problem of credit risk described above—there are many ways to do so, but they haven't been applied yet to this population where security is so important. "Old people, in a sense, are like people who live next to a nuclear plant; chances are that nothing will happen, but if something goes wrong, it's a disaster."[11]

Are there examples of the future which exist today, which might give us insight into cultures which favor the old? In other societies, it is not until quite late in life that positions of power and authority are attained.

> A society ruled by the old is called a gerontocracy. Gerontocrats acquire power in a variety of ways, in agricultural and pastoral societies. Although the US is far more complex than pastoral or primitive societies, elite families apparently control power in ways that resemble those used in clans in tribal societies. Senior family members typically control decisions about economic resources, determining to which of the younger family members or others they wish to grant power. Many members of the US Congress live to an advanced age, and perhaps it is not surprising that Congress has a seniority system that increases the power of older members. This system is not at all unlike the power systems found in primitive societies. It should be noted, however, that the existence of a gerontocracry does not necessarily ensure the well being of older people in general. Government by the old is not necessarily government for the old.[12]

Looking for cultural values in the long sweep of history, we recall that, although many baby boomers tend to value themselves based on how much they can do for their children, the Ten Commandments decree, "Honor thy father and thy mother." Indeed, for the religions based upon that tradition, the obligations of children to their parents far outweigh the obligations of parents to their children. Could that view become part of popular culture as well?

Reconfiguring Values and Institutions

In considering the coming cultural changes, and the potential institutional responses, let me suggest four areas to watch.

First, how much can we hope for from technology? That is, if loneliness and isolation are two of the key factors behind dependency, can technology actually provide more of the connectivity and community that people crave, in a way that is truly responsive to the underlying need?

Second is the increasing emphasis on financial advice and guidance. Right now, these systems are not designed for people living in the "foreign country" of the elderly. Can systems emerge that will help people make better decisions under conditions of stress and despair?

Third, will new cultural values come into

---

[10] *Pipher (1999), pp. 30–31.*

[11] *Schaie and Willis (1996), p. 85.*

[12] *Schaie and Willis (1996), p. 99.*

vogue that are perhaps better suited to the stage of life that baby boomers will find themselves in? Will dependency become more socially desirable?

Fourth, what new financial structures will emerge that are responsive to these other trends? Many of the financial building blocks, of course, are here already, so that individuals can move from direct market exposure to more protected structures, like annuitization and so on. But the fit isn't necessarily right and the complexity is high, and I am certain new innovations will occur.

Bibliography

K. Warner Schaie and Sherry L. Willis. *Adult Development and Aging*. New York: Harper Collins College Publishers, 1996).

Mary Pipher. Another Country: Navigating the Emotional Terrain of Our Elders. New York: Riverhead Books, 1999.

3

Overview of the U.S. Employment-Based Retirement Income System

by Paul Yakoboski, EBRI

The retirement income system in the United States is a dynamic, continually evolving structure. It looks very different today than it did 25 years ago at the passage of the Employee Retirement Income Security Act (ERISA), and it will surely look very different 25 years from now on the 50th anniversary of ERISA. This paper provides background on the voluntary, employment-based retirement income security system in the United States and an overview of ERISA, the 1974 federal law that governs the operation of private retirement plans in the nation. The article also examines worker coverage and participation in retirement plans, as well as the typical features of plans today. The appendix contains a history of retirement plan legislation.

The Employee Retirement Income Security Act of 1974 (ERISA)

President Gerald Ford signed the Employee Retirement Income Security Act (ERISA) into law on Labor Day, September 2, 1974. The crafting and passage of ERISA has a long history. President John F. Kennedy appointed a cabinet-level committee in 1962 to study private pension plans. In releasing its report, the committee concluded "that private pension plans should continue as a major element in the nation's total retirement security program. Their strength rests on the supplementation they can provide to the basic public system." But the committee also noted that the pension system was inadequate in certain areas, such as participant rights, funding, benefit protection, and oversight. The report led to investigations by various congressional committees that spanned nearly 10 years.

During its examinations, Congress found that most plans were operated for the benefit of participants and beneficiaries, but that a small number were not. Congress determined that participants generally received insufficient information about their benefit plans and that there was inadequate protection of their rights.

In designing ERISA, Congress wanted to address these problems but at the same time promote "a renewed expansion of private retirement plans" and increase the number of participants receiving benefits in the voluntary employment-based system. ERISA established standards that employee benefit plans must follow to obtain and maintain their tax-favored status, such as standards for reporting and disclosure, funding, fiscal responsibility, and employee eligibility and vesting. ERISA set up a new government agency to insure most vested benefits against plan termination and established contribution and benefit limits for retirement plans. Although the "R" in ERISA and most of the law's provisions refer to "retirement," during final deliberations over the legislation Congress also included provisions affecting employment-based health benefits as well.

The U.S. Departments of Labor (DOL) and the Treasury have primary responsibility for administering ERISA. DOL has primary jurisdiction over reporting, disclosure, and fiduciary matters, while the Treasury Department has primary jurisdiction over eligibility, vesting, and funding. The Pension Benefit Guaranty Corporation (PBGC), a federal agency, administers the plan termination insurance program.

ERISA's standards are set out in four titles to the act: Title I—Reporting, Disclosure, and Minimum Standards Administered by the Labor Department; Title II—Minimum Standards Administered by the Treasury Department (Internal Revenue Code provisions); Title III—Jurisdiction and Administration; and Title IV—Plan Termination Insurance.

Reporting and Disclosure

Employee benefit plan sponsors subject to ERISA are required to provide summary plan descriptions (SPDs) to plan participants and beneficiaries. The summary must be written so that the average participant can understand it, and must be accurate and detailed enough to reasonably inform participants and beneficiaries of their rights and obligations.

While the law does not dictate the exact form the SPD should take, it does require inclusion of specific information. For example, among other things, an SPD must include:

- Name and address of the employer or employee organization maintaining the plan.
- Name and/or title and business address of each trustee.
- Plan requirements for participation and benefit accrual eligibility.
- A description of provisions for nonforfeitable pension benefits.
- Information regarding credited service and breaks in service.
- A description of situations that may result in disqualification, denial, loss, or forfeiture of benefits.

In addition to the SPD, each participant and beneficiary must have access to financial information about the plan. This information is provided in summary form (summary annual report), drawn from a more extensive annual report (Form 5500 series) filed with the Internal Revenue Service (IRS). Such information is intended to give participants and beneficiaries an awareness of the plan's financial status. (The full annual report, which IRS sends to DOL, includes detailed information on the number of plan participants; plan benefit obligations; distributions made to participants and beneficiaries; financial, actuarial, and insurance data; and the amount and nature of the plan's assets. Participants may obtain the full report from DOL.)

Participants are also entitled to see other documents relating to the plan (e.g., insurance contracts, trustee reports, etc.). Once a year, participants and beneficiaries may request a written statement of accrued and vested benefits. A plan participant who terminates service with vested benefits that are not paid at that time must be given a statement showing the amount of accrued and vested benefits.

Other reports must be filed when certain events occur. DOL, for example, must be notified when a new plan is established (through the SPD) or when an existing plan is revised (through the Summary of Material Modifications). PBGC must be notified when private defined benefit plans are terminated.

Fiduciary Requirements

Employers who sponsored retirement plans before ERISA was enacted were subject to one general fiduciary standard: Plans had to be operated for the exclusive benefit of participants and beneficiaries. ERISA expanded this principle. Fiduciaries are broadly defined as those who exercise control or discretion in managing plan assets; those who render investment advice to the plan for direct or indirect compensation or have authority to do so; and those who have discretionary authority in administering the plan.

In fulfilling their responsibilities, fiduciaries must act in the exclusive interest of plan participants and plan beneficiaries, diversify the plan's assets to minimize risk of large losses, and act in accordance with documents that govern the plan.

Fiduciaries must act with the care, skill, prudence, and diligence under the circumstances then prevailing that a "prudent man" acting in a like capacity and familiar with such matters would use in the conduct of an enterprise of a like character and with like aims. This standard is frequently referred to as ERISA's "prudent man" rule. Because the performance standard is so high, the prudent man rule is often referred to as the "prudent expert" rule.

Fiduciaries must meet this test in performing any aspect of plan operation for which they are responsible—from selecting the individual or institution that will handle plan asset investments to setting investment objectives.

■ Minimum Standards and Other Qualified Plan Rules

ERISA also sets specific standards for eligibility, coverage, participation, vesting, benefit accrual, and funding of retirement plans. Most of these represent minimum requirements (thus the term *minimum standards*); employers may adopt plans with more liberal standards.

General Eligibility

A pension plan may require that an employee meet an age and service requirement before becoming eligible for participation. However, the employer cannot require the employee to be over age 21 or to have completed more than one year of service with the employer, typically defined as at least 1,000 hours of work, in a 12-month period.[1]

Coverage and Participation

An employer has some flexibility in determining who will be covered under the pension plan(s). For example, employee groups may be defined on the basis of pay (hourly vs. salaried), job location, or unionization. An employer may have one plan covering all these types of groups (and others), or separate plans for each. However, tax-qualified plan(s) must generally satisfy a set of nondiscrimination rules (under Internal Revenue Code Sec. 401(a)(4), 410(b), and, in some cases, 401(a)(26)), which are designed to ensure that the plan arrangement does not discriminate in favor of highly compensated employees[2] in coverage, participation, and benefits provided.[3]

Vesting

Participants generally attain nonforfeitable and nonrevocable—vested—rights to pension benefits after satisfying specific service (or years of participation) or age and service requirements. Once vested, an employee's rights generally cannot be revoked. ERISA requires a plan to adopt vesting standards for the employee's benefit (the account balance under a defined contribution plan or the accrued benefit under a defined benefit plan) at least as liberal as one of the following two schedules: full vesting (100 percent) after five years of participation in the plan (with no vesting prior to that time, known as "cliff vesting") or graded (gradual) vesting of 20 percent after three years of service and an additional 20 percent after each subsequent year of service until 100 percent vesting is reached at the end of seven years of service. These rules apply to benefits attributable to employer contributions to a single-employer pension plan. Benefits attributable to employee contributions to either defined contribution or defined benefit plans and investment income earned on employee contributions to defined contribution plans are immediately vested.[4]

Multiemployer plans, which cover the workers of two or more unrelated companies under a collective bargaining agreement, currently may use a 10-year cliff vesting schedule. This schedule means that employees do not attain vested rights to benefits attributable to employer contributions until they have completed 10 years of service, at which point they become 100 percent vested. However, effective for plan years beginning on or after the earlier of (1) January 1, 1997, or expiration of the collective bargaining agreement under which the plan is maintained, whichever is later; or (2) January 1, 1999, multiemployer plans will be subject to these same vesting rules as other qualified plans. Multiemployer plans may provide for cancellation of part of a vested benefit when the participant's employer withdraws.

---

[1] *An exception applies to plans with immediate vesting; such plans may require completion of up to two years of service.*

[2] *For discussion of what constitutes a highly compensated employee, see chapter 4 of* Fundamentals of Employee Benefit Programs, *5th edition (Washington, DC: Employee Benefit Research Institute, 1997).*

[3] *For more information on coverage and participation requirements, see chapter 12 of* Fundamentals of Employee Benefit Programs, *5th edition (Washington, DC: Employee Benefit Research Institute, 1997).*

[4] *Full vesting must also occur when a participant reaches the plan's normal retirement age (commonly age 65, but sometimes earlier) or (to the extent the benefit is then funded) if the plan is terminated; some plans provide for it on early retirement, death, or disability.*

Form of Benefit Payment

ERISA requires retirement plans that offer an annuity as a payment option to provide a qualified joint and survivor (J&S) annuity for married participants as the normal method of benefit payment. This provides the surviving spouse with a lifetime monthly income equal to at least one-half the amount of the employee's benefit. To pay for this protection, the employee's benefit usually is reduced. In order to select a pension paid over the duration of the participant's life only (or any other payment form), both the participant and the spouse must refuse the J&S option in writing. The J&S need not be provided unless the participant has been married at least one year.[5]

Benefit Accrual

ERISA requires that plans use one of three alternative formulas to determine the minimum speed at which defined benefit pension benefits accrue to participants. In general, benefit amounts in a defined benefit plan accrue over the period of an employee's plan participation, but they do not have to accrue evenly over that time. The law focuses only on the rate of benefit accrual, generally forbidding benefits to accrue disproportionately at the end of an employee's career; it does not mandate any specific benefit levels. However, benefit accruals may not be reduced or discontinued because of age. Thus, employees who work beyond normal retirement age will continue to receive credit for time worked and contributions made to their plan, but the employer is allowed to restrict the number of years of benefit accrual.

Funding

Assets in qualified pension plans must be kept separate from the employer's general assets. A plan may be maintained through one of a number of vehicles. One method is to establish a trust agreement with a bank or similar financial institution. A plan may also be maintained with an insurance company through allocated or unallocated accounts. Pension plans may also be maintained through individual policies issued on each participant's life. Sometimes both arrangements are used.

To ensure that pension plans have sufficient assets to pay benefits when participants retire, ERISA established minimum funding standards for defined benefit and some defined contribution plans. Money purchase and target benefit plans are covered under these requirements, but profit-sharing, stock bonus, or most employee stock ownership plans are not. For money purchase and target benefit plans, the minimum contribution is the amount set out in the plan formula. Single-employer defined benefit plans must make at least a minimum contribution equal to the normal cost of the plan plus amounts necessary to amortize in equal installments any unfunded past service liabilities, any experience gains or losses, any waived funding deficiencies, any changes in actuarial assumptions, and other items.[6]

There are also maximum funding limits on tax-deductible contributions, and there is a 10 percent excise tax on nondeductible employer contributions. The funding rules for multiemployer plans are somewhat different from those for single-employer plans.

Contributions and Benefits

ERISA also sets maximum limits on annual contributions and benefits that qualified retirement plans may provide for each participant. The limits are known as Sec. 415 limits, referring to the Internal Revenue Code (IRC) section that defines

---

[5] *Most plans must also provide preretirement survivor benefits to the spouse of a vested participant who dies before retirement. The benefit is payable in the form of an annuity for the life of the surviving spouse beginning at what would have been the employee' normal retirement date or, at the election of the surviving spouse, as early as the employee' earliest retirement date or death, whichever is later. (Profit-sharing plans generally do not have to comply with spousal provisions, if the surviving spouse is the beneficiary.) Unless both spouses waive this benefit option in writing, these benefits will be provided to the surviving spouse even if the participant had named someone else as his or her heir.*

[6] *The normal cost equals the cost of pension benefits earned that year and administrative costs. Past service liabilities occur when credit for an employee's past service prior to the inception of the plan is granted. Experience gains or losses result from changes in actuarial assumptions or methods.*

them. There are separate limits for defined benefit and defined contribution plans.[7]

Plan Termination Insurance

Title IV of ERISA established the Pension Benefit Guaranty Corporation (PBGC) to insure payment of certain pension plan benefits in the event a covered (i.e., private-sector defined benefit) plan terminates with insufficient funds to pay the benefits. Covered plans or their sponsors must pay annual premiums to PBGC to provide funds from which guaranteed benefits can be paid. Both single-employer and multiemployer plans are covered under Title IV, but under separate insurance programs.[8]

ERISA originally set the premium for single-employer plans at $1 per plan participant per year. PBGC premium rates, which must be legislated by Congress, have been increased a number of times over the years, and the Omnibus Budget Reconciliation Act of 1987 (OBRA '87) not only increased the premium but significantly changed the premium structure for single-employer pension plans. Certain provisions of OBRA '87, also known as the Pension Protection Act, raised the base premium to $16 per participant. In addition, for plans with more than 100 participants, a variable-rate premium of $6 was imposed for each $1,000 of unfunded vested benefits, rising to a maximum total premium of $50 per participant per year.

The Omnibus Budget Reconciliation Act of 1989 (OBRA '89) made further modifications. For plan years beginning after 1990, the single-employer flat-rate per-participant premium was increased to $19. The additional premium required of underfunded plans was increased to $9 per $1,000 of unfunded vested benefits, rising to a maximum additional premium of $53 per participant per year. The Retirement Protection Act of 1994 will gradually eliminate this cap.

Multiemployer premium rates, originally set at $0.50 per plan participant per year, were raised by the 1980 Multiemployer Pension Plan Amendments Act (MPPAA) to $1.40, with scheduled increases reaching $2.60 in 1989.

Termination Policy

Voluntary terminations of single-employer plans are restricted to two types: a standard termination and a distress termination.[9] A standard termination is permitted only if the plan has sufficient assets to pay all of the plan's benefit liabilities. The term *benefit liabilities* is defined by IRS, although it is a key element in PBGC's insurance program.

Underfunded plans may only terminate in a distress situation, which is allowed only if the entire corporate (controlled) group would not be able to pay its debts pursuant to a plan of reorganization without the termination or would be unable to continue business outside the Chapter 11 reorganization process. A distress termination is only possible with the approval of the bankruptcy court or PBGC.

Covered Plans and Benefits

PBGC guarantees certain nonforfeitable retirement benefits, and any death, survivor, or disability benefit either owed or in payment status at plan termination, under defined benefit plans covered by Title IV should such a plan terminate. There are certain restrictions on the monthly benefit amount PBGC will pay.[10] In general, payment of guaranteed benefits is limited to a maximum dollar amount that is adjusted annually to reflect increases in workers' wages. In November 1999, the PBGC approved a 6 percent increase in the maxi-

---

[7] *For a description of these limits, see chapter 4 of* Fundamentals of Employee Benefit Programs, *5th edition (Washington, DC: Employee Benefit Research Institute, 1997).*

[8] *Coverage is mandatory if the employer is in interstate commerce or the plan has been determined to be qualified for tax-favored status. Certain plans are exempt, including defined contribution plans, government and church plans, plans established by fraternal societies to which no employer contributions are made, and plans established and maintained by a professional service employer with 25 or fewer participants in the plan.*

[9] *PBGC may, at its discretion, force a termination in certain situations. This is known as an involuntary termination.*

[10] *Insurance on new benefit provisions (i.e., benefits resulting from newly established plans or recent plan amendments) is phased in at 20 percent per year (or $20 per month if higher).*

mum monthly benefit, from $3,051 in 1999 to $3,221 in 2000. The new yearly maximum payment in 2000 will be $38,659.

For multiemployer plans, MPPAA established a level of guaranteed benefits that is much lower than single-employer plan benefit guarantees. No portion of a multiemployer plan benefit is guaranteed until it has been in effect for five years; the maximum amount guaranteed per year of service is 100 percent of the first $5 in monthly benefit rate plus 75 percent of the lesser of the next $15 of the accrual rate in excess of $5 (i.e., a maximum of $20 per month for each year of service, or $600 per month for a 30-year employee). For a multiemployer plan, the guarantee applies only at the point of plan insolvency.

Employer Liability to PBGC

If a plan terminates in a distress situation with insufficient assets to meet all benefit liabilities, the contributing plan sponsor and each member of the controlled group is jointly and severally liable to PBGC for the total amount of unfunded liabilities, plus interest on such liabilities from the termination date.

Different rules apply for multiemployer plans. MPPAA imposes liability, payable to the plan, on an employer for withdrawal from a multiemployer plan that is less than fully funded for vested benefits. Withdrawal liability is a legal obligation requiring an employer that discontinues or sharply reduces its contributions to a multiemployer plan to pay for its share of the plan's unfunded vested benefits. The employer must continue to make annual payments for 20 years or until the liability is satisfied, whichever occurs first.

Coverage, Participation, and Vesting

Pre-ERISA

Over the 30-year period leading up to ERISA, participation rates in employment-based retirement plans were growing. Participation rates in private employment-based retirement plans among nonagricultural wage and salary workers increased steadily over the period 1940 to 1974, rising from 14.6 percent to 46.5 percent (table 3.1). The number of workers participating in these plans rose from 4.1 million to 29.8 million over this time period.

Table 3.1
Private Retirement Plan Participation Trends, All Private Nonagricultural Wage and Salary Workers, Selected Years 1940–1974

	Total Workers (thousands)	Plan Participants (thousands)	Participation Rate (percentage)
1940	28,159	4,100	14.6%
1945	34,431	6,400	18.6
1950	39,170	9,800	25.0
1955	43,727	14,200	32.5
1960	45,836	18,700	40.8
1965	50,689	21,800	43.0
1970	58,325	26,100	44.7
1974	64,095	29,800	46.5

Source: Alfred Skolnik, "Private Pension Plans, 1950–1974," *Social Security Bulletin* (June 1976): 3–17; and U.S. Department of Labor, Bureau of Labor Statistics, *Employment and Earnings* (Washington, DC: U.S. Government Printing Office, March issues).

Post-ERISA

After a well-documented drop in the early and mid-1980s, retirement plan coverage and participation rates reversed direction or, at minimum, ceased their decline. According to EBRI tabulations of the Current Population Survey (CPS) employee benefit supplements, between 1988 and 1993 the pension coverage rate among all civilian workers ages 16 and over stayed flat, at 57 percent, while the total number of individuals working for an employer where a plan was sponsored increased from 65 million to 67 million (table 3.2).[11] The participa-

[11] Data for 1988 were tabulated under two methodologies to allow for comparability with earlier years' surveys. Workers who reported that their employer or union did not have a pension plan or retirement plan for any of its employees were not counted as working for an employer where a plan was sponsored in the first line of 1988 data reported in table 2 even if they did report that their employer offered a profit sharing plan or a stock plan in a follow up question. Additionally, participants who reported not being able to receive some benefits at retirement age if they were to leave the plan now were not counted as vested, even if they later responded that they could receive a lump sum distribution if their left their plan now. Data for 1988 reported above, and in the second line of 1988 data in table 3.2 includes these individuals.

Table 3.2

TRENDS IN RETIREMENT PLAN SPONSORSHIP, PARTICIPATION, AND VESTING AMONG CIVILIAN WORKERS AGES 16 AND OVER, 1979, 1983, 1988, 1993

	Workers (millions)	Covered Workers (millions)	Plan Participants (millions)	Vested Participants (millions)	Sponsorship Rate	Participation Rate	Vesting Rate
All Civilian Workers							
1979	95	53	44	23	56%	46%	24%
1983	99	52	43	24	52	43	24
1988[a]	114	62	47	32	55	42	28
1988[b]	114	65	49	38	57	43	34
1993	118	67	51	44	57	44	38
All Males							
1979	56	33	29	16	59	51	28
1983	56	30	26	16	54	47	28
1988[a]	63	35	28	20	55	45	31
1988[b]	63	36	29	23	58	46	36
1993	64	36	30	25	56	45	39
All Females							
1979	39	21	15	7	52	38	18
1983	43	21	16	8	50	38	20
1988[a]	51	27	19	13	54	38	25
1988[b]	51	29	20	15	57	40	30
1993	54	32	23	19	58	42	36
Nonagricultural Wage and Salary							
1979	85	52	42	21	61	50	25
1983	88	50	41	22	56	46	25
1988[a]	102	60	45	30	59	44	29
1988[b]	102	63	47	36	62	46	35
1993	106	66	50	43	62	47	40

Source: EBRI Tabulations of the May 1979, May 1983, May 1988 and April 1993 Current Population Survey employee benefit supplements.

[a]The fraction of workers whose employer or union sponsors a plan for any of the employees at the worker's place of employment.

[b]The fraction of workers participating in a plan among those whose employer or union sponsors a plan for any of the employees at the worker's place of employment.

[c]Workers who reported that their employer or union did not have a pension plan or retirement plan for any of its employees were not counted as working for an employer where a plan was sponsored, even if they reported that their employer offered a profit-sharing plan or a stock plan in a followup question. Participants who reported not being able to receive some benefits at retirement age if they were to leave the plan now were not counted as vested, even if they later responded that they could receive a lump-sum distribution if they left their plan now. This allows comparability with the tabulations from earlier years.

[d]Workers who reported that their employer or union did not have a pension plan or retirement plan for any of its employees were counted as working for an employer where a plan was sponsored if they reported that their employer offered a profit-sharing plan or a stock plan in a followup question. Participants who reported not being able to receive some benefits at retirement age if they were to leave the plan now were counted as vested if they later responded that they could receive a lump-sum distribution if they left their plan now. This allows comparability with the tabulations from 1993.

tion rate and vesting rates increased from 43 percent to 44 percent and from 34 percent to 38 percent, respectively.

The percentage of male workers working for an employer where a plan was sponsored decreased between 1988 and 1993, from 58 percent to 56 percent (table 3.2). Over the same period, the male participation rate fell from 46 percent to 45 percent, but the male vesting rate rose from 36 percent to 39 percent. Female coverage rates increased from 57 percent to 58 percent between 1988 and 1993. Over the same period, the female participation rate rose from 40 percent to 42 percent and the female vesting rate increased from 30 percent to 36 percent (table 3.2).

Although the overall increases between 1988 and 1993 are not always sizable, they are notable in view of the attention that was focused on the decline in retirement plan coverage and participation rates that occurred during the 1980s. Especially notable was the strong growth rate for females, a group that historically has received little income from employment-based retirement plans in their older years.

Recent Data

According to the Bureau of Labor Statistics (BLS), as of 1997, 71.6 percent of employees at medium and large private establishments (100 or more employees) participated in some form of employment-based retirement plan. A little over one-half (51.4 percent) of workers at these establishments participated in some form of defined contribution plan, and 44.6 percent participated in a defined benefit plan.

At small private establishments (fewer than 100 employees) in 1996, BLS found that 37.3 percent of workers participated in some form of retirement plan. Almost one-third (30.7 percent) of workers at small private establishments participated in some form of defined contribution, and 12.1 percent participated in a defined benefit plan.

These figures highlight an important point: While the voluntary retirement income system in the United States has been a success for workers at large employers, workers at small enterprises have not shared this success to the same degree. This matters, since small employers employ 38 percent of all workers in the nation. Why is plan sponsorship not higher among small employers given the attention that policymakers have devoted to the issue over time? Conventional wisdom holds that low plan sponsorship rates among small employers are driven by high administrative burden and cost placed on small employers. Findings from the 1999 Small Employer Retirement Survey (SERS) reveal that this view, while true for some small employers, is often too simplistic, and that the long-term solution to low coverage is not simply "building a better mousetrap" of new retirement programs. Plan nonsponsors responding to the survey report that employee-related reasons and revenue uncertainty are often more important reasons than red tape for not sponsoring a plan.

Nineteen percent of nonsponsors said that the most important reason for not offering a plan was that revenue is too uncertain to permit the company to commit to a plan. One-half (50 percent) of all nonsponsors said that this was a major reason they do not sponsor a plan.

Having a large portion of workers who are seasonal, part time, or high turnover was cited by 19 percent as the most important reason for not sponsoring a plan. An additional 17 percent said employee preferences for wages and/or other benefits was the most important reason. Therefore, 36 percent of those without retirement plans cited some sort of employee-related reason as the most important reason for not offering a plan.

Twelve percent said the most important reason was that it cost too much to set up and administer a plan. Ten percent said the most important reason was that required company contributions are too expensive;[12] for 3 percent, the most important reason was "too many government regulations." Therefore, 25 percent of nonsponsors cited a cost and/or administration-related reason as the most important reason for not offering a plan.

Private Plan Trends

Between 1975, when ERISA became effective, and 1995, the most recent year for which these data are available, the total number of private tax-qualified employer-sponsored plans more than doubled, from 311,000 to 693,000 (table 3.3). The total number of participants in these plans, including active workers, separated vested, survivors, and retirees rose from 45 million to 87 million over the same period. Data on active participants in private primary plans show similar trends. The number of active participants increased from 31 million in 1975 to 47 million in 1995. Total assets in private plans increased from $260 billion to $2.7 trillion over the same time period.

While the number of private employer-sponsored pension plans and plan participants has been increasing, proportionately fewer of these plans are defined benefit plans. An increasing number of employers have been offering primary and supplemental defined contribution plans as well as an array of hybrid plans. The total number of private defined benefit plans increased from 103,000 in 1975 to 175,000 in 1983, then decreased sharply to 69,000 in 1995. The total number of private defined contribution plans increased from

[12] *Plans exist in which employers as plan sponsors are not legally required to make contributions. For example, employer contributions are not required with a 401(k) plan—the sponsor could choose not to match participant contributions and to pass the administrative costs on to the plan. However, if the 401(k) is established as a SIMPLE plan, then company contributions are required.*

Table 3.3

PRIVATE PENSION PLANS AND PARTICIPANTS

SUMMARY OF PRIVATE-SECTOR QUALIFIED DEFINED BENEFIT AND DEFINED CONTRIBUTION PLANS AND PARTICIPANTS, SELECTED YEARS 1975–1995

	1975	1980	1981	1982	1983	1984	1985	1986	1987	1988	1989	1990	1991	1992	1993	1994	1995
	(thousands)																
Total Plans[a,b]	311	489	546	594	603	604	632	718	733	730	731	712	699	708	702	690	693
Defined benefit[a]	103	148	167	175	175	168	170	173	163	146	132	113	102	89	84	74	69
Defined contribution[a]	208	341	378	419	428	436	462	545	570	584	599	599	598	620	619	616	624
Defined contribution as percentage of total	67%	70%	69%	71%	71%	72%	73%	76%	78%	80%	82%	84%	85%	87%	88%	89%	90%
	(millions)																
Total Participants[b,c]	45	58	61	63	69	74	75	77	78	78	76	77	78	82	84	85	87
Defined benefit[c]	33	38	39	39	40	41	40	40	40	41	40	39	39	40	40	40	40
Defined contribution[c]	12	20	22	25	29	33	35	37	38	37	36	38	39	42	44	45	48
Defined contribution as percentage of total	26%	34%	36%	39%	42%	45%	47%	48%	49%	48%	48%	50%	50%	52%	52%	53%	55%
Active Participants	31	36	37	37	39	40	40	41	42	42	43	42	43	45	45	46	47
Primary plan is defined benefit[d]	27	30	30	29	30	30	29	29	28	28	27	26	26	25	25	25	24
Primary plan is defined contribution[d]	4	6	7	8	9	10	12	13	13	14	15	16	17	19	19	21	23
Defined Contrbution as percentage of total	13%	16%	19%	22%	23%	25%	30%	32%	31%	33%	35%	38%	40%	42%	42%	46%	49%
	($ billions)																
Assets[b,e]	$260	$564	$629	$789	$923	$1,045	$1,253	$1,383	$1,402	$1,504	$1,676	$1,674	$1,936	$2,094	$2,316	$2,299	$2,724
Defined benefit	186	401	444	553	642	701	826	895	877	912	988	962	1,102	1,147	1,248	1,211	1,402
Defined contribution	74	162	185	236	281	344	427	488	525	592	688	712	834	947	1,068	1,088	1,322
Defined contribution as percentage of total	28%	29%	29%	30%	30%	33%	34%	35%	37%	39%	41%	43%	43%	45%	46%	47%	49%

Source: Employee Benefit Research Institute tabulations based on U.S. Department of Labor, Pension and Welfare Benefits Administration, Private Pension Plan Bulletin (Spring 1999).

[a]Excludes single participant plans.

[b]Due to rounding, sums of individual items may not equal totals.

[c]Includes active, retired, and separated vested participants not yet in pay status. Not adjusted for double counting of individuals participating in more than one plan.

[d]For workers covered under both a defined benefit and a defined contribution plan, the defined benefit plan is designated as the primary plan unless the plan name indicates it provides supplemental or past service benefits.

[e]Excludes funds held by life insurance companies under allocated group contracts for payment of reitrement benefits. These funds make up roughly 10 to 15 percent of total

208,000 to 624,000 between 1975 and 1995, increasing from 67 percent to 90 percent of total private retirement plans.

The number and percentage of individuals participating in private defined contribution plans is increasing relative to the number and percentage participating in defined benefit plans. The total number of participants in all defined benefit plans was 33 million in 1975. Participation increased to 40 million in 1983 and has remained in the 39 million–41 million range since that time. By contrast, the total number of participants in defined contribution plans increased from 12 million in 1975 to 48 million in 1995.

The trends for active participants in private primary plans are similar to those for total partici-

Table 3.4
401(k) Trends

Summary of Private-Sector Qualified 401(k) Cash or Deferred Arrangement Trends, 1984–1995

	1984	1985	1986	1987	1988	1989	1990	1991	1992	1993	1994	1995
Plans[a]	17,303	29,869	37,420	45,054	68,121	83,301	97,614	111,394	139,704	154,527	174,945	200,813
Percentage of all private plans	3%	5%	5%	6%	9%	11%	14%	16%	20%	22%	25%	29%
Percentage of all private DC plans	4%	6%	7%	8%	12%	14%	16%	19%	23%	24%	28%	32%
						(thousands)						
Active Participants[b]	7,540	10,339	11,559	13,131	15,203[c]	17,337[c]	19,548	19,126	22,404	23,138	26,206	28,061
Percentage of all active participants[d]	12%	17%	18%	21%	24%	28%	32%	31%	35%	36%	40%	42%
						($ millions)						
Assets[a]	$91,754	$143,939	$182,784	$215,477	$276,995	$357,015	$384,854	$440,259	$552,959	$616,316	$674,681	$863,918
Percentage of all private assets	9%	11%	13%	15%	18%	21%	23%	23%	26%	27%	29%	32%
Percentage of all private defined contribution assets	27%	34%	37%	41%	47%	52%	54%	53%	58%	58%	62%	65%
Contributions[a]	$16,291	$24,322	$29,226	$33,185	$39,412	$46,081	$48,998	$51,533	$64,345	$69,322	$75,878	$87,416
Percentage of all private contributions	18%	26%	32%	36%	43%	47%	50%	46%	50%	45%	53%	55%
Percentage of all private defined contribution contributions	38%	46%	50%	53%	61%	63%	65%	64%	69%	68%	72%	74%
Benefit Payments[a]	$10,617	$16,399	$22,098	$22,215	$25,235	$30,875	$32,028	$32,734	$43,166	$44,206	$50,659	$62,163
Percentage of all private benefits	13%	16%	17%	18%	21%	23%	25%	24%	28%	28%	31%	34%
Percentage of all private defined contribution benefits	33%	35%	35%	40%	43%	47%	51%	51%	58%	57%	62%	64%

Source: Employee Benefit Research Institute tabulations based on U.S. Department of Labor, Pension and Welfare Benefits Administration, Private Pension Plan Bulletin (Spring 1999).
[a]Excludes single-participant plans.

pants.[13] In 1975, there were 27 million active participants in primary defined benefit plans. This number decreased to 24 million by 1995. By contrast, between 1975 and 1995 the number of active participants with a primary defined contribution plan significantly increased, from 4 million to 23 million.

In 1975, total assets were $186 billion in defined benefits plans and $74 billion in defined contribution plans. By 1995, assets were $1.4 trillion in defined benefit plans and $1.3 trillion in defined contribution plans. Therefore, over those 20 years, defined contribution assets rose from 28 percent of the private-sector total to 49 percent.

The tremendous growth of the defined contribution sector is largely a product of the 401(k) phenomena. The number of 401(k) plans has increased from 17,000 in 1984 to 201,000 in 1995 (table 3.4). The number of active participants in 401(k) plans has increased from 8 million to 28 million over this time period. 401(k) assets increased from $92 billion to $864 billion between 1984 and 1995.

Though still relatively rare, hybrid retirement plans (such as cash balance plans) are gaining attention and are blurring the nonfundamental distinctions between defined benefit and defined contribution plan types.[14] According to data from KPMG, 4 percent of employers with 200 or more employees sponsored a cash balance plan in 1998, compared with 2 percent in 1993. While hybrid plans are either fundamentally defined benefit or defined contribution in nature, they combine features of both. Cash balance is the best-known type of hybrid plan, but others include age-weighted profit-sharing plans, target benefit plans, and life-cycle pension plans. The existence of hybrid plans shows that not all benefits and shortfalls attributed to traditional defined benefit or traditional defined contribution plans are inherent to these plans.

Putting the Past in Perspective

An examination of the change in the aggregate number of private pension plans and participants masks trends in plans by size. Examining defined benefit and defined contribution plans by plan size allows us to determine the number of participants being affected by trends in plan sponsorship.

Examining private primary defined benefit plan trends by plan size shows that the vast majority of plan terminations were very small plans: those with two to nine active participants. Between 1985 and 1993, there was a net decrease in the total number of primary defined benefit plans of 51 percent, or 86,000 plans. The net number of plans with two to nine active participants decreased by about 56,000 plans, and accounted for 65 percent of the total reduction in defined benefit plans (table 3.5). It has been suggested that very small plans were often top-heavy plans used by employers as tax shelters. After enactment of the Tax Equity and Fiscal Responsibility Act of 1982 (TEFRA), which imposed penalties on top-heavy plans, and the Tax Reform Act of 1986 (TRA '86), which lowered basic income tax rates and imposed faster minimum vesting standards, there was less incentive for these employers to maintain their defined benefit pension plans. TRA '86 also included a provision that eliminated the tax qualification of some small defined benefit plans, primarily single-participant plans.

Between 1985 and 1993, the net change in the number of primary defined benefit plans was generally greater for plans with fewer active participants. The number of defined benefit plans with 10–24 active participants decreased 55 percent between 1985 and 1993, while the number of defined benefit plans with 500–999 active participants decreased 22 percent. Some of the change in the number of plans by plan size is due to changes in individual plans' demographics. For example, a

---

[13] *There is little difference between the total number of participants and the number of active participants included in defined contribution plans. These participants represent individuals other than active participants who are still included in the plan, such as retired participants, participants who have separated from service and are vested in the plan, or survivors. Fewer individuals remain participants in a defined contribution plan than remain in a defined benefit plan after terminating employment with the plan sponsor because most defined contribution participants receive lump-sum distributions on leaving.*

[14] *For a full discussion see Sharyn Campbell, "Hybrid Retirement Plans: The Retirement Income System Continues to Evolve,"* EBRI Issue Brief *no. 171 (Employee Benefit Research Institute, March 1996).*

Table 3.5

PRIMARY PLAN TRENDS BY PLAN SIZE

PRIMARY DEFINED BENEFIT AND DEFINED CONTRIBUTION PLAN AND ACTIVE PARTICIPANT TRENDS, SELECTED YEARS 1985–1993

Active Participants	Primary Plans							Active Participants (thousands)						
						Net Change	Net Change						Net Change	Net Change
	1985	1990	1991	1992	1993	1985–1993	1992–1993	1985	1990	1991	1992	1993	1985–1993	1992–1993
Defined Benefit Plans														
2–9	88,124	45,796	38,424	34,316	32,121	–56,003	–2,195	353	189	168	147	141	–212	–6
10–24	24,267	15,624	18,095	12,452	10,903	–13,364	–1,549	369	244	273	191	168	–201	–23
25–49	14,178	8,605	7,374	7,745	7,252	–6,927	–494	491	304	255	271	252	–239	–19
50–99	11,303	8,346	8,060	8,114	7,499	–3,804	–615	808	599	585	588	537	–271	–51
100–249	9,534	6,563	6,183	6,290	6,209	–3,325	–81	1,498	1,040	979	995	978	–520	–17
250–499	4,670	3,647	3,514	3,447	3,444	–1,226	–3	1,651	1,293	1,245	1,220	1,224	–427	4
500–999	3,149	2,463	2,328	2,378	2,450	–699	72	2,222	1,751	1,655	1,686	1,751	–471	65
1,000–2,499	2,360	2,090	2,028	2,065	2,122	–238	57	3,636	3,221	3,119	3,180	3,285	–351	105
2,500–4,999	847	798	780	796	790	–57	–6	2,930	2,802	2,704	2,797	2,790	–140	–7
5,000–9,999	455	434	469	445	428	–27	–17	3,141	3,015	3,261	3,033	2,966	–175	–67
10,000–19,999	198	223	219	224	223	25	–1	2,749	3,134	3,134	3,132	3,088	339	–44
20,000 or more	175	161	167	167	167	–8	0	8,985	8,711	8,324	8,073	7,912	–1073	–161
None or None Reported	10,280	18,139	13,944	9,960	9,909	–371	–51	–	–	–	–	–	–	–
Total[a]	169,540	112,890	101,585	88,400	83,517	–86,023	–4,883	28,834	26,303	25,701	25,313	25,091	16,257	–222
Defined Contribution Plans														
2–9	199,704	266,129	266,298	270,764	266,284	66,580	–4,480	852	1,127	1,151	1,180	1,165	313	–15
10–24	70,424	97,054	99,188	112,560	112,889	42,465	329	1,056	1,476	1,508	1,737	1,735	679	–2
25–49	31,406	45,737	49,132	54,488	55,094	23,688	606	1,091	1,584	1,695	1,889	1,915	824	26
50–99	17,620	27,446	29,528	32,548	33,835	16,215	1,287	1,224	1,911	2,067	2,273	2,374	1,150	101
100–249	8,878	13,658	13,890	16,187	16,902	8,024	715	1,331	2,071	2,117	2,466	2,572	1,241	106
250–499	2,552	4,144	4,314	5,051	5,187	2,635	136	737	868	1,428	1,488	1,786	1,049	298
500–999	1,185	1,838	1,952	2,242	2,376	1,191	134	808	1,266	1,345	1,532	1,632	824	100
1,000–2,499	784	1,103	1,169	1,332	1,400	616	68	1,194	1,671	1,790	2,028	2,144	950	116
2,500–4,999	219	310	325	355	372	153	17	752	1,072	1,124	1,199	1,272	520	73
5,000–9,999	97	130	126	156	148	51	–8	683	869	850	1,048	984	301	–64
10,000–19,999	34	44	47	50	50	16	0	460	626	644	694	683	223	–11
20,000 or more	29	27	31	40	35	6	–5	1,100	1,151	1,361	1,704	1,518	418	–186
None or None Reported	13,082	40,473	40,067	34,855	37,970	24,888	3,115	–	–	–	–	–	–	–
Total[a]	346,014	498,093	506,066	530,627	532,542	186,528	1,915	11,420	16,251	17,141	19,486	19,779	18,359	293

Source: Employee Benefit Research Institute tabulations of 1985, 1990, 1991, 1992 and 1993 Form 5500 annual reports filed with the Internal Revenue Service.

[a]Total may not equal the sum of individual items due to rounding.

plan that had 400 participants in 1985 may have had 600 participants in 1993. The number of large primary defined benefit plans remained relatively stable between 1985 and 1993. In fact, the number of plans with 10,000 or more active participants increased 5 percent over this time period.

Because most of the decline in primary defined benefit plans occurred in plans with two to nine participants, the decline in the number of employees covered by a primary defined benefit plans is relatively small. Approximately 80 percent of active participants in primary defined benefit plans in 1993 were in plans with 1,000 or more active participants. Even if the 70,000 plans with fewer than 1,000 participants in 1993 were to terminate, 80 percent of active participants with primary defined benefit plans would continue to accrue benefits in their pension plans, while 20 percent of defined benefit participants (5 million) would have their pension benefits frozen. Many of these latter employees would still be covered by an existing defined contribution plan or contribute to another retirement arrangement.

Between 1985 and 1993, there was a net increase in the number of private primary defined contribution plans of 54 percent, or 187,000 plans. However, most of this increase was in plans with two to nine active participants. The net number of such plans increased by 67,000 plans, or 36 percent of the total increase in primary defined contribution plans (table 3.5).

The net increase in the number of primary defined contribution plans becomes smaller as plan size increases. Primary defined contribution plans with 10–24 active participants increased by 42,000 plans, while plans with 100–249 active participants increased by 8,000 plans. The increase in primary defined contribution plans with 1,000 or more active participants was 800 plans, or 3.3 percent of the total increase.

Much of the growth in defined contribution plans has been through primary and supplemental 401(k) plans. Unlike some other defined contribution plans, these plans generally require employee contributions as a condition of participation, and it is often up to the employee to decide how much current pay to defer (within plan and legal limits). Many 401(k) plan participants also receive employer contributions that match all or a fraction of the employees' contribution (see discussion below regarding plan features). These defined contribution plans, while providing an effective means for individuals to save, require individuals to bear most of the funding and investment responsibility in their retirement planning, especially compared with employer-funded and directed defined benefit plans.

Typical Retirement Plan Features[15]

Defined Benefit

Based on its annual survey of retirement benefits, KPMG finds that the "typical" defined benefit plan bases benefits on a formula of final average earnings times years of service. The formula is likely to be at least 2 percent of final average pay, without a limit on the number of years of service counted for benefits, and without integration of Social Security benefits. Full vesting occurs after five years. Normal retirement age is 65, and early retirement age is 55.

Seventy percent of defined benefit plans use a final average earnings formula, 22 percent use a career average formula, and 4 percent use a flat-dollar amount formula. Sixty-three percent of defined benefit plans vest fully after five years, while 8 percent vest earlier. Seventy percent of plans are not integrated with Social Security. The median reported early retirement benefit was 56 percent of benefit paid at normal retirement age. Thirty-eight percent of survey respondents reported exercising their early retirement option. Twenty-eight percent of plans reported automatic cost-of-living adjustments. Fifty-three percent of defined benefit plans offered a lump-sum distribution option for benefit amounts in excess of $3,500.

401(k) Plans

Based on its annual survey of retirement benefits, KPMG finds that the "typical" 401(k) plan offers an

---

[15] *Data in this section are from* Retirement Benefits in the 1990s: 1998 Survey Data, *KPMG Peat Marwick LLP, 1998. Data is based on a survey of 1,292 employers with 200 or more employees (95 percent of which offer retirement benefits to their workers). The survey is random and thus weighting allows generalization of the results to the national level.*

employer matching contribution (but not other employer contributions). It offers between four and nine investment options and permits daily changes to contribution levels and investment allocations.

Eighty-seven percent of 401(k) plans provide employer matching contributions, 30 percent provide other employer contributions, and 36 percent permit employee after-tax contributions. The most common match rate is 50 cents per dollar of worker contributions, with almost all sponsors limiting the percent of employee compensation matched. Among plans that match, 87 percent do it in the form of cash and 6 percent use stock. Among plans that match, 31 percent vest fully after five years and 37 percent vest quicker. Twenty-nine percent of plans provide 10 or more options, 38 percent provide seven to nine options, and 30 percent provide four to six options. Sixty-eight percent of plans allow participants to change investments on a daily basis, 9 percent on a monthly basis, and 17 percent on a quarterly basis. Ninety-one percent of plans permit hardship withdrawals and 82 percent permit loans.

Conclusion

In one sense, the private retirement plan system in the United States has always been dominated by defined contribution plans. Even in 1975, two-thirds (67 percent) of all private plans were defined contribution; today, that has grown to 90 percent. On the other hand, in 1975 the minority of plan participants was in defined contribution plans (26 percent), and now it is the majority (55 percent in 1995).[16] What is unmistakable is that the private retirement system is moving in the direction of defined contribution plans and individual account plans. This trend has been driven largely by the 401(k) phenomena, and today it is manifested by the conversion of traditional final-average pay defined benefit plans into cash balance arrangements with "individual accounts."

On balance, such changes can be viewed as a plus for workers. Today's plans better match the reality of the work experience—job mobility—than plans did for past generations of workers who were also quite mobile.[17] This means enhanced portability of retirement benefits and greater opportunities for wealth accumulation among today's workers relative to the past.

Of course, today's environment also requires very explicit decision-making responsibility on the part of workers that will directly affect their ultimate level of retirement income security (in the case of 401(k) plans, such decisions involve participation, contribution levels, asset allocation, and preservation of account balances upon job change). This explains why one of the primary (if not *the* primary) area of focus today for policymakers, plan sponsors, and service providers is worker education regarding planning and saving for retirement. Worker education was an overriding theme at the National Summit on Retirement Savings held in June of 1998, and is certain to be stressed again at the ensuing national summits scheduled for 2001 and 2005.

Appendix – Retirement Plan Legislation

Revenue Act of 1921
Exempted interest income on trusts for stock bonus or profit-sharing plans from current taxation. Trust income was taxed as it was distributed to employees only to the extent that it exceeded employees' own contributions; did not authorize deductions for past service contributions.

Revenue Act of 1926
Income of pension trusts exempted from current taxation.

Revenue Act of 1928
Allowed employers to take tax deductions for reasonable amounts paid into a qualified trust in excess of the amounts required to fund current liabilities. Changed the taxation of trust distributions so that individuals are taxed only on distributions that are attributable to employer contributions and earnings.

Social Security Act of 1935
Enacted Social Security.

---

[16] *Not adjusted for double counting of individuals participating in more than one plan.*

[17] *See "Male and Female Tenure Continues to Move in Opposite Directions,"* EBRI Notes *no. 2 (Employee Benefit Research Institute, February 1999): 1–4.*

Revenue Act of 1938
Enacted nondiversion rule. Made pension trusts irrevocable.

Investment Advisers Act of 1940
Required delegation of investment responsibilities only to an adviser registered under the act or to a bank or an insurance company (qualified under the laws of two or more states).

Revenue Act of 1942
Tightened coverage standard qualification, limited allowable deductions, and allowed integration with Social Security.

Labor-Management Relations Act of 1947
Sec. 302 provided fundamental guidelines for the establishment and operation of pension plans administered jointly by an employer and a union.

Revenue Act of 1950
Restricted stock options.

Social Security Amendments of 1950, 1952, 1954, 1958, and 1967
Affected pension integration provisions.

Welfare and Pension Plans Disclosure Act of 1958
Established disclosure requirements to limit fiduciary abuse.

Revenue Act of 1961
Amended Sec. 403(b) to extend tax deferral for annuity purchases to employees of public school systems.

Welfare and Pension Plans Disclosure Act Amendments of 1962
Revised the 1958 act; shifted responsibility for protection of plan assets from participants to federal government to prevent fraud and poor administration.

Self-Employed Individual Retirement Act of 1962
Also known as the Keogh Act; adopted and subsequently liberalized by amendment. Made available qualified pension plans for self-employed persons, unincorporated small businesses, farmers, professionals, and their employees.

Tax Reform Act of 1969
Sec. 302 provided fundamental guidelines for the establishment and operation of pension plans administered jointly by an employer and a union. Provided that part of a lump-sum distribution received from a qualified employee trust within one taxable year (on account of death or other separation from service) was to be given ordinary income treatment instead of the capital gains treatment it had been given under prior law. Under this act, the bargain element on the exercise of statutory options is a tax preference item, unless the stock option is disposed of in the same year the option is exercised.

Employee Retirement Income Security Act of 1974 (ERISA)
Signed into law September 2, 1974, ERISA was designed to secure the benefits of participants in private pension plans through participation, vesting, funding, reporting, and disclosure rules, and established the Pension Benefit Guaranty Corporation. Provided added pension incentives for the self-employed (through changes in Keoghs) and to persons not covered by pensions (through individual retirement accounts (IRAs)). Established legal status of employee stock ownership plans (ESOPs) as an employee benefit; codified stock bonus plan under Internal Revenue Code. Established requirements for plan implementation and operation.

Tax Reduction Act of 1975
Established the Tax Reduction Act stock ownership plan (TRASOP) as employee benefit. Provided additional 1 percent of investment tax credit for acquisitions, construction, and other capital expenditures made between February 1975 and January 1977, if employer sets up a TRASOP.

Tax Reform Act of 1976
Extended availability of TRASOP credit from February 1977 to January 1981 and added another 0.5 percent credit for employer-employee matching contributions.

Revenue Act of 1978
Extended TRASOP tax credit provisions through December 31, 1983, and required all TRASOPs to be tax-qualified if employee contributions were made for plan years beginning after December 11,

1978. Established qualified deferred compensation plans (Sec. 401(k)) under which employees are not taxed on the portion of income they elect to receive as deferred compensation rather than direct cash payments. Created simplified employee pensions (SEPs). Changed IRA rules. Established nondiscrimination rules for cafeteria plans.

Miscellaneous Revenue Act of 1980
Permitted tax-qualified ESOPs to provide cash distribution to participants.

Economic Recovery Tax Act of 1981 (ERTA)
Raised contribution limits on IRAs and Keogh plans and extended IRA eligibility to persons covered by employer pension plans. Also authorized qualified voluntary employee contributions. Permitted payroll-based tax credit instead of investment-based TRASOPs. Repealed qualified stock options. Established incentive stock options (ISOs) subject to taxation, modification, and reporting.

Tax Equity and Fiscal Responsibility Act of 1982 (TEFRA)
TEFRA changed Keogh plan contribution limitations, established a new category of plans known as top-heavy plans, and imposed more stringent Sec. 415 funding and benefit limitations. Altered provisions allowing loans to plan participants. Changed rules governing integration with Social Security. Reduced estate tax exclusion for proceeds of qualified retirement plans, set age limits for plan distributions, and established various rules aimed at personal service corporations.

Social Security Amendments of 1983
Prohibited further pullouts of state and local government employer associations after effective date of law. Included amounts in salary reduction plans as taxable compensation for payroll tax purposes. Increased payroll taxes for self-employed persons. Required gradual increase of Social Security normal retirement age.

Tax Reform Act of 1984 (also see DEFRA)
Made substantial changes to rules governing IRAs, SEPs, ESOPs, ISOs, top-heavy plans, and golden parachutes.

Deficit Reduction Act of 1984 (DEFRA) (included in Tax Reform Act of 1984)
Froze TEFRA's maximum annual pension benefit and contribution limits through 1987. Modified TEFRA's top-heavy provisions and definition of key employees, and exempted government plans from top-heavy requirements. Made changes affecting 401(k) plans, including the nondiscrimination test. Substantially changed TEFRA's rules on distribution limits from qualified plans. Established additional tax incentives to encourage the formation of ESOPs.

Retirement Equity Act of 1984 (REA)
Changed the age requirements for purposes of enrollment and vesting in pension plans. Permitted certain breaks in service without loss of pension credits. Changed treatment of pension benefits for widowed and divorced spouses.

Consolidated Omnibus Budget Reconciliation Act of 1985 (COBRA) (included in Single-Employer Pension Plan Amendments Act of 1986)
Significantly restricted the definition of insured termination for purposes of Pension Benefit Guaranty Corporation (PBGC) coverage. Raised the employer's annual PBGC premium rate.

Tax Reform Act of 1986
Established faster minimum vesting schedules, changed rules for integration of private pension plans with Social Security, and mandated broader and more comparable minimum coverage of rank-and-file employees. Restricted 401(k) salary reduction contributions, tightened nondiscrimination rules, required inclusion of all after-tax contributions to defined contribution plans as annual additions under Sec. 415 limits. Extended the limit on amount of compensation that may be taken into account under all qualified plans, imposed new excess benefit tax on distributions over a certain amount, and reduced maximum benefits payable to early retirees under defined benefit plans. Restricted the allowable tax-deductible contributions to IRAs for individuals who participate in employer-sponsored pension plans and whose income exceeds a specified threshold. Imposed excise tax on lump-sum distributions

received before age 59 1/2. Created SEP salary reduction option for firms with 25 or fewer employees. Subjected loans above a certain amount to current income tax.

Omnibus Budget Reconciliation Act of 1986 (OBRA '86)
Required that employers with pension plans provide pension accruals or allocations for employees working beyond age 64 and for newly hired employees who are within five years of normal retirement age.

Omnibus Budget Reconciliation Act of 1987 (OBRA '87)
Changed funding rules governing underfunded and overfunded pension plans and PBGC premium levels and structure. Increased per-participant premiums for single-employer defined benefit plans, and established variable rate surcharge for underfunded plans. Established maximum funding limit of 150 percent of current liability, beyond which employer contributions are not deductible. Tightened minimum funding requirements for underfunded plans; required quarterly premium payment for single-employer plans. Amended Age Discrimination in Employment Act (ADEA) and the Employee Retirement Income Security Act (ERISA) to require full pension service credits for participants employed beyond normal retirement age.

Technical and Miscellaneous Revenue Act of 1988 (TAMRA)
Increased excise tax on excess pension assets upon termination of qualified plans.

Omnibus Budget Reconciliation Act of 1989 (OBRA '89)
Partially repealed the interest exclusion on ESOP loans. Imposed mandatory Labor Department civil penalties on violations by qualified plan fiduciaries and created a tax penalty for substantial overstatement of pension liabilities in determining deductibility. Required that various forms of deferred compensation be included in determination of average compensation and, in turn, the Social Security taxable wage base.

Omnibus Budget Reconciliation Act of 1990 (OBRA '90)
Increased the excise tax on asset reversions from 15 percent to 20 percent in certain cases. Increased the excise tax to 50 percent if the employer does not maintain a qualified replacement plan or provide certain pro rata increases. Allowed the limited use of qualified transfers of excess pension assets to a 401(h) account to fund current retiree health benefits. Raised the PBGC flat premium and increased the variable premium. Extended Social Security coverage to states and local government employees who are not participating in a state or local public employee retirement system.

Older Workers Benefit Protection Act of 1990
Amended the Age Discrimination in Employment Act (ADEA) to apply to employee benefits. Restored and codified the equal-benefit-for-equal-cost principle. Set a series of minimum standards for waivers of rights under ADEA in early retirement situations.

The Comprehensive Deposit Insurance Reform and Taxpayer Protection Act of 1991
To reform the banking industry. Included provisions to eliminate pass-through coverage for benefit-responsive bank investment contracts (BICs) and to limit federal deposit insurance to $100,000 per individual per institution.

Unemployment Compensation Amendments of 1992
Imposed a 20 percent mandatory withholding tax on lump-sum distributions that are not rolled over into qualified retirement accounts; liberalized rollover rules; and required plan sponsors to transfer eligible distributions directly to an eligible plan if requested by the participant.

Pension Benefit Guaranty Corporation (PBGC) Lease Settlements Act of 1993
Solidified a settlement made by PBGC and Continental Airlines clarifying that PBGC will be protected in the event of a future Continental Airlines bankruptcy.

Omnibus Budget Reconciliation Act of 1993 (OBRA '93)
Reduced the compensation limit for qualified plans (Sec. 401(a)(17)) from $235,840 to $150,000. Increased the amount of Social Security benefits subject to taxation from 50 percent to 85 percent for single individuals with incomes above $34,000 ($44,000 for married individuals filing jointly). Placed a cap on the deduction of executive compensation in excess of $1 million that is not tied to performance.

Social Security Administrative Reform Act of 1994
Established the Social Security Administration as an independent federal agency effective March 31, 1995.

Pension Annuitants Protection Act of 1993
Clarified that, in cases where a pension plan fiduciary purchases insurance annuities in violation of ERISA rules, a court may award appropriate relief, including the purchase of backup annuities, to remedy the breach.

Uniformed Services Employment and Reemployment Rights Act of 1993
Guaranteed a veteran's right to pension benefits that would have accrued during military service. Pension plans would not have to pay earnings or forfeitures on make-up contributions. Repayment of employee contributions can be made over a period of three times the period of military service, not to exceed five years. If the service member elects not to be re-employed, no pension rights accrue for the period of military service, but the person's vested interest prior to entering military service would remain intact.

Bankruptcy Reform Act of 1994
Gave the PBGC and state and local government pension plans seats on creditors' committees in corporate bankruptcies.

Social Security Act Amendments of 1994
Simplified employment taxes for domestic services. Reallocated a portion of the Social Security tax to the Disability Insurance trust fund.

Uruguay Round Agreements Act of 1994
Included provisions from the Retirement Protection Act of 1993 to require greater contributions to underfunded plans. Limited the range of interest rate and mortality assumptions used to establish funding targets, phased out the variable rate premium cap, modified certain rules relating to participant protections, and required private companies with underfunded pension plans to notify the PBGC before engaging in a large corporate transaction. Slowed pension cost-of-living adjustments. Extended through the year 2000 a tax provision that allows excess pension assets in certain defined benefit plans to be transferred into a 401(h) retiree health benefits account.

The Small Business Job Protection Act of 1996
Created the savings incentive match plan for employees (SIMPLE) for small establishments. Created a new nondiscrimination safe harbor, repealed Sec. 415(e) limits, created a new definition of highly compensated employees, modified plan distribution rules, repealed family aggregation rules, made USERRA technical changes, and required that Sec. 457 plan assets be held in trust. Additionally, allowed nonworking spouses to contribute up to $2,000 to an individual retirement account (IRA) if the working spouse is eligible, clarified employment tax status for independent contractors, and temporarily reinstated the Sec. 127 education deduction.

Source Tax' Repeal of 1996
Amended the Internal Revenue Code to eliminate state taxation of pension income received by individuals who no longer reside in the state where they earned their pensions.

Taxpayer Relief Act of 1997
Pensions: Increased the full-funding limit from 150 percent to 170 percent over time. Repealed the 15 percent excise tax on excess distributions. Increased the cash-out limit from $3,500 to $5,000, applicable to both defined benefit (DB) and defined contribution (DC) plans. Increased the prohibited transaction tax from 10 percent to 15 percent. The bill also made numerous modifications to the administrative rules governing qualified plans. *Individual Retirement Accounts*: Doubled the

income thresholds for individuals and couples for deductible IRAs. The limits rise in increments of $5,000 and $10,000, respectively, in 1998, 2002, 2003, and 2004, eventually bringing the income limits to $50,000 for singles and $80,000 for couples. Created back-loaded "Roth IRA" accounts in which contributions are made with after-tax money, but earnings within the account accumulate tax-free. Income limits are $95,000–110,000 for individuals and $150,000–160,000 for couples. Also repealed the spousal eligibility rules based on participation in a qualified retirement plan. Authorized penalty-free withdrawals for first-time home purchases and for educational expenses from conventional or Roth IRA accounts.

Education IRAs: Created new tax-free accounts with maximum contributions of $500 per child annually. Income limits are $95,000–110,000 for individuals and $150,000–160,000 for couples.

Savings Are Vital for Everyone's Retirement (SAVER) Act of 1997

Authorized the National Summit on Retirement Savings, held in June 1998, in Washington, DC. Subsequent summits will be held in 2001 and 2005. Also requires the Department of Labor to set up a retirement savings Web site, and carry out an ongoing effort to educate the public about the need for retirement planning and saving.

4

Current Provisions and Recent Trends in Qualified Single-Employer Defined Contribution Plans in the Private Sector

by Jack VanDerhei, Temple University and EBRI Fellow, and Ken McDonnell, EBRI

Introduction

The first pension plan in the United States was established in 1759 to benefit widows and children of Presbyterian ministers. But it was more than a century later, in 1875, before the American Express Company established a formal corporate plan (Allen et al., 1997). During the next century, some 400 plans were established, primarily in the railroad, banking, and public utility industries. The most significant growth has occurred since the mid-1940s. By 1995, there were more than 693,000 private pension plans. Defined benefit plans accounted for approximately 10 percent of all plans and covered more than 23 million active participants. Defined contribution plans accounted for 90 percent of all plans (more than 623,000 plans) and covered more than 42 million active participants (U.S. Department of Labor, Pension and Welfare Benefits Administration, 1999).[1]

The tax treatment accorded qualified plans provides incentives both for employers to establish such plans and for employees to participate in them. In general, a contribution to a qualified plan is immediately deductible in computing the employer's taxes but only becomes taxable to the employee on subsequent distribution from the plan. In the interim, investment earnings on the contributions are not subject to tax. This preferential tax treatment is contingent on the employer's compliance with rules set out in the Employee Retirement Income Security Act of 1974 (ERISA)[2] and administered by the U.S. Department of the Treasury (under the Internal Revenue Code) and the U.S. Department of Labor (under ERISA). Plans not meeting ERISA qualification requirements may also be used to provide retirement income. Nonqualified plans are generally governed by trust law rather than the tax code.

The statutory tax treatment of pensions was formally legislated through the Revenue Act of 1921, which exempted interest income of stock bonus and profit-sharing plans from current taxation and deferred taxation of income to employees until distribution. Statutes enacted since 1921 have permitted employers to deduct a reasonable amount in excess of the amount necessary to fund current pension liabilities (1928); made pension trusts irrevocable (1938); and established nondiscriminatory eligibility rules for pension coverage, contributions, and benefits (1942). These provisions were incorporated into the IRC of 1954 and, along with major modifications made by the Tax Reform Act of 1986 (TRA '86), constitute the basic rules governing the tax qualification of pension plans. The purpose of this paper is to provide an overview of qualified, single-employer defined contribution plans in the private sector and to review how they have changed.[3] However, the most important plan

---

[1] *The number of participants includes double counting of workers in more than one plan.*

[2] *For a discussion of the original goals and spirit of ERISA and what it has accomplished, see Gordon (1999).*

[3] *The discussion in this paper focuses on qualified private single-employer plan rules. See Chapter 41 of Employee Benefit Research Institute (1997) for a description of defined contribution plans in the public sector, including Sec. 403(b) and 457 plans. A summary of multiemployer defined contribution plans is contained in VanDerhei and Yakoboski (1999). For a review of nonqualified plans, see Rosenbloom (1996).*

design innovation (the introduction of the 401(k) plan) did not take place until after proposed regulations were released in November of 1981 and design constraints for many other plan features were substantively restricted as a result of the TRA '86 modifications. For these reasons, as well as a desire to focus on the most consistent time series available,[4] this paper will focus primarily on the time period from 1989 (when most of the TRA '86 provisions were effective) to 1997—the most recent data available from the U.S. Bureau of Labor Statistics (BLS) Employee Benefits Survey (EBS) of medium and large firms.[5]

Types of Defined Contribution Plans[6]

The percentage of full-time employees participating in retirement benefit programs in medium and large private establishments has remained relatively constant from 1989–1997 (Table 4.1), declining slightly from 81 percent in 1989 to 79 percent in 1997. Olsen and VanDerhei (1997) document the substitution in participation from defined benefit to defined contribution through 1993, and it is apparent that this trend has continued at least for this segment of the plan universe. Half of all full-time employees in medium and large private establishments were enrolled in defined benefit plans in 1997, compared with 56 percent in 1993. In contrast, 57 percent were in enrolled in defined contribution plans in 1997, compared with 49 per-cent in 1989.

There are several types of defined contribution plans. Although two of these are explained more thoroughly below, the definitions used by BLS are:

- *Savings and thrift plans.* Under these retirement plans, employees may contribute a predetermined portion of earnings to an individual account, all or part of which the employer matches. Employers may match a fixed percent of employee contributions or a percent that varies by length of service, the amount of employee contribution, or other factors. Contributions are invested as directed by the employee or employer. Although usually designed as a long-term savings vehicle, savings and thrift plans may allow pre-retirement withdrawals and loans.
- *Deferred profit-sharing plans.* This is a retirement plan under which a company credits a portion of company profits to employees' accounts. Plans may set a fixed formula for sharing profits, but this is not a requirement. Most plans hold money in employee accounts until retirement, disability, or death.
- *Money purchase pension plans.* Under these retirement plans, fixed employer contributions (usually calculated as a percentage of employee earnings) are allocated to individual employee accounts. Some of these plans may allow employee contributions, but employees are usually not required to make any contributions. Employers may also make profit-sharing contributions to these plans at their discretion.[7]
- *Employee Stock Ownership Plan (ESOP).* Under ESOP retirement plans, the employer pays a designated amount, often borrowed, into a fund which then invests primarily in company stock. Any debt incurred in the purchase of the stock is repaid by the company. The stocks are then distributed to employees according to an allocation formula.[8]

---

[4] *See pg. 12 of Mitchell (2000) for an explanation of the time series consistency in BLS.*

[5] *The most recent survey provides representative data for 46 million employees in the nation's private nonagricultural industries. It reports on benefits provided to employees in establishments with 100 or more workers in all private nonfarm industries. Currently, small private establishments and state and local governments are surveyed in even-numbered years and medium and large private establishments are surveyed in odd-numbered years. Therefore, the time series analyzed in this paper is typically limited to 1989, 1991, 1993, 1995 and 1997. For a thorough analysis of the BLS time series from 1980–1989, see Mitchell (1992).*

[6] *The descriptive sections of this paper borrow heavily from materials previously prepared by the author in Chapters 6–8 of* Fundamentals of Employee Benefit Programs, *Fifth Edition (Employee Benefit Research Institute, 1997).*

[7] *See chapter 7 of Allen, Melone, Rosenbloom and VanDerhei (1997) for more information on money purchase plans.*

[8] *See Chapter 9 of Employee Benefit Research Institute (1997) for more information on ESOPs.*

Table 4.1

PARTICIPATION IN RETIREMENT BENEFITS, FULL-TIME EMPLOYEES, 1989–1997

PERCENTAGE OF FULL-TIME EMPLOYEES PARTICIPATING[a] IN RETIREMENT BENEFIT PROGRAMS: MEDIUM AND LARGE PRIVATE ESTABLISHMENTS, SELECTED YEARS 1989–1997

Retirement Income Benefit Program[b]	1989	1991	1993	1995	1997
			(percentage)		
All Retirement Income Benefit Programs	81%	78%	78%	80%	79%
Defined benefit pension	63	59	56	52	50
Defined contribution	48	48	49	55	57
types of plans					
savings and thrift	30	29	29	41	39
money purchase pension	5	7	8	7	8
deferred profit sharing	15	16	13	13	13
employee stock ownership	3	3	3	5	4
stock bonus	c	c	c	2	1
tash or deferred arrangements					
with employer contributions	d	d	36	45	46
salary reduction	d	d	35	44	44
savings and thrift	d	d	29	37	38
deferred profit sharing	d	d	4	5	3
other[e]	d	d	3	2	2
deferral of profit–sharing allocation	d	d	1	2	3
no employer contributions	d	d	7	9	9

Source: U.S. Department of Labor, Bureau of Labor Statistics, *Employee Benefits in Medium and Large Private Establishments*, 1989, 1991, 1993, 1995, and 1997 (Washington, DC: U.S. Government Printing Office, 1991, 1993, 1995, 1997, and 1999).

Note: Because of rounding, sums of individual items may not equal totals.

[a]Includes workers covered but not yet participating due to minimum service requirements. Does not include workers offered but not electing contributory benefits.

[b]Includes defined benefit pension plans and defined contribution retirement plans. The total is less than the sum of the individual items because many employees participated in both types of plans.

[c]Less than 0.5 percent.

[d]Data not available.

[e]Includes money purchase pension and employee stock ownership plans.

- *Stock Bonus Plans.* A stock bonus plan specifies employer or employee and employer contributions to a trust fund that invests in various securities.

In 1997, 39 percent of full-time employees in medium and large private establishments participated in savings and thrift plans, up from 30 percent in 1989 (Table 4.1). Deferred profit sharing plans declined slightly during this period, from 15 percent to 13 percent of full-time employees, while money purchase plans increased slightly from 5 percent to 8 percent. Fifty-five percent of full-time employees deferred a portion of their current earnings (and sheltered the income from current income taxes) by contributing to a cash or deferred arrangement (a 401(k) plan).[9] 401(k) plans constituted 43 percent of the DB market in 1993.

Profit-Sharing Plans

There are three basic types of profit-sharing plans:

- *Cash Plan.* At the time profits are determined, contributions are paid directly to employees in the form of cash, checks, or stock. The amount is taxed as ordinary income when distributed.
- *Deferred Plan.* Profit-sharing contributions are not paid out currently but rather are deferred to individual accounts set up for each employee. Benefits—and any investment earnings accrued—are distributed at retirement, death, disability, and sometimes at separation from service and other events.

[9] *In the Employee Benefits Surveys, similar arrangements authorized under Sec. 403(b) of the Internal Revenue Code are also tabulated as 401(k) plans. Foster (1996a).*

- *Combination Plan.* In this type of plan the participant has the option of deferring all or part of the profit-sharing allocation. That portion taken as a deferral is placed into the participant's account, where it and investment earnings accrue tax-free until withdrawal. Any amount taken in cash is taxed currently. For tax purposes, Internal Revenue Service (IRS) qualification of profit-sharing plans is restricted to deferred or combination plans. Therefore, the remainder of this section will focus primarily on these two types of profit-sharing arrangements.

Plan Qualification Rules

Profit-sharing plans, as other retirement plans, must meet a variety of requirements to qualify for preferential tax treatment. These rules, created under ERISA, are designed to protect employee rights and to guarantee that pension benefits will be available for employees at retirement. The rules govern requirements for reporting and disclosure of plan information, fiduciary responsibilities, employee eligibility for plan participation, vesting of benefits, form of benefit payment, and funding. In addition, qualified plans must satisfy a set of IRS nondiscrimination rules (under IRC Secs. 401(a)(4), 410(b), and, in some cases, 401(a)(26)) designed to insure that a plan does not discriminate in favor of highly compensated employees (HCEs).[10]

Contributions

Employer Contributions—Plans must define how employer contributions will be allocated to employee accounts. The allocation formula is generally based on compensation. Sometimes the allocation is a flat percentage of pay, or it may be determined by calculating the proportion of each employee's compensation relative to the total compensation of all plan participants. For example, if the employee earns $15,000 annually and total annual compensation for all participants is $300,000, he or she would receive 5 percent of the employer's annual contribution.

Some plans base their allocations on compensation and service credits. These plans must be careful to assure that the wage/service formula meets the regulatory scheme for demonstrating that the formula does not discriminate in favor of highly compensated employees. Whether a plan uses compensation or both compensation and service in determining allocations depends on an employer's objectives. If employee retention is a primary goal, this can be reflected in a pay-and-service allocation formula. Allocation formulas may be integrated with Social Security within prescribed limits.[11] Panel B of table 4.2 shows that allocation based exclusively on earnings has been by far the most common method of allocating profits to employees.

Maximum annual contributions (employer and employee, if any) on behalf of each plan participant are limited by the defined contribution limits under IRC Sec. 415—the lesser of 25 percent of compensation or $30,000.[12] But the total amount of contributions for all employees that an employer may deduct for federal tax purposes is limited to 15 percent of all covered employees' compensation. At one time, an employer's contribution to a profit-sharing plan was limited to the extent of an employer's current or accumulated profits. Currently, an employer does not have to have profits to establish a profit-sharing plan, and total contributions are not restricted to total profits. However, plan documents must specify that the plan is a profit-sharing plan. Panel A of table 4.2 shows the percentage of full-time employees participating in deferred profit sharing plans, by employer contribution, for medium and large private establishments from 1989–1997. It appears that the percentage of participants in plans where the employer contribution is either a fixed percentage of profits or a variable percentage of profits has increased substantially during that time (from 28 percent to 47 percent).

If an employer's contribution for a particular year is less than the maximum amount for

---

[10] *In general, employees earning more than $80,000 in 1999 will be considered HCEs. See Chapter 4 of Employee Benefit Research Institute (1997) for a definition of highly compensated employees. This limit is scheduled to increase to $85,000 starting Jan. 1, 2000.*

[11] *For more information about integration with Social Security, see Chapter 13 of Employee Benefit Research Institute (1997).*

[12] *For further details on contribution limits, including future increases in the dollar amount, see Chapter 4 of Employee Benefit Research Institute (1997).*

Table 4.2
PROVISIONS OF DEFERRED PROFIT-SHARING PLANS, 1989–1997

PERCENTAGE OF FULL-TIME EMPLOYEES PARTICIPATING[a] IN DEFERRED PROFIT SHARING PLANS, BY EMPLOYER CONTRIBUTION, ALLOCATION OF PROFITS, AND LOANS PERMITTED, MEDIUM AND LARGE PRIVATE ESTABLISHMENTS, SELECTED YEARS, 1989–1997

Type of Provision	1989	1991	1993	1995	1997
			(percentage)		
Panel A: Type of Formula					
Employer Contributions:					
Based on stated formula	60%	52%	40%	62%	62%
fixed percentage of profits	10	10	11	28	20
variable percentage of profits	18	24	15	25	27
other formulas	33	17	15	12	15
No formula	40	48	60	38	38
Panel B: Allocation of Profits to Employees					
Equally to all	1	2	7	6	18
Based on earnings	64	52	52	56	49
Based on earnings and service	9	13	11	7	8
Other	26	33	30	31	24
Panel C: Loans Permitted					
Permitted	19	27	23	33	32
Not permitted	81	73	77	67	68

Source: U.S. Department of Labor, Bureau of Labor Statistics, *Employee Benefits in Medium and Large Private Establishments*, 1989, 1991, 1993, 1995, and 1997 (Washington, DC: U.S. Government Printing Office, 1991, 1993, 1995, 1997, and 1999).
[a]Includes workers covered but not yet participating due to minimum service requirements. Does not include workers offered but not electing contributory benefits.

which a deduction is allowed, the unused limit may not be carried forward to subsequent years unless the carryforward existed as of Dec. 31, 1986. These limit carryforwards may be used to increase the general deduction limit to 25 percent until the carryforwards are exhausted.

A deduction carryforward of contributions in excess of the deduction limit for a particular year may be deductible in succeeding taxable years to the extent allowed. However, such contributions may be subject to a 10 percent nondeductible excise tax. Excess contributions are defined as the sum of total amounts contributed for the taxable year over the amount allowable as a deduction for that year plus the amount of excess contributions for the preceding year, reduced by amounts returned to the employer during the year, if any, and the portion of the prior excess contribution that is deductible in the current year. In other words, if an excess contribution is made during a taxable year, the excise tax would apply for that year and for each succeeding year to the extent that the excess is not eliminated. Excess contributions for a year are determined at the close of the employer's taxable year, and the tax is imposed on the employer.

Employee Contributions—Pure profit-sharing plans do not require employee contributions, but some may permit voluntary employee contributions up to certain limits. The plan then generally looks more like a thrift plan (discussed below). Employee contributions in the form of a salary reduction are becoming increasingly popular. When pretax salary reduction is allowed, the plan must follow rules for 401(k) arrangements (explained below).

Taxation—Employer contributions to a profit-sharing plan are deductible by the company as a business expense (up to the limits noted previously). Employees are not taxed on the deferred contributions—and any interest accrued—until distribution. Any allocation (all or part) taken in cash is taxed on a current basis.

Distributions

Retirement, Disability, and Death Benefits—The law requires that participants' account balances fully vest at retirement. In addition, plans generally provide for benefits on death and disability. The plan's vesting provisions determine whether an employee will receive full or partial benefits on other types of employment termination. Participants generally attain nonforfeitable and nonrevocable—vested—rights to pension benefits after satisfying specific service (or years of participation) or age and service requirements. Once vested, an employee's rights generally cannot be revoked. ERISA requires a plan to adopt vesting standards for the employee's benefit (the account balance under a defined contribution plan or the accrued benefit under a defined benefit plan) at least as liberal as one of the following two schedules: full vesting (100 percent) after five years of participation in the plan (with no vesting prior to that time, known as cliff vesting), or graded (gradual) vesting of 20 percent after three years of service and an additional 20 percent after each subsequent year of service until 100 percent vesting is reached at the end of seven years of service. Benefits attributable to employee contributions to either defined contribution or defined benefit plans, and investment income earned on employee contributions to defined contribution plans, are immediately vested.

Panel B of table 4.3 shows the time series of vesting requirements for employer contributions in profit-sharing plans for full-time employees participating in plans sponsored by medium and large establishments. With the exception of what may be an anomalous result in 1993, there appears to be a very recent trend to provide less liberal vesting. The percentage of these participants with immediate full vesting is reported to have deceased from 37 percent in 1995 to 29 percent in 1997. There has been a continuing increase in the percentage of participants subject to cliff vesting, increasing form 12 percent in 1989 to 30 percent in 1997. Moreover, the percentage required to complete at least five years of service has increased from 8 percent to 21 percent.

Profit-sharing plans typically give retiring participants and beneficiaries of deceased participants a choice between a lump-sum payment and installments. Usually, those who terminate employment for reasons other than retirement, death, or disability receive lump-sum distributions, although if the benefit exceeds $5,000, the participant cannot be forced to take an immediate benefit. Distributions from profit-sharing accounts must follow the distribution rules for all qualified retirement plans. Distributions must generally begin by the year following the attainment of age 70½, unless the individual has not retired. There are minimum and maximum limits on the amount of annual distribution, both subject to penalty taxes if not followed.[13]

In-Service Withdrawals—Some profit-sharing plans provide for partial account withdrawals during active employment. Plans allowing participants to elect account withdrawals impose certain conditions, which vary widely. But generally the funds must be held in the plan for two years before a withdrawal is allowed.

A 10 percent additional income tax applies to most early distributions made before age 59½. The 10 percent additional tax does not apply to distributions that are: (1) due to the participant's death or disability; (2) in the form of an annuity or installments payable over the life or life expectancy of the participant (or joint lives or life expectancies of the participant and the participant's beneficiary); (3) made after the participant has separated from service on or after age 55; (4) used for payment of medical expenses deductible under federal income tax rules; (5) made to or on behalf of an alternate payee pursuant to a qualified domestic relations order; or (6) rolled over to an individual retirement account (IRA) or another qualified plan within 60 days.

Loans—Some plans permit employees to borrow a portion of their vested benefits. In general, the employee must repay the loan according to a level amortization schedule, with payments made at least quarterly. If loans are permitted, they must be available to all participants on a comparable basis

---

[13] *See Chapter 4 of Employee Benefit Research Institute (1997) for a complete description of pension plan distributions.*

[14] *For a detailed explanation of loan requirements, see Chapter 4 of Employee Benefit Research Institute (1997).*

Table 4.3

VESTING PROVISIONS OF SAVINGS AND THRIFT, DEFERRED PROFIT SHARING, AND 401(K) PLANS, 1989–1997

PERCENTAGE OF FULL-TIME EMPLOYEES PARTICIPATING[a] IN SAVINGS AND THRIFT, DEFERRED PROFIT SHARING, AND 401(K) PLANS, BY TYPE OF VESTING PROVISION, MEDIUM AND LARGE PRIVATE ESTABLISHMENTS, SELECTED YEARS, 1989–1997

Retirement Plan and Vesting Provision	1989	1991	1993	1995	1997
			(percentage)		
Panel A: Savings and Thrift Plans					
Immediate full vesting	30%	31%	34%	33%	29%
Cliff vesting	24	31	29	25	30
with full vesting after:					
1–2 years' service	2	2	2	1	3
3–4 years' service	11	9	9	5	6
5 or more years' service	12	19	18	18	21
Graduated vesting	30	35	33	24	33
with full vesting after:					
4 years' service or less	4	3	5	3	10
5 years' service	19	21	18	12	15
6–9 years' service	5	10	10	8	9
Panel B: Deferred Profit Sharing Plans					
Immediate full vesting	37	40	18	37	29
Cliff vesting	12	18	21	22	30
with full vesting after:					
1–2 years' service	b	b	b	2	3
3–4 years' service	4	1	6	2	6
5 or more years' service	8	16	15	17	21
Graduated vesting	50	41	55	34	33
with full vesting after:					
4 years' service or less	2	2	2	1	10
5 years' service	6	4	16	4	15
6–9 years' service	28	37	37	28	9
10 years' service or more	15	b	1	1	b
Panel C: 401(k) Plans					
Immediate full vesting	b	b	34	39	34
Cliff vesting	b	b	26	24	27
with full vesting after:					
1–2 years' service	b	b	2	1	3
3–4 years' service	b	b	8	5	5
5 or more years' service	b	b	16	18	19
Graduated vesting	b	b	37	27	32
with full vesting after:					
4 years' service or less	b	b	4	3	11
5 years' service	b	b	18	13	13
6–9 years' service	b	b	14	10	9

Source: U.S. Department of Labor, Bureau of Labor Statistics, *Employee Benefits in Medium and Large Private Establishments*, 1989, 1991, 1993, 1995, and 1997 (Washington, DC: U.S. Government Printing Office, 1991, 1993, 1995, 1997, and 1999).

[a]Includes workers covered but not yet participating due to minimum service requirements. Does not include workers offered but not electing contributory benefits.

[b]Data not available.

and must bear a reasonable interest rate.[14]

Panel C of table 4.2 shows an increasing trend in the provision of plan loans for profit sharing plans, increasing from 19 percent of the participants in 1989 to 32 percent in 1997.

Thrift Plans

A thrift, or savings, plan is a type of defined contribution plan. The IRC qualifies thrift plans as a type of profit-sharing plan, and they are similar in many ways, including the plan qualification rules that must be satisfied. The chief differences from an employer's perspective are that thrift plans generally require participants to make contributions, while profit-sharing plans do not. Employees generally make periodic contributions to thrift plans. Employee contributions are sometimes matched (completely or in part) by employer contributions. These contributions are placed in a trust fund and invested. For recordkeeping purposes, each participant's savings and earnings are assigned to an individual account. The tax-favored treatment of employer contributions and employer and employee investment gains make these plans attractive and effective vehicles for retirement savings.

Contributions

Employee Contributions—Most thrift plans are contributory; i.e., to participate, eligible employees agree to make voluntary contributions. Employee contributions to thrift plans are of two types: basic contributions, which are sometimes matched by employer contributions; and supplemental contributions, which are not matched by employer contributions. Depending on the plan's structure, the employee's contributions can be made from after-tax income or through pretax income in the form of salary reduction. Employee contributions are generally made through payroll deductions. If the thrift plan utilizes this salary reduction feature, the plan must follow special rules for 401(k) arrangements (explained below). Sometimes the employer requires participants to contribute a specified percentage of pay. Alternately, the employee may be able to choose a contribution level between certain limits, e.g., between 1 percent and 10 percent of pay. Employees are usually permitted to change or suspend contributions at some time during the plan year.

Employer Contributions—Employers can make contributions to a thrift plan through a number of arrangements. Employer contributions usually are defined as a fixed percentage of each dollar of basic employee contributions up to some maximum percentage of compensation (e.g., the employer matches 50 percent of employee compensation up to 6 percent). The matching percentage may be the same for all employees, or it may increase with years of service or participation.[15] Employer matching contributions, together with employee contributions, are subject to a special nondiscrimination rule under IRC Sec. 401(m). Under a different approach, employers may provide a contribution matched (partially or fully) to an employee's contribution and a supplemental contribution based on profits. Under a relatively uncommon approach, employer contributions are based entirely on profits.[16] Many surveys suggest that the level of the employer's matching contribution is an important factor in determining employees' participation and their level of contributions. Table 4.4 shows the percentage distribution of full-time employees participating in savings and thrift plans with specified employer matching contributions for medium and large private establishments from 1989–1997.[17] The distribution has varied over time but it appears that the percentage of participants in plans matching on a full dollar-for-dollar basis has decreased significantly (from 22 percent in 1989 to 15 percent in 1997) and that those in plans matching on less than a 50 percent basis has increased (from 11 percent to 23 percent in the same time period).

However, looking only at the matching percentage may give only part of the answer in looking at trends in employer contributions. For example, an employer matching 100 percent of the first 3 percent of compensation would be providing the same contribution as one that matched 50 per-

---

[15] *In 1997, 5 percent of full-time employees participating in savings and thrift plans sponsored by medium and large establishments had employer matching contributions that varied by service (U.S. Department of Labor, Bureau of Labor Statistics, 1999).*

[16] *In 1997, only 3 percent of full-time employees participating in savings and thrift plans sponsored by medium and large establishments had employer matching contributions that varied by profit level (U.S. Department of Labor, Bureau of Labor Statistics, 1999).*

[17] *In 1997, 81 percent of full-time employees participating in savings and thrift plans sponsored by medium and large establishments had employer matching contributions with a specified matching percent (U.S. Department of Labor, Bureau of Labor Statistics, 1999).*

Table 4.4

EMPLOYER MATCHING CONTRIBUTIONS TO SAVINGS AND THRIFT PLANS, 1989–1997

PERCENTAGE DISTRIBUTION OF FULL-TIME EMPLOYEES PARTICIPATING[a] IN SAVINGS AND THRIFT PLANS WITH SPECIFIED EMPLOYER MATCHING CONTRIBUTIONS, MEDIUM AND LARGE PRIVATE ESTABLISHMENTS, SELECTED YEARS, 1989–1997

		Specified Matching Percentage[b]			
Year	"Average" Maximum Employer Contribution	1–49 percent	50 percent	51–99 percent	100 percent
		(percentage)			
1989	3.19%	11%	60%	6%	22%
1991	3.13	14	58	5	24
1993	3.11	21	44	11	24
1995	2.94	22	45	14	17
1997	2.98[e]	23	47	13	15

Source: Author's tabulations based on U.S. Department of Labor, Bureau of Labor Statistics, *Employee Benefits in Medium and Large Private Establishments*, 1989, 1991, 1993, 1995, and 1997 (Washington, DC: U.S. Government Printing Office, 1991, 1993, 1995, 1997, and 1999). See text for description of the "average" maximum employer contribution calculation.

[a]Includes workers covered but not yet participating due to minimum service requirements. Does not include workers offered but not electing contributory benefits.

[b]The percentage of matchable employee contributions added by employers. Some plans specified a maximum annual employer contribution.

[c]Data not available.

[d]Less than 0.5 percent.

[e]Distributions above 6 percent were assumed to follow the 1995 distribution.

cent on the first 6 percent of compensation, assuming that the employee contributed at least up to the maximum amount of compensation being matched. Therefore, we computed an "average" maximum employer contribution in each year to proxy for any trend.[18] This number, which proxies the average maximum contribution employers would pay each year if each eligible employee contributed at least up to the maximum amount of compensation being matched, decreased from 3.19 percent in 1989 to 2.94 percent in 1995 before increasing to 2.98 percent in 1997.[19]

---

[18] *Specifically, the interplay between the matching rate and the maximum amount of compensation matched is approximated as an average maximum cost to the employers over time. The second column in Table 4 is derived from EBS time series by multiplying the relative frequency of the population each year by the rate (25 percent and 75 percent for the first and third intervals) by the upper boundary for the compensation rate (i.e., 2.01-3.0 would be expressed as 3.0). The products were summed over all match rates / maximum amount of compensation matched combinations to estimate what employers would pay on average if all eligible employees contributed at least up to the maximum amount of compensation being matched. Obviously, this is not what actually occurs in practice, and EBRI is currently analyzing contribution behavior of more than 6 million participants from over 27,000 plans to determine the behavioral aspects of contribution activity and the impact of match rates as well as the maximum amount of compensation matched.*

[19] *Employee participation in savings and thrift plans would also be expected to be impacted by the presence of an employer match and, perhaps, the level of the match. Foster (1996b) uses the 1993 EBS to show that employee participation averaged 69 percent that year, but that plans with employer matching contributions averaged 80 percent; those with no employer matching contribution averaged 51 percent. However, the differential based on level of contribution was less pronounced with those employees with an "effective" match of 2 percent of salary or less, who had an average participation of 74 percent compared with 80percent to 84 percent for higher rates. The effective match is defined as the product of the match rate times the maximum amount of employee contribution matched.*

Papke (1995) used Form 5500 data to analyze 401(k) participation rates and concluded they are sensitive both to the presence and level of the employer match rate. She found substantial increases in employee contributions occur when a plan moves from a zero to a small or moderately sized match rate; however, once the employer provides at least 10 cents on the dollar, the marginal effect of increasing the match rate is small.

Limits—As with other defined contribution plans, annual employer and employee contributions to thrift plans are limited under IRC Sec. 415. Annual contributions per participant cannot exceed 25 percent of compensation, or $30,000, whichever is less. Compensation up to $160,000 (indexed) is used in computing the limit. The $30,000 will also be indexed.[20] A further limit applies if an employee participates in both a defined benefit and a defined contribution plan. Employee contributions are limited separately. In practice, any employee contributions—and matching employer contributions—are limited by nondiscrimination rules under IRC Sec. 401(m) unless a safe harbor test is satisfied (explained below).[21] These rules limit the employee after-tax contributions of highly compensated employees and the employer contributions for highly compensated employees to a proportion of the amount nonhighly compensated employees contribute. The rules are very similar to those for 401(k) cash or deferred arrangements and include a prescribed method for distributing to highly compensated participants amounts exceeding the permitted limits (explained below). An employer is also limited in the amount of contributions that are eligible for a tax deduction. Each year, total employer contributions are deductible as a business expense up to 15 percent of total employee compensation (IRC Sec. 404).

Employees in these plans may also face plan-specific limits on employee contributions (often as a method to help mitigate problems with 401(m) testing). Panel A of table 4.5 shows what appears to be a gradual trend to loosening these restrictions. Of those with an identifiable constraint, 69 percent of employees were allowed to make contributions of 15 percent or more in 1997, an increase from 56 percent in 1989.[22]

Taxation—Employer contributions to a thrift plan are deductible by the company as a business expense up to the limits noted above. If employees make contributions with after-tax money, federal income, Social Security, and other payroll taxes apply. However, any employer contributions and investment earnings on all contributions accrue tax-free until distribution.

Distributions

Retirement, Disability, and Death Benefits—The law requires that participants' account balances fully vest at retirement. In addition, plans generally provide for benefits on death and disability. The plan's vesting provisions determine whether an employee will receive full or partial benefits on other types of employment termination. However, if the plan is contributory (i.e., employees make contributions), the employee will always receive the benefits that are attributable to his or her own contributions.

Panel A of table 4.3 shows the distribution of types of vesting requirements have been relatively constant since 1989. The most recent data shows that 29 percent of participants were immediately vested in 1997, 30 percent were subject to cliff vesting (most commonly at least five years) and 33 percent had some type of graduated vesting. Usually, those who terminate employment for reasons other than retirement, death, or disability receive lump-sum distributions. Panel A of table 4.6 shows the percentage of full-time employees participating in savings and thrift plans, by method of account distribution at retirement for medium and large private establishments from 1989–1997. While the time series do not appear to have any significant trends, it is obvious that a significantly larger percentage of participants had a lump sum option available in 1997 (91 percent) than a lifetime annuity (25 percent).

Distributions from profit-sharing accounts must follow the general distribution rules for all qualified retirement plans. Distributions generally must begin by the April 15 following the attainment of age 70½ unless the individual has not retired. There are minimum limits on the amount of annual distribution, subject to penalty taxes if not followed.[23]

---

[20] *For further discussion of contribution limits, see Chapter 4 of Employee Benefit Research Institute (1997).*

[21] *The safe harbor is available for years beginning after Dec. 31, 1998.*

[22] *Bucci (1990) analyzed the individual constraints placed upon savings and thrift plans in the 1989 EBS and devised a model to project expected retirement accumulations at retirement.*

[23] *For a complete description of distribution rules, see Chapter 4 of Employee Benefit Research Institute (1997).*

Table 4.5

EMPLOYEE CONTRIBUTIONS TO SAVINGS AND THRIFT AND 401(K) PLANS, 1989–1997

PERCENTAGE OF FULL-TIME EMPLOYEES PARTICIPATING[a] IN SAVINGS AND THRIFT AND 401(K) PLANS, BY MAXIMUM EMPLOYEE CONTRIBUTION ALLOWED, MEDIUM AND LARGE PRIVATE ESTABLISHMENTS, SELECTED YEARS, 1989–1997

Retirement Plan and Type of Contribution Formula	1989	1991	1993	1995	1997
			(percentage)		
Panel A: Savings and Thrift Plans					
Basis of Maximum Contribution:					
Specified dollar amount	1%	1%	2%	1%	1%
Percentage of earnings	97	93	91	83	89
less than 5 percent	2	5	5	2	2
6–9 percent	9	7	10	5	4
10 percent	12	12	19	10	7
11–14 percent	20	11	15	13	15
15 percent	17	20	19	21	33
16 percent	21	22	16	18	17
17–19 percent	9	10	4	7	8
20 percent or more	7	5	2	6	3
Other	2	5	7	16	10
Tax Status of Contribution:					
Pre–tax contribution					
not allowed	8	2	b	b	b
allowed	92	98	b	b	b
Panel B: 401(k) Plans					
Basis of Maximum Contribution:					
Specified dollar amount	b	b	2	1	1
Percentage of earnings	b	b	91	83	87
less than 5 percent	b	b	5	4	4
6–9 percent	b	b	8	10	5
10 percent	b	b	19	12	11
11–14 percent	b	b	15	13	11
15 percent	b	b	19	20	31
16 percent	b	b	16	12	11
17–19 percent	b	b	4	7	7
20 percent or more	b	b	2	5	3
Other	b	b	7	16	12

Source: U.S. Department of Labor, Bureau of Labor Statistics, *Employee Benefits in Medium and Large Private Establishments*, 1989, 1991, 1993, 1995, and 1997 (Washington, DC: U.S. Government Printing Office, 1991, 1993, 1995, 1997, and 1999).

[a]Includes workers covered but not yet participating due to minimum service requirements. Does not include workers offered but not electing contributory benefits.

[b]Data not available.

In-Service Withdrawals—Some profit-sharing plans provide for partial account withdrawals during active employment. Plans allowing participants to elect account withdrawals impose certain conditions, which vary widely, but generally, the funds must be held in the plan for two years before a withdrawal is allowed. A 10 percent additional income tax applies to most early distributions made before age 59½. The 10 percent additional tax does not apply to distributions that are: (1) due to the participant's death or disability, (2) in the form of an annuity or installments payable over the life or life expectancy of the participant (or joint lives or life expectancies of the participant and the participant's beneficiary); (3) made after the participant has separated from service on or after age 55; (4) used for payment of medical expenses deductible under federal income tax rules; (5) made to or on behalf of an alternate payee pursuant to a qualified domestic relations order; or (6) rolled over to an individual retirement account or another qualified plan within 60 days.

Table 4.7 shows a significant decrease in the percentage of participants eligible for early

Table 4.6

METHOD OF ACCOUNT DISTRIBUTION AT RETIREMENT: SAVINGS AND THRIFT AND 401(K) PLANS, 1989–1997

PERCENTAGE OF FULL-TIME EMPLOYEES PARTICIPATING[a] IN SAVINGS AND THRIFT AND 401(K) PLANS, BY METHOD OF ACCOUNT DISTRIBUTION AT RETIREMENT, MEDIUM AND LARGE PRIVATE ESTABLISHMENTS, SELECTED YEARS, 1989–1997

Type of Distribution	1989	1991	1993	1995	1997
			(percentage)		
Panel A: Savings and Thrift Plans					
Cash Distribution[b]	97%	99%	c	c	c
Lifetime annuity	28	30	30%	17%	25%
Installments	52	52	48	30	41
Lump sum	96	99	98	85	91
Panel B: 401(k) Plans					
Cash Distribution[b]	c	c	c	c	c
Lifetime annuity	c	c	34	21	27
Installments	c	c	49	34	41
Lump sum	c	c	98	92	91

Source: U.S. Department of Labor, Bureau of Labor Statistics, *Employee Benefits in Medium and Large Private Establishments*, 1989, 1991, 1993, 1995, and 1997 (Washington, DC: U.S. Government Printing Office, 1991, 1993, 1995, 1997, and 1999).

[a]Includes workers covered but not yet participating due to minimum service requirements. Does not include workers offered but not electing contributory benefits.

[b]Many plans offer more than one form of cash distribution so sums of individual items exceed total.

[c]Data not available.

Table 4.7

EARLY WITHDRAWALS FROM SAVINGS AND THRIFT PLANS, 1989–1997

PERCENTAGE OF FULL-TIME EMPLOYEES PARTICIPATING[a] IN SAVINGS AND THRIFT PLANS, BY PROVISIONS FOR WITHDRAWAL OF EMPLOYER CONTRIBUTIONS PRIOR TO RETIREMENT, DISABILITY, OR TERMINATION, MEDIUM AND LARGE PRIVATE ESTABLISHMENTS, SELECTED YEARS, 1989–1997

Type of Provision	1989	1991	1993	1995	1997
			(percentage)		
No Withdrawals Permitted	29%	50%	51%	43%	48%
Withdrawals Permitted	71	50	47	43	52
For any reason	37	24	29	16	18
no penalty	17	16	b	b	b
some penalty	18	8	b	b	b
For hardship reasons	34	26	18	28	35
no penalty	27	17	b	b	b
some penalty	7	9	b	b	b

Source: U.S. Department of Labor, Bureau of Labor Statistics, *Employee Benefits in Medium and Large Private Establishments*, 1989, 1991, 1993, 1995, and 1997 (Washington, DC: U.S. Government Printing Office, 1991, 1993, 1995, 1997, and 1999).

[a]Includes workers covered but not yet participating due to minimum service requirements. Does not include workers offered but not electing contributory benefits.

[b]Data not available.

withdrawals in these plans, from 71 percent in 1989 to 52 percent in 1997. It appears that most of this decrease took place in those plans offering early withdrawals for any reason (decreasing from 37 percent to 18 percent), while those eligible for early withdrawals subject to satisfaction of the plan's hardship criteria actually increased nominally from 34 percent to 35 percent.

Loans—Some plans permit employees to borrow a portion of their vested benefits. In general, the employee must repay the loan according to a level amortization schedule with payments made at least quarterly. If loans are permitted, they must be available to all participants on a comparable basis, and must bear a reasonable interest rate.

401(k) Cash or Deferred Arrangements

Introduction

A qualified cash or deferred arrangement under Sec. 401(k) of the IRC allows an employee to elect to have a portion of his or her compensation (otherwise payable in cash) contributed to a qualified retirement plan. The employee contribution is treated not as current income but most commonly as a pretax reduction in salary, which is then paid into the plan by the employer on behalf of the employee. In some cases, an employer allows employees to elect to have profit-sharing allocations contributed to the plan. In both instances, the employee defers income tax on the 401(k) plan contribution until the time of withdrawal. Whatever portion is not contributed to the 401(k) arrangement may be taken in cash, which is considered current income and taxed accordingly.

Various forms of deferred compensation have existed for many years. As early as the mid-1950s, cash or deferred profit-sharing plans using pretax employee contributions were permitted by the IRS as long as at least one-half of the participants electing to defer were in the lowest paid two-thirds of all plan participants. It was not until the late 1970s that the Congress acted to sanction cash or deferred arrangements, formalize their design, and provide for regular guidance. The Revenue Act of 1978 added Sec. 401(k) to the IRC—hence the commonly used reference to this type of arrangement as a 401(k) plan. These arrangements are a popular vehicle for retirement savings. They provide employees the ability to save on a tax-effective basis by deferring current taxes until a future time when taxes might be lower, and also permit employers some flexibility in pension plan design and contribution levels.

Eligibility

Most private firms may establish 401(k) arrangements. Employees become eligible to participate in 401(k) arrangements usually after meeting a service requirement. For a 401(k) arrangement, the maximum service period is one year.

Vesting

The employee's attainment of nonforfeitable rights to benefits—of employee contributions and some employer contributions[24] —must be immediate. Other types of contributions, including employer matching contributions, are subject to minimum vesting standards under ERISA. Panel C of table 4.3 shows a fairly stable trend in vesting provisions for 401(k) participants. In 1997, 34 percent were immediately vested, 27 percent were subject to cliff vesting (about two-thirds of these had to wait until at least five years of service was completed before they were vested) and 32 percent has some type of graduated vesting.

Types of 401(k) Arrangements

There are essentially two ways a 401(k) arrangement can be designed: through an actual salary reduction or through a profit-sharing distribution. In a salary reduction arrangement, the employee may elect to have a percentage of salary contributed to the plan (otherwise payable in cash), thereby reducing current salary and reducing the base on which federal income and some state taxes are calculated. These arrangements must be included in an employer's profit-sharing, stock bonus, pre-ERISA money-purchase, or rural electric cooperative plan. They can be designed to include employee contributions only, employer contributions only, or both employee and employer contribu-

---

24 *Specifically, those used as qualified nonelective contributions to satisfy the ADP test.*

tions.[25] In a cash or deferred profit-sharing arrangement, the employee is offered the option of deferring a profit-sharing distribution (or some portion of it) to a trust account or taking the distribution in cash. In both arrangements, the deferral and any income thereon accrue tax free until distribution. Any distribution taken in cash from the profit-sharing arrangement is currently taxed.

Contributions

Four types of contributions are normally paid to 401(k) plans.

- *Elective.* Tax-deferred employee contributions (made by the employer on behalf of the employee) in the form of a salary reduction.
- *Matching.* Employer contributions that match employee contributions, although the employer does not always provide a full dollar-for-dollar match.
- *Nonelective.* Contributions other than matching made by the employer from employer funds. Sometimes these are made to help satisfy nondiscrimination tests (see following discussion).
- *Voluntary.* After-tax employee contributions not made through salary reduction.

Employee elective contributions to a 401(k) arrangement are limited (to $10,000 in 1999) and are coordinated with elective contributions to simplified employee pensions, Sec. 457 state and local government plans, tax-deferred 403(b) annuities, and Sec. 501(c)(18) trusts. The limit is adjusted for inflation to reflect changes in the consumer price index. Employee after-tax contributions and employer matching contributions may be limited under IRC Sec. 401(m).

The limit on total employer and employee contributions to a qualified 401(k) plan is governed by the same rules as other defined contribution plans under IRC Sec. 415. In general, the sum of the employer's contribution (including the amount the employee elected to contribute through salary reduction plus any employer matching contributions), any after-tax employee contributions, and any additions from former employee's forfeitures[26] may not exceed the lesser of 25 percent of an employee's compensation or $30,000 (indexed). Only compensation up to $160,000 (in 1999, indexed) is used in determining the limit. Employees may also be subject to a plan-specific limit on the percentage of compensation they may contribute to a 401(k) plan. This is often imposed to mitigate actual deferral percentage (ADP) problems (discussed below) that might otherwise occur as a result of the tendency for HCEs to defer a larger percentage of their compensation than non-highly compensated employees (NHCEs). Panel B of table 4.5 shows a fairly diverse distribution of these maxima across the universe of defined contribution plans but the modal percentage is 15 percent and appears to be adopted by an increasing percentage of sponsors. In 1997, 31 percent of all 401(k) participants had such a constraint.

Nondiscrimination Requirements

Like other qualified retirement plans, 401(k) arrangements must be designed to ensure that a plan does not discriminate in favor of highly compensated employees in terms of coverage and participation in the plan and contributions provided. The rules for coverage and participation are the same as those for other qualified retirement plans (under Secs. 410(b) and 401(a)(26)). However, a special test for 401(k)s that limits elective contributions of highly compensated employees replaces the general plan rules prohibiting discrimination in contributions and benefits (under Sec. 401(a)(4)). The test, known as the ADP (or actual deferral percentage) test, must be run annually. Effective for taxable years beginning after 1996, 401(k) nondiscrimination requirements may be satisfied by adopting a savings incentive match plan for employees (SIMPLE) plan.[27] Effective for years beginning after Dec. 31, 1998,

---

[25] *The Employee Benefits Survey collects detailed information only on defined contribution plans (with or without 401(k) features) with an employer contribution (Foster, 1996b).*

[26] *If a plan participant terminates, the nonvested benefits are forfeited and become available for other plan uses. They may be reallocated among employees or used to reduce employer contributions. For further discussion of Sec. 415 limits, see Chapter 4 on pension plans, Employee Benefit Research Institute (1997).*

[27] *See Tacchino and Littell (1997) for a detailed discussion of SIMPLE plans.*

two alternative safe-harbor methods of meeting the ADP tests became available.[28]

The ADP test works this way: The eligible group of employees (defined as those employees who are eligible for employer contributions under the plan for that year) is divided into the highly compensated and the nonhighly compensated. Then, within each group, the percentage of compensation that is contributed on behalf of each employee is determined.[29] The percentages for the employees are totaled and averaged to get an ADP for the group. The ADP for the highly compensated group is then compared with the ADP for the nonhighly compensated group. The ADP test may be satisfied in one of two ways.

Test 1: The ADP for the eligible highly compensated may not be more than the ADP of the other eligible employees multiplied by 1.25 (the basic test).

Test 2: The excess of the ADP for the highly compensated over the nonhighly compensated may not be more than 2 percentage points, and the ADP for the highly compensated may not be more than the ADP of the nonhighly compensated multiplied by 2 (the alternative test).

For example, if the ADP for the nonhighly compensated group is 4 percent, and the ADP for the highly compensated group is 6 percent, are the nondiscrimination rules satisfied?

Test 1: Because 6 percent (the ADP of the highly compensated) is greater than 5 percent (4 percent x 1.25), test 1 is not satisfied.

Test 2: Because 6 percent (the ADP of the highly compensated) is not more than 2 percentage points more than 4 percent (the ADP of the nonhighly compensated) and 6 percent is not more than 8 percent (the ADP of the nonhighly compensated multiplied by 2), test 2 is satisfied.

Because one of the tests has been satisfied, the nondiscrimination rules are, therefore, satisfied. As mentioned earlier, these rules apply to employee elective deferrals. Employee after-tax and employer matching contributions in 401(k) arrangements and any other qualified retirement plan are subject to a parallel rule called the actual contribution percentage (ACP) test under IRC Sec. 401(m). The test is essentially the same as the ADP test applied to elective contributions. If the 401(k) arrangement consists of both elective and nonelective contributions, there are further tests that must be satisfied.[30]

Table 4.8 illustrates the maximum ADPs allowed for the highly compensated employees, assuming various ADPs for the nonhighly compensated.

Table 4.8
Maximum Actual Deferral Percentages (ADP) for HCEs[a]

Maximum ADP Allowed Under Current Law

If the Average ADP for the NHCE[b] is:	The Maximum Average ADP for the HCE Will Be: Test 1	Test 2
0.5 percent	5/8%	1%
1 percent	1-1/4	2
2 percent	2-1/2	4
3 percent	3-3/4	5
4 percent	5	6
5 percent	6-1/4	7
6 percent	7-1/2	8
7 percent	8-3/4	9
8 percent	10	10
9 percent	11-1/4	11
10 percent	12-1/4	12

Source: Author's calculations.
[a]Highly compensated employees, earning $85,000 or more annually in 2000.
[b]Non-highly compensated employee, earning less than $85,000 annually in 2000.

Distributions

Withdrawals—The ability to withdraw funds is more restricted in a 401(k) arrangement than in

28 IRS Notice 98–52 provides guidance on the design-based alternative or "safe harbor" methods in Sec. 401(k)(12) and Sec. 401(m)(11) of the Internal Revenue Code for satisfying the Sec. 401(k) and Sec. 401(m) nondiscrimination tests.

29 The permitted deferrals for highly compensated employees may be based on the preceding year's deferrals of the nonhighly compensated employees, rather than the current year's deferrals.

30 If a plan must meet both the actual deferral percentage and actual contribution percentage tests, there is a restriction on the multiple use of the alternative limitation. For more details, see VanDerhei (1996).

other types of pension plans. In general, distributions of employee elective contributions (and any nonelective or matching contributions used to satisfy the ADP test) may be made before age 59½ only in the case of death, disability, separation from service, plan termination if there is no establishment or maintenance of another defined contribution plan (other than an employee stock ownership plan), sale of a subsidiary or substantially all the business' assets (as long as the employee remains in employment with the corporation acquiring the assets), or financial hardship. Voluntary employee after-tax contributions, matching employer contributions, and applicable earnings are not subject to these rules.

Hardship Defined—When the term financial hardship was originally defined in 1981 by the IRS in proposed regulations, a two-part definition was set out that said that the participant must (1) have an "immediate and heavy" financial need and (2) have no other resources "reasonably" available. These rules required the employer to investigate the individual circumstances of the hardship applicant. Until 1988, the only other regulatory guidance came from individual plan IRS revenue rulings. In August 1988, IRS issued final regulations in which it retained the two-part definition of hardship but clarified the conditions under which each of these would be met. Each part may be satisfied through either a "facts and circumstances" test or safe harbor rules. The safe harbors provide a set of events that may be deemed automatically to cause an "immediate and heavy financial need" and that would satisfy the "other resources" provision.

Immediate and Heavy Need—Under the facts and circumstances rule, a need is defined as immediate and heavy if the need can be determined by the facts and circumstances surrounding the hardship request. Under the safe harbor test, a distribution will be deemed to be immediate and heavy if it is for medical expenses; purchase of a principal residence for the employee; tuition for post-secondary education, but only for the next quarter or semester; and prevention of eviction or mortgage foreclosure.

Determining Financial Need From Reasonably Available Resources—To determine that a financial need cannot be met by other reasonably available resources under the facts and circumstances test, the employee must show that (1) the distribution does not exceed the amount required to meet the need and (2) the need cannot be met from other reasonably available resources (including assets of the employee's spouse and minor children). An employer may demonstrate that these provisions are met without an independent investigation of the applicant's financial affairs if the employer reasonably relies on the participant's representation that the need cannot be relieved by insurance, reasonable liquidation of other assets, the cessation of employee contributions under the plans, and other plan distributions or loans from either the plan or commercial sources.

The safe harbor rules for establishing financial need are satisfied if:

- The hardship withdrawal does not exceed the amount needed;
- The employee has obtained all distributions (other than for hardship) and all nontaxable loans available from all of the employer's plans;
- The employee's contributions under all other employer plans are suspended for 12 months after the hardship withdrawal; and
- The dollar limit on pretax contributions for the year after the hardship withdrawal is reduced by the amount of pretax contributions made during the year in which the hardship occurred.

Furthermore, the amount available for a hardship distribution consists only of employee elective contributions and investment earnings that have accrued through December 31, 1988. Most hardship withdrawals are subject to the early distribution penalty tax, discussed later in this section.

Incidence of Early Withdrawal Provisions—Panel B of table 4.9 shows the percentage of full-time employees participating in 401(k) plans, by provisions for early withdrawals for medium and large private establishments in 1993, 1995, and 1997. For those participants with available data, this suggests a slight increase in early withdrawal eligibility from 42 percent in 1993 to 54 percent in 1997. However, the reversal in whether hardship is a necessary condition for the withdrawal has been dramatic. Those eligible for 401(k) withdrawals for any reason have declined from 26 to 18 percent for

Table 4.9

Loan and Early Withdrawal Provisions in 401(k) Plans, 1993, 1995, and 1997

Percentage of Full-Time Employees Participating[a] in 401(k) Plans, by Provisions for Loans and Early Withdrawals, Medium and Large Private Establishments, 1993, 1995, and 1997

Type of Provision	1993	1995	1997
		(percentage)	
Panel A: Loans			
Loans Permitted	43%	49%	51%
Hardship only	3	4	6
Any reason	39	44	45
Loans Not Permitted	56	46	40
Not Determinable	1	15	9
Panel B: Withdrawals			
Withdrawals Permitted	41	46	50
For any reason	25	16	17
For hardship reasons	16	30	33
Data not available	2	5	8

Source: U.S. Department of Labor, Bureau of Labor Statistics, *Employee Benefits in Medium and Large Private Establishments*, 1993, 1995, and 1997 (Washington, DC: U.S. Government Printing Office, 1995, 1997, and 1999).

[a]Includes workers covered but not yet participating due to minimum service requirements. Does not include workers offered but not electing contributory benefits.

those with available data, while those permitted to take an early withdrawal only for hardship reasons increased from 16 to 36 percent during this period.

Loans—An employee may be able to borrow funds from the plan if the plan permits. The rules governing loans from a 401(k) are essentially the same as those for other qualified plans.

Table 4.9 show the percentage of full-time employees participating in 401(k) plans, by provisions for loans, for medium and large private establishments from 1993–1997. The time series suggest a large increase for the percentage of those whose loan eligibility status was determinable, from 43 percent in 1993 to 56 percent in 1997.[31]

Method of Account Distribution—Panel B of table 4.10 shows the percentage of full-time employees

[31] The 1997 figure is slightly larger than the 52 percent determined using individual observations on more than 6 million 401(k) participants from the 1996 EBRI/ICI database. However, nearly 10 percent of the sample represented participants of plans with fewer than 100 participants, and this study confirmed a positive relationship between plan size and loan eligibility (VanDerhei, Galer, Quick and Rea, 1999).

Table 4.10

Method of Account Distribution at Retirement: Savings and Thrift and 401(k) Plans, 1989–1997

Percentage of Full-Time Employees Participating[a] in Savings and Thrift and 401(k) Plans, by Method of Account Distribution at Retirement, Medium and Large Private Establishments, Selected Years, 1989–1997

Type of Distribution	1989	1991	1993	1995	1997
			(percentage)		
Panel A: Savings and Thrift Plans					
Cash Distribution[b]	97%	99%	c	c	c
Lifetime annuity	28	30	30%	17%	25%
Installments	52	52	48	30	41
Lump sum	96	99	98	85	91
Panel B: 401(k) Plans					
Cash Distribution[b]	c	c	c	c	c
Lifetime annuity	c	c	34	21	27
Installments	c	c	49	34	41
Lump sum	c	c	98	92	91

Source: U.S. Department of Labor, Bureau of Labor Statistics, *Employee Benefits in Medium and Large Private Establishments*, 1989, 1991, 1993, 1995, and 1997 (Washington, DC: U.S. Government Printing Office, 1991, 1993, 1995, 1997, and 1999).

[a]Includes workers covered but not yet participating due to minimum service requirements. Does not include workers offered but not electing contributory benefits.

[b]Many plans offer more than one form of cash distribution so sums of individual items exceed total.

[c]Data not available.

participating in savings and thrift plans, by method of account distribution at retirement for medium and large private establishments from 1989–1997. While the time series do not appear to have any significant trends, it is obvious that a significantly larger percentage of participants have a lump sum option available in 1997 (91 percent) than a lifetime annuity (27 percent).

Taxation

Contributions—Elective, nonelective, and matching contributions to a qualified Sec. 401(k) arrangement are excludable from the employee's gross income until distribution. The employee thus defers federal income tax until the time the benefit is distributed. The deferral of taxation applies also to some states and municipality tax provisions but not to Social Security and unemployment taxes. Voluntary employee after-tax contributions are taxable on a current basis. Earnings generated by any of these contributions are not taxed until withdrawal.

An employer may claim a business deduction for contributions to a 401(k) plan up to statutory limits defined under IRC Sec. 404(a). If the 401(k) is part of a profit-sharing plan, the maximum annual deduction is generally limited to 15 percent of the total compensation of participating employees.

Distributions—Distributions of 401(k) funds prior to age 59½ are subject to a 10 percent penalty tax (in addition to regular income tax) unless the distribution is (1) on the participant's death or disability, (2) in the form of an annuity payable over the life or life expectancy of the participant (or the joint lives or life expectancies of the participant and the participant's beneficiary), (3) made after the participant has separated from service after attainment of age 55, (4) made to or on behalf of an alternate payee pursuant to a qualified domestic relations order, (5) for payment of a medical expense to the extent deductible for income tax purposes under IRC Sec. 213 (expenses that exceed 7.5 percent of adjusted gross income), or rolled over to an IRA or another qualified plan within 60 days. Hardship distributions are subject to the 10 percent penalty tax unless for medical expenses to the extent deductible for federal income tax purposes. Distributions of 401(k) accumulations received after the attainment of age 59½ are taxed just as other qualified plan distributions. [32]

Investments

Plan participants may be allowed to direct the investment of plan contributions (sometimes just their own contributions, and sometimes the employer contributions as well). Investment options commonly include: a fixed (or guaranteed investment contract—GIC—) fund, which invests in a guaranteed interest contract with an insurance company; a balanced fund, which is designed to provide stability as well as growth through an investment mix of stocks and bonds; and an equity fund, which historically has demonstrated the most potential for growth but also the most risk. Investments in this fund are made in common stocks. The different funds allow the participant the option to direct investments toward his or her individual retirement planning goal. Other options sometimes available include bond funds, money market funds, fixed income securities, and company stock.

In general, retirement plans may not hold more than 10 percent of their assets in employer securities. However, an exception exists for profit-sharing plans, stock bonus plans, thrift plans, and employee stock ownership plans, as well as money purchase plans that were in existence before ERISA's enactment and invested primarily in employer securities at that time. Therefore, contributions are frequently invested in employer securities. This practice may give participants an increased interest in the firm's success.[33]

---

[32] *For a detailed discussion of these rules, see Chapter 4 of Employee Benefit Research Institute (1997).*

[33] *Under the Taxpayer Relief Act of 1997, any 401(k) plan that requires the employee's pretax contributions to be invested in employer stock is subject to the rule forbidding the plan to hold more than 10 percent of its assets in employer stock or real property. The change does not apply to employer matching contributions. There are several exceptions to this rule: The restriction does not apply to ESOPs. It does not apply if all the individual account plans sponsored by the employer have no more than 10 percent of all the assets of all the pension plans sponsored by the employer. And it does not apply if not more than 1 percent of the employee's deferrable compensation is required to be invested in the employer's securities. This change applies to elective deferrals for plan years beginning after 1998.*

Table 4.11

INVESTMENT CHOICES IN SAVINGS AND THRIFT PLANS, 1989, 1993, AND 1997

PERCENTAGE OF FULL-TIME EMPLOYEES PARTICIPATING[a] IN SAVINGS AND THRIFT PLANS, BY INVESTMENT CHOICES, MEDIUM AND LARGE PRIVATE ESTABLISHMENTS, 1989, 1993, AND 1997

	1989		1993		1997	
Investment Choices	Employee Contributions	Employer Contributions	Employee Contributions	Employer Contributions	Employee Contributions	Employer Contributions
			(percentage)			
Employee Permitted to Choose Investments	90%	53%	86%	58%	87%	65%
1–2 choices	25	22	12	7	2	2
3 choices	36	40	21	13	11	3
4 choices	23	20	30	17	21	14
5 or more choices	15	16	24	21	47	34
Employee Not Permitted to Choose Investments	b	b	7	35	6	27

Source: U.S. Department of Labor, Bureau of Labor Statistics, *Employee Benefits in Medium and Large Private Establishments*, 1989, 1993, and 1997 (Washington, DC: U.S. Government Printing Office, 1991, 1995, and 1999).

[a]Includes workers covered but not yet participating due to minimum service requirements. Does not include workers offered but not electing contributory benefits.

[b]Data not available.

Individual account assets can be held in one fund or in several funds. The plan sponsor usually has responsibility for developing broad investment policies. The trustee (e.g., a bank) is usually responsible for the actual investment of plan assets. Some employers permit participants to select among several investment options. In addition, participants may be given individual direction within certain limits set forth in Department of Labor regulations.

Table 4.11 shows the percentage of full-time employees participating in savings and thrift plans, by investment choices, for medium and large private establishments in 1989, 1993, and 1997. While the percentage of employees not permitted to choose investments for their own contributions has remained relatively small (7 percent in 1993 and 6 percent in 1997), the percentage of participants that were not able to direct the investment of employer contributions was significantly greater (35 percent in 1993 and 27 percent in 1997). Table 4.12 shows similar findings for 401(k) plans in 1993, 1995, and 1997.

■ Bibliography

Allen, Everett T., Jr., Joseph J. Melone, Jerry S. Rosenbloom, and Jack L. VanDerhei. *Pension Planning: Pensions, Profit-Sharing, and Other Deferred Compensation Plans.* Eighth edition. Homewood, IL: Richard D. Irwin, Inc., 1997.

Bucci, Michael. "Contributions to Savings and Thrift Plans." *Monthly Labor Review* (November 1990): 28–36.

Bureau of National Affairs. *Non-Traditional Incentive Pay Programs.* Washington, DC: Bureau of National Affairs, 1991.

Burkhauser, Richard V., and Dallas L. Salisbury, eds. *Pensions in a Changing Economy.* Washington, DC: Employee Benefit Research Institute/National Academy on Aging, 1993.

Employee Benefit Research Institute. *Fundamentals of Employee Benefit Programs.* Fifth Edition. Washington, DC: Employee Benefit Research Institute, 1997.

________. *EBRI Databook on Employee Benefits.* Third edition. Washington, DC: Employee Benefit Research Institute, 1995.

Foster, Ann C. "Defined Contribution Retirement Plans Become More Prevalent." *Compensation and Working Conditions* (June 1996a): 42–44.

________. "Employee Participation in Savings and Thrift Plans, 1993." *Monthly Labor Review* (March 1996b): 17–22.

________. "Public and Private Sector Defined Benefit Pension Plans: A Comparison." *Compen-*

Table 4.12
INVESTMENT CHOICES IN 401(K) PLANS, 1993, 1995, AND 1997

PERCENTAGE OF FULL-TIME EMPLOYEES PARTICIPATING[a] IN 401(K) PLANS, BY INVESTMENT CHOICES, MEDIUM AND LARGE PRIVATE ESTABLISHMENTS, 1993, 1995, AND 1997

	1993		1995		1997	
Investment Choices	Employee Contributions	Employer Contributions	Employee Contributions	Employer Contributions	Employee Contributions	Employer Contributions
			(percentage)			
Employees Permitted to Choose Investments	86%	58%	83%	64%	86%	65%
1–2 choices	11	8	4	3	3	2
3 choices	23	13	15	11	11	8
4 choices	28	16	26	16	21	14
5 or more choices	25	22	37	35	31	24
Employee not permitted to choose investments	7	35	8	26	6	27

Source: U.S. Department of Labor, Bureau of Labor Statistics, *Employee Benefits in Medium and Large Private Establishments*, 1993, 1995, and 1997 (Washington, DC: U.S. Government Printing Office, 1995, 1997, and 1999).
[a]Includes workers covered but not yet participating due to minimum service requirements. Does not include workers offered but not electing contributory benefits.

sation and Working Conditions (Summer 1997): 37–43.

Gordon, Michael S. "Twenty-fifth Anniversary Reflections on ERISA." *Benefits Quarterly* (Fourth Quarter 1999): 6–15.

Kruse, Douglas L. *Does Profit Sharing Affect Productivity?* Cambridge, MA: Bureau of Economic Research, 1993.

Mitchell, Olivia S., and Erica L. Dykes. "New Trends in Pension Benefit and Retirement Provisions." *Pension Research Council Working Paper 2000-01.* Philadelphia: Pension Research Council (January 2000).

Mitchell, Olivia S. "Trends in Pension Benefit Formulas and Retirement Provisions." In J. Turner and D. Beller, eds., *Trends in Pensions, 1992.* Washington, DC: U.S. Department of Labor, Pension and Welfare Benefits Administration, 1992.

Mitchell, Olivia S., and Rebecca Luzadis. "Changes in Pension Incentives Through Time." *Industrial and Labor Relations Review 42* (October 1988): 100–108.

Olsen, Kelly A., and Jack L. VanDerhei. "Defined Contribution Plan Dominance Grows Across Sectors and Employer Sizes, While Mega Defined Benefit Plans Remain Strong: Where We Are and Where We Are Going." In Dallas Salisbury, ed., *Retirement Prospects in a Defined Contribution World.* Washington, DC: Employee Benefit Research Institute, 1997.

Papke, Leslie E. "Participation In and Contributions To 401(k) Pension Plans: Evidence from Plan Data." *Journal of Human Resources* (Spring 1995): 311–325.

Rosenbloom, Jerry S., ed. *Handbook of Employee Benefits.* Third edition. Homewood, IL: Dow Jones-Irwin, 1996.

Salisbury, Dallas L. "Individual Saving for Retirement: The 401(k) and IRA Experiences." *EBRI Issue Brief* no. 95 (Employee Benefit Research Institute, October 1989).

Tacchino, Kenn Beam and David A Littell, "Comparing 401(k) Plans With SIMPLEs—Which is Best for Your Organization?" *Benefits Quarterly* (First Quarter 1997): 54–68.

U.S. Department of Labor. Bureau of Labor Statistics. *Employee Benefits in Medium and Large Private Establishments,* various years. Washington, DC: U.S. Government Printing Office, various years.

U.S. Department of Labor. Pension and Welfare Benefits Administration. "Abstract of 1995 Form 5500 Annual Reports." *Private Pension Plan*

Bulletin No. 8 (Spring 1999).

VanDerhei, Jack L. "Cash or Deferred Plans." In Jerry S. Rosenbloom, ed., *Handbook of Employee Benefits.* Third edition. Homewood, IL: Dow Jones-Irwin, 1996.

VanDerhei, Jack, Russell Galer, Carol Quick, and John Rea. "401(k) Plan Asset Allocation, Account Balances, and Loan Activity." *EBRI Issue Brief* no. 205 (Employee Benefit Research Institute, January 1999).

VanDerhei, Jack, and Paul Yakoboski. "Multiemployer Pension Plans." *EBRI Notes* (Employee Benefit Research Institute, June 1999): 1–4.

Weinstein, Harriet G. "Linking Retirement Plan Measures." *Compensation and Working Conditions* (Spring 1998): 52–55.

Wiatrowski, William J. "Family Retirement Benefits." *Compensation and Working Conditions* (Spring 1998): 12–17.

5

Overview of the Defined Benefit System

by Paul Yakoboski, EBRI

The continuing evolution of the U.S. retirement income system has had a tremendous impact on the defined benefit (DB) pension sector. By 1995, the aggregate number of defined benefit plans had declined by 61 percent from its peak in 1983. The number of participants in defined benefit plans has held steady over this time period, however, as most terminations involved smaller plans. But the large end of the market is also experiencing change, as a growing number final average pay DB plans are converted to cash balance arrangements. This paper provides background on the defined benefit system in the United States and focuses on trends in the number of plans and participants, typical features of plans today, and the emergence of cash balance and other hybrid arrangements.

Understanding Defined Benefit Plans

In a traditional defined benefit plan, each employee's future benefit is determined by a specific formula, and the plan provides a nominal level of benefits on retirement. Usually, the promised benefit is tied to the employee's earnings, length of service, or both. For example, an employer may promise to pay each participant a benefit equal to a percentage of the employee's final five-year average salary times number of years of service at retirement, or the employer may pay a flat dollar amount per year of service. A defined benefit plan is typically not contributory—i.e., there are usually no employee contributions, as the employer pays all the costs. And there are usually no individual accounts maintained for each employee. The employer makes regular contributions to the plan to fund the participants' future benefits. The employer bears the risk of providing the guaranteed level of retirement benefits. There are three major ways that defined benefit plans calculate contributions and benefits:

- *Flat-Benefit Formulas*—These formulas pay a flat dollar amount for each year of service recognized under the plan.
- *Career-Average Formulas*—There are two types of career-average formulas. Under the first type, participants earn a percentage of the pay recognized for plan purposes in each year they are plan participants. The second type of career-average formula averages the participant's yearly earnings over the period of plan participation. At retirement, the benefit equals a percentage of the career-average pay, multiplied by the participant's number of years of service.
- *Final-Pay Formulas*—These plans base benefits on average earnings during a specified number of years at the end of a participant's career; this is presumably the time when earnings are highest. The benefit equals a percentage of the participant's final average earnings, multiplied by the number of years of service. This formula provides preretirement inflation protection to the participant but can represent a higher cost to the employer.

Flat-benefit formulas are common in collectively bargained plans or plans covering hourly paid employees. Career-average and final-pay formulas are most common in plans covering nonunion employees. Under pay-related formulas, an employer has some discretion in defining pay for plan purposes, provided the definition does not discriminate in favor of highly compensated employees, subject to the statutory and regulatory definition of compensation used in testing for nondiscrimination. Under the minimum standards established by the Employee Retirement Income Security Act of 1974 (ERISA), there is also some leeway in determining what employment period will be recognized in the benefit formula. The benefit may reflect only the plan participation period or may be based on the entire employment period.

Defined Benefit Plan Trends

Between 1975, when ERISA became effective, and 1995, the latest year for which these data are available, the number of private employer-sponsored pension plans and plan participants continued to increase, but proportionately fewer of these plans were defined benefit plans. The total number of private-sector defined benefit plans increased from 103,000 in 1975 to 175,000 in 1983, then decreased to 69,000 in 1995 (table 5.1). While defined benefit plans accounted for 33 percent of all private plans in 1975, they accounted for only 10 percent by 1995.

The total number of participants in all defined benefit plans was 33 million in 1975. Participation increased to 40 million in 1983 and has remained in the 39 million–41 million range since that time. The trends for active participants in private primary plans are similar to those for total participants. In 1975, there were 27 million active participants in primary defined benefit plans, and this number decreased to 24 million by 1995.

For 87 percent of all active participants in 1975, the primary retirement plan type was defined benefit. By 1995, this figure had decreased to 51 percent.

In 1975, defined benefits plans had $186 billion in total assets, and this amount grew to $1.4 trillion by 1995. But over this 20-year period, defined benefit assets declined as a percentage of total private-sector pension assets from 72 percent to 51 percent.

Though still relatively rare, cash balance plans are gaining attention and are blurring the non-fundamental distinctions between defined benefit and defined contribution plan types.[1] According to data from KPMG, 4 percent of employers with 200 or more employees sponsored a cash balance plan in 1998, compared with 2 percent in 1993. While cash balance plans are legally considered defined benefit plans, they combine features of both defined benefit and defined contribution plans, and consequently are referred to as "hybrid plans."[2]

[1] *For a full discussion, see Sharyn Campbell, "Hybrid Retirement Plans: The Retirement Income System Continues to Evolve,"* EBRI Issue Brief *no. 171 (Employee Benefit Research Institute, March 1996).*

[2] *Other common hybrid plans include age-weighted profit-sharing plans, target benefit plans, and life-cycle pension plans.*

Putting the Past in Perspective

An examination of the change in the aggregate number of private pension plans and participants masks trends in plans by size. Examining private primary defined benefit plan trends by plan size shows that the vast majority of plan terminations were very small plans: those with two to nine active participants. Between 1985 and 1993, there was a net decrease in the total number of primary defined benefit plans of 51 percent, or 86,000 plans. The net number of plans with two to nine active participants decreased by about 56,000 plans, and accounted for 65 percent of the total reduction in defined benefit plans (table 5.2). It has been suggested that very small plans were often top-heavy plans used by employers as tax shelters. After enactment of the Tax Equity and Fiscal Responsibility Act of 1982 (TEFRA), which imposed penalties on top-heavy plans, and the Tax Reform Act of 1986 (TRA '86), which lowered basic income tax rates and imposed faster minimum vesting standards, there was less incentive for these employers to maintain their defined benefit pension plans. TRA '86 also included a provision that eliminated the tax qualification of some small defined benefit plans, primarily single-participant plans.

Between 1985 and 1993, the net change in the number of primary defined benefit plans was generally greater for plans with fewer active participants. The number of defined benefit plans with 10–24 active participants decreased 55 percent between 1985 and 1993, while the number of defined benefit plans with 500–999 active participants decreased 22 percent. Some of the change in the number of plans by plan size is due to changes in individual plans' demographics. For example, a plan that had 400 participants in 1985 may have had 600 participants in 1993. The number of large primary defined benefit plans remained relatively stable between 1985 and 1993. In fact, the number of plans with 10,000 or more active participants increased 5 percent over that time period.

Table 5.1

PRIVATE PENSION PLANS AND PARTICIPANTS

SUMMARY OF PRIVATE-SECTOR QUALIFIED DEFINED BENEFIT AND DEFINED CONTRIBUTION PLANS AND PARTICIPANTS, SELECTED YEARS 1975–1995

	1975	1980	1981	1982	1983	1984	1985	1986	1987	1988	1989	1990	1991	1992	1993	1994	1995
								(thousands)									
Total Plans[a,b]	311	489	546	594	603	604	632	718	733	730	731	712	699	708	702	690	693
Defined benefit[a]	103	148	167	175	175	168	170	173	163	146	132	113	102	89	84	74	69
Defined contribution[a]	208	341	378	419	428	436	462	545	570	584	599	599	598	620	619	616	624
Defined contribution as percentage of total	67%	70%	69%	71%	71%	72%	73%	76%	78%	80%	82%	84%	85%	87%	88%	89%	90%
								(millions)									
Total Participants[b,c]	45	58	61	63	69	74	75	77	78	78	76	77	78	82	84	85	87
Defined benefit[c]	33	38	39	39	40	41	40	40	40	41	40	39	39	40	40	40	40
Defined contribution[c]	12	20	22	25	29	33	35	37	38	37	36	38	39	42	44	45	48
Defined contribution as percentage of total	26%	34%	36%	39%	42%	45%	47%	48%	49%	48%	48%	50%	50%	52%	52%	53%	55%
Active Participants	31	36	37	37	39	40	40	41	42	42	43	42	43	45	45	46	47
Primary plan is defined benefit[d]	27	30	30	29	30	30	29	29	28	28	27	26	26	25	25	25	24
Primary plan is defined contribution[d]	4	6	7	8	9	10	12	13	13	14	15	16	17	19	19	21	23
Defined Contrbution as percentage of total	13%	16%	19%	22%	23%	25%	30%	32%	31%	33%	35%	38%	40%	42%	42%	46%	49%
								($ billions)									
Assets[b,e]	$260	$564	$629	$789	$923	$1,045	$1,253	$1,383	$1,402	$1,504	$1,676	$1,674	$1,936	S2,094	$2,316	$2,299	$2,724
Defined benefit	186	401	444	553	642	701	826	895	877	912	988	962	1,102	1,147	1,248	1,211	1,402
Defined contribution	74	162	185	236	281	344	427	488	525	592	688	712	834	947	1,068	1,088	1,322
Defined contribution as percentage of total	28%	29%	29%	30%	30%	33%	34%	35%	37%	39%	41%	43%	43%	45%	46%	47%	49%

Source: Employee Benefit Research Institute tabulations based on U.S. Department of Labor, Pension and Welfare Benefits Administration, Private Pension Plan Bulletin (Spring 1999).

[a]Excludes single participant plans.

[b]Due to rounding, sums of individual items may not equal totals.

[c]Includes active, retired, and separated vested participants not yet in pay status. Not adjusted for double counting of individuals participating in more than one plan.

[d]For workers covered under both a defined benefit and a defined contribution plan, the defined benefit plan is designated as the primary plan unless the plan name indicates it provides supplemental or past service benefits.

[e]Excludes funds held by life insurance companies under allocated group contracts for payment of reitrement benefits. These funds make up roughly 10 to 15 percent of total private pension plan assets.

Table 5.2

PRIMARY PLAN TRENDS BY PLAN SIZE

PRIMARY DEFINED BENEFIT AND DEFINED CONTRIBUTION PLAN AND ACTIVE PARTICIPANT TRENDS, SELECTED YEARS 1985–1993

	Primary Plans							Active Participants (thousands)						
						Net Change	Net Change						Net Change	Net Change
Active Participants	1985	1990	1991	1992	1993	1985–1993	1992–1993	1985	1990	1991	1992	1993	1985–1993	1992–1993
							Defined Benefit Plans							
2–9	88,124	45,796	38,424	34,316	32,121	–56,003	–2,195	353	189	168	147	141	–212	–6
10–24	24,267	15,624	18,095	12,452	10,903	–13,364	–1,549	369	244	273	191	168	–201	–23
25–49	14,178	8,605	7,374	7,745	7,252	–6,927	–494	491	304	255	271	252	–239	–19
50–99	11,303	8,346	8,060	8,114	7,499	–3,804	–615	808	599	585	588	537	–271	–51
100–249	9,534	6,563	6,183	6,290	6,209	–3,325	–81	1,498	1,040	979	995	978	–520	–17
250–499	4,670	3,647	3,514	3,447	3,444	–1,226	–3	1,651	1,293	1,245	1,220	1,224	–427	4
500–999	3,149	2,463	2,328	2,378	2,450	–699	72	2,222	1,751	1,655	1,686	1,751	–471	65
1,000–2,499	2,360	2,090	2,028	2,065	2,122	–238	57	3,636	3,221	3,119	3,180	3,285	–351	105
2,500–4,999	847	798	780	796	790	–57	–6	2,930	2,802	2,704	2,797	2,790	–140	–7
5,000–9,999	455	434	469	445	428	–27	–17	3,141	3,015	3,261	3,033	2,966	–175	–67
10,000–19,999	198	223	219	224	223	25	–1	2,749	3,134	3,134	3,132	3,088	339	–44
20,000 or more	175	161	167	167	167	–8	0	8,985	8,711	8,324	8,073	7,912	–1073	–161
None or None Reported	10,280	18,139	13,944	9,960	9,909	–371	–51	–	–	–	–	–	–	–
Total[a]	169,540	112,890	101,585	88,400	83,517	–86,023	–4,883	28,834	26,303	25,701	25,313	25,091	16,257	–222
							Defined Contribution Plans							
2–9	199,704	266,129	266,298	270,764	266,284	66,580	–4,480	852	1,127	1,151	1,180	1,165	313	–15
10–24	70,424	97,054	99,188	112,560	112,889	42,465	329	1,056	1,476	1,508	1,737	1,735	679	–2
25–49	31,406	45,737	49,132	54,488	55,094	23,688	606	1,091	1,584	1,695	1,889	1,915	824	26
50–99	17,620	27,446	29,528	32,548	33,835	16,215	1,287	1,224	1,911	2,067	2,273	2,374	1,150	101
100–249	8,878	13,658	13,890	16,187	16,902	8,024	715	1,331	2,071	2,117	2,466	2,572	1,241	106
250–499	2,552	4,144	4,314	5,051	5,187	2,635	136	737	868	1,428	1,488	1,786	1,049	298
500–999	1,185	1,838	1,952	2,242	2,376	1,191	134	808	1,266	1,345	1,532	1,632	824	100
1,000–2,499	784	1,103	1,169	1,332	1,400	616	68	1,194	1,671	1,790	2,028	2,144	950	116
2,500–4,999	219	310	325	355	372	153	17	752	1,072	1,124	1,199	1,272	520	73
5,000–9,999	97	130	126	156	148	51	–8	683	869	850	1,048	984	301	–64
10,000–19,999	34	44	47	50	50	16	0	460	626	644	694	683	223	–11
20,000 or more	29	27	31	40	35	6	–5	1,100	1,151	1,361	1,704	1,518	418	–186
None or None Reported	13,082	40,473	40,067	34,855	37,970	24,888	3,115	–	–	–	–	–	–	–
Total[a]	346,014	498,093	506,066	530,627	532,542	186,528	1,915	11,420	16,251	17,141	19,486	19,779	18,359	293

Source: Employee Benefit Research Institute tabulations of 1985, 1990, 1991, 1992 and 1993 Form 5500 annual reports filed with the Internal Revenue Service.
[a]Total may not equal the sum of individual items due to rounding.

Because most of the decline in primary defined benefit plans occurred in plans with two to nine participants, the decline in the number of employees covered by a primary defined benefit plans is relatively small. Approximately 80 percent of active participants in primary defined benefit plans in 1993 were in plans with 1,000 or more active participants. Even if the 70,000 plans with fewer than 1,000 participants in 1993 were to terminate, 80 percent of active participants with primary defined benefit plans would continue to accrue benefits in their pension plans, while 20 percent of defined benefit participants (5 million) would have their pension benefits frozen. Many of these latter employees would still be covered by an existing defined contribution plan or contribute to another retirement arrangement.

Defined Benefit Funding

As of 1998, 84 percent of large defined benefit plans were fully funded on a termination basis, i.e., they had assets greater than total current liability for accrued benefits (table 5.3).[3, 4] While this figure is unchanged over the past 10 years (85 percent in 1993 and 83 percent in 1988), it represents a marked improvement in funding relative to the situation at the beginning of the 1980s (45 percent in 1981). However, it should also be noted that the percentage of plans that are "very" overfunded (a funding ratio of 150 percent or more) has decreased from 48 percent in 1987 to 24 percent in 1998. The median accrued benefit ratio for 1998 was 123 percent. In 1998, 24 percent of plans had a benefit ratio of 150 percent or more, 23 percent had a ratio of 125 percent–149 percent, 37 percent had a ratio of 100 percent–124 percent, 14 percent had a ratio of 75 percent–99 percent, and 2 percent had a ratio of 1 percent–74 percent (table 5.3 presents trends for these data).

Ippolito[5] documents that aggregate funding ratios generally increased in the early 1980s, flattened out in the latter 1980s, and began falling after 1990. He finds that the reduction is not attributable to changing interest rates used to discount pension annuities nor is it explained by poor investment performance. He argues such a funding ratio pattern is suggestive of some stimulus that explains rapid and systematic change throughout the industry over a short time period. He presents evidence that plan sponsors have voluntarily reduced pension plan funding levels, and that most plans reduced their funding status well below the levels affected by the new maximum funding limits.[6] He argues that the most likely underlying reason for this change is the introduction by Congress of a sequence of reversion taxes starting at 10 percent in 1986 and reaching 50 percent in 1990, since these taxes effectively increased the sponsor's legal pension liability beyond termination values if it maintained an overfunded plan. Therefore, most sponsors have shed a large percentage of the excess assets in their defined benefit plan as a result.

In the aggregate, multiemployer defined benefit plans are well-funded, as can be seen from the two time series in chart 5.1. The first line (plans fully funded for vested benefits) depicts the percentage of plans that had plan assets at least equal to their participants' vested benefits. The sample includes more than 450 multiemployer plans (representing approximately 40 percent of all participants in multiemployer plans) surveyed by the Segal Company for the last five years. In the most recent plan valuations, 74 percent of plans were fully funded for vested benefits. Moreover, as can be seen from the second (average funded ratio) line, even plans that were not fully funded were not far from this target, as evidenced by the fact that the ratio for all surveyed plans was 96 percent.[7]

---

[3] *See* 1998 Survey of Actuarial Assumptions and Funding, Pension Plans with 1,000 or More Active Participants *(Watson Wyatt Worldwide, 1998).*

[4] *Ninety-one percent of plans have assets greater than the vested portion of current liability, and 99 percent of plans have assets greater than the current liability for retiree benefits.*

[5] *See Richard A. Ippolito,* The New Pension Economics: Defined Contribution Plans and Sorting, *unpublished manuscript, November 1999.*

[6] *The 150 percent full-funding limit was imposed by the Omnibus Budget Reconciliation Act of 1987. In addition, the Tax Reform Act of 1986 prohibited the value of projected wage increases from exceeding $200,000 in nominal terms. This limit was further reduced to $150,000 in 1992.*

[7] *Assets in excess of 100 percent of vested benefits are excluded from the calculation.*

Table 5.3

FUNDED RATIOS OF SURVEYED PRIVATE PENSION PLANS

SURVEYED FIRMS' FUNDED RATIOS, BY PERCENTAGE OF ALL DEFINED BENEFIT PENSION PLANS, 1981-1998

	1981	1983	1985	1986	1987	1988	1989	1990	1991	1992	1993	1994	1995	1996	1997	1998
Ratio of Assets Over Accrued Benefits	All Defined Benefit Pension Plans															
Less than 75%	34%	19%	9%	7%	6%	6%	7%	4%	5%	4%	3%	3%	4%	6%	2%	2%
75%–99%	21	17	13	14	10	11	11	11	10	11	12	15	20	24	17	14
100%–124%	23	25	21	17	16	16	18	20	25	24	26	30	35	34	37	37
125%–149%	11	18	19	21	20	20	19	20	22	24	27	26	23	20	24	23
150% or More	11	21	38	41	48	47	45	45	38	37	32	26	18	16	20	24
100% or More	45	64	78	79	84	83	82	85	85	85	85	82	76	70	81	84
Number of Plans[a]	575	695	912	836	799	720	786	787	781	748	695	722	663	619	588	540

Source: The Wyatt Company, Survey of Actuarial Assumptions and Funding: Pension Plans with 1,000 or More Active Participants, 1983, 1988, 1994 and 1998) and unpublished data from The Wyatt Company's Survey of Actuarial Assumptions and Funding: Pension Plans with 1,000 or More Active Participants, 1981–1995.

Note: Data from The Wyatt Company are based on a survey of pension plans covering 1,000 or more active employees. The 1994 survey contained single-employer plans (91 percent) and multiemployer plans (9 percent)

[a]The number of plans surveyed is greater than the actual number of plans providing complete funding information.

■ PBGC's Financial Status

The Pension Benefit Guaranty Corporation (PBGC) was established by ERISA to provide timely and uninterrupted payment of benefits. PBGC protects the retirement incomes of about 42 million American workers in more than 44,000 defined benefit pension plans.

As of 1998, PBGC assets in the single-employer program exceeded liabilities by $5.0 billion (assets of $17.6 billion and liabilities of $12.6 billion). PBGC has had a surplus for three consecutive years after running a deficit for more than 20 straight years. At its depth in 1986, the PBGC single-employer program deficit was $3.8 billion. In the multiemployer program, net

Chart 5.1

FUNDED POSITION OF MULTIEMPLOYER PENSION PLANS

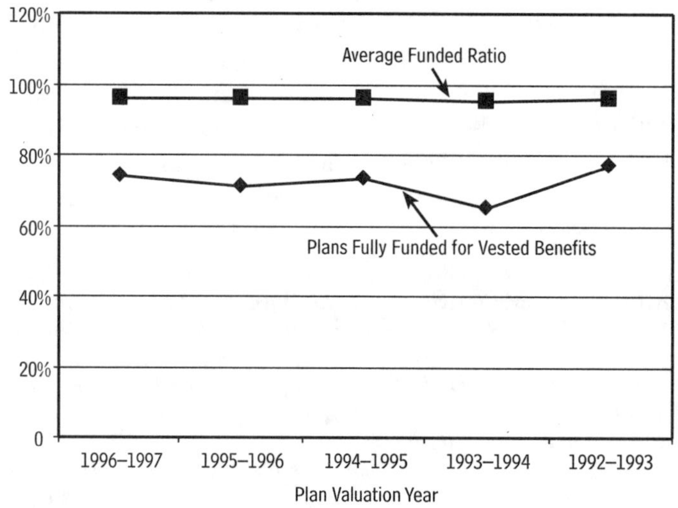

Source: The Segal Company Newsletter, U.S. Edition, Vol. 43, No. 1, January 1999, pp. 1–2.

assets were positive at $0.3 billion as of 1998. In 1998 PBGC paid $848 million in pension benefits to 209,300 individuals and became trustee for 160 terminated plans. An additional 263,000 individuals will receive benefits from PBGC in the future when they retire.

"Typical" Defined Benefit Plan Features[8]

Based on its annual survey of retirement benefits, KPMG finds that the "typical" defined benefit plan bases benefits on a formula of final average earnings times years of service. The formula is likely to be at least 2 percent of final average pay, without a limit on the number of years of service counted for benefits, and without integration of Social Security benefits. Full vesting occurs after five years. Normal retirement age is 65 and early retirement age is 55.

Seventy percent of defined benefit plans use a final average earnings formula, 22 percent use a career average formula, and 4 percent use a flat-dollar amount formula. Sixty-three percent of defined benefit plans vest fully after five years, while 8 percent vest earlier. Seventy percent of plans are not integrated with Social Security. The median reported early retirement benefit was 56 percent of benefit paid at normal retirement age. Thirty-eight percent of survey respondents reported exercising their early retirement option. Twenty-eight percent of plans reported automatic cost-of-living adjustments. Fifty-three percent of defined benefit plans offered a lump-sum distribution option for benefit amounts in excess of $3,500.

Cash Balance Plans

The trend among large companies toward conversion from traditional final-average defined benefit plans to cash balance plans has precipitated one of the most complex pension-related controversies of the late 1990s. Current debate appears to focus on both the effects of these conversions on expected retirement incomes and on the manner and extent to which companies must disclose these effects to participants. This section provides background information on issues surrounding cash balance plans, and is based on EBRI testimony on hybrid pension plans, submitted Sept. 21, 1999, at the request of the Senate Health, Education, Labor and Pensions Committee; and on the cover story in the fourth quarter 1999 *ACA Journal,* "The Controversy of Traditional vs. Cash Balance Plans," by Jack VanDerhei, Temple University and EBRI Fellow.

The recent trend among large employers toward conversion of traditional final-average and career-average defined benefit plans to cash balances has raised a controversial and complex set of issues. A cash balance plan is a "hybrid" type of pension plan—i.e., one that takes on the characteristics of both a defined benefit plan and a defined contribution plan. Legally, a cash balance plan is a defined benefit plan. A cash balance plan offers some of the popular advantages of a defined benefit plan but is designed to look more like a defined contribution plan, with an individual "hypothetical" account that appears to accumulate assets for each participant. Cash balance plan accounts are a record-keeping feature only, as these plans are funded on an actuarial basis, in the same way that defined benefit pension plans are funded. Therefore, at any point in time, the benefits promised to a participant are based on the plan formulae and not on the assets in his or her "account."

In a typical cash balance plan, a participant's retirement account grows by earning annual credits that may be based on a flat percentage of pay but that might be integrated with Social Security benefits.[9] However, it is also possible to provide age or service-weighted pay credits under these plans, even though a cursory examination of Internal Revenue Code (IRC) Sec. 411(b) would suggest that this violates the 133-1/3 percent rule.[10] Cash balance plans also provide a yield on

---

[8] *Data in this section are from* Retirement Benefits in the 1990s: 1998 Survey Data *(KPMG Peat Marwick LLP, 1998). Data are based on a survey of 1,292 employers with 200 or more employees (95 percent of whom offer retirement benefits to their workers). The survey is random and thus weighting allows generalization of the results to the national level.*

[9] *See Carol Quick, "An Overview of Cash Balance Plans,"* EBRI Notes *no. 7 (Employee Benefit Research Institute, July 1999): 1–8.*

[10] *The plan design constraints otherwise provided via the anti-backloading provisions appear to be mitigated due to the assumption that early pay credits will earn more interest credits by retirement age.*

the hypothetical account that is typically defined as either the 30-year Treasury rate or the one-year T-bill rate plus a stated percentage[11, 12]

Cash Balance Trends

Large employers that continue to sponsor defined benefit plans are less frequently utilizing "traditional" benefit formulas, such as "final-average" and "career-average pay" formulas. Table 5.4 below demonstrates that for respondents to a survey of the large U. S. employers offering a defined benefit plan, the percentage utilizing a final-average formula decreased from 85 percent to 72 percent over the last 14 years. Similarly, the percentage utilizing a career-average pay formula declined from 15 percent in 1985 to 9 percent in 1999. During that same period of time, utilization of cash balance plans increased dramatically, with most of the growth occurring after 1994 (when the number of cash balance plans increased from 6 percent to 16 percent of all large defined benefit plans).

Questions often arise as to what forces have caused this acceleration over the last four years. The Employee Benefit Research Institute (EBRI) surveyed current, future, and potential hybrid retirement plan sponsors in June 1995,[13] and no similar survey appears to have been published subsequently. However, it is likely that regulatory clarifications of certain technical aspects of cash balance plans (such as those provided in 1996 when the Internal Revenue Service (IRS) issued Notice 96-8[14]) were important catalysts for many of the more recent conversions from "traditional" defined benefit plans to those of the cash balance variety.

Table 5.4
PRIMARY TYPE OF DEFINED BENEFIT FORMULA, 1985–1999

	1985	1990	1995	1999
Number of Employers	740	806	836	773
Highest Average Pay	85%	81%	82%	72%
5-year average	71	63	62	55
3-year average	12	16	17	15
Other (e.g., 10-year average)	2	3	3	2
Career Average Pay	15	14	12	9
Cash Balance	0	2	6	16
Pension Equity	0	0	0	3
Other (e.g., fixed dollar only)	<1	2	<1	<1

Source: Hewitt Associates SpecBook™

Final-Average vs. Cash Balance Plans

Under either the final-average or cash balance plans illustrated in chart 5.2, an employee starting at age 25 will obtain the same benefit value at age 65 if he or she remains with the same employer for a full career. However, the accrual rates under each plan differ fundamentally. The annual increase in benefit value (meaning how much additional retirement income an employee will earn by working one more year) tends to be much higher for young employees under the cash balance plan and

11 *See Ron Gebhardtsbauer, "Testimony on Cash Balance Plans, Conversions and Disclosure," ERISA Advisory Council (U.S. Department of Labor, May 6 and June 9, 1999).*

12 *One factor that may be a constraint on adoption of these plans in the current financial markets is that many participants in defined contribution plans have come to expect annual returns far in excess of these rates (approximately 6 percent currently). However, for technical reasons enumerated in IRS Notice 96-8, employers providing a rate of return in excess of one of these indices would be subject to the "whipsaw" problem. In brief, this would potentially require the plan sponsor to pay lump-sum distributions (LSDs) that were larger than the hypothetical account balance (significantly so for young employees, as a percentage of the account balance) because Internal Revenue Code (IRC) requirements appear to require account balances to be accumulated out to retirement age and then discounted back to the current age at the 417(e) discount rate (Demby, May 1999).*

13 *See Sharyn Campbell, "Hybrid Retirement Plans: The Retirement Income System Continues to Evolve,"* EBRI Issue Brief *no. 171 (Employee Benefit Research Institute, March 1996).*

14 *IRS Notice 96-8 provided proposed guidance on applying IRC Secs. 411 and 417(e) to cash balance plans. In order to comply with these sections in determining the amount of a single-sum distribution, the balance of an employee's hypothetical account under a cash balance plan has to be projected to normal retirement age, and then the employee must be paid at least the present value of that projected hypothetical account (White 1999).*

Chart 5.2
Illustration of a Conversion From a Hypothetical Traditional Final-Average Defined Benefit Plan to a Hypothetical Service-Weighted Cash Balance Plan (without transition credits) at Age 55

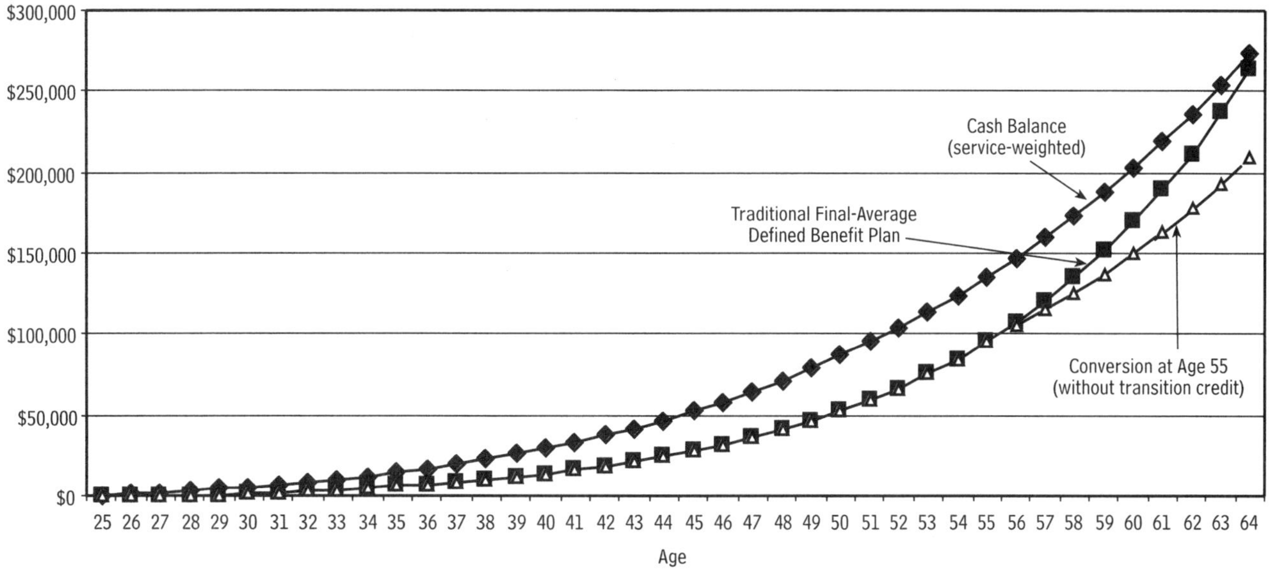

Source: Author's tabulations based on assumptions in Purcell (1999) with the following modification: the benefit accrual rate was decreased to 0.91 to allow for benefit equivalence of the two programs assuming 40 years of participation in the same program.

much higher for older employees under the final-average plan. This is true even though the cash balance plan illustrated in this chart adopts a service-weighted pay credit schedule.[15]

A difference in accrual rates between older and younger workers upon conversion from a final-average to a cash balance plan is likely to exist whether or not a so-called wear-away provision (explained below) is included in the plan. The difference is conceptually similar to the effects of changing a final-average plan to a career-average plan or, more drastically, terminating a defined benefit plan and establishing a defined contribution plan. However, the magnitude of the difference is influenced by plan-specific design parameters.[16]

Employees faced with the type of graph shown in chart 5.2 are likely to wonder why the shapes look different. The difference essentially lies in the different determinants of benefit value under each type of plan. Under a final-average plan, the present value of the annual accrual of pension wealth at any point in time is expressed as a percentage of compensation that depends on age, service, and pay. However, under a cash balance plan it depends predominantly on pay and service (and to a lesser extent on age). Therefore, even if the overall generosity of a plan remains the same after conversion to a cash-balance formula, higher accruals for young employees means that accruals for older employees will likely decrease unless some type of grandfathering or transition provisions (explained below) are provided to older workers.

For example, a 30-year employee participating in the hypothetical *final-average* defined benefit plan in chart 5.2 would have a present value from his or her defined benefit plan at age 55 of approximately $95,000, as opposed to approximately $135,000 for a similar employee who had participated in the hypothetical *cash balance* plan

---

[15] *All assumptions for this chart replicate those in Purcell (1999) with the exception of the benefit accrual rate, which was decreased to 0.91 percent to allow for benefit equivalence of the two programs assuming 40 years of participation in the same program. The pay credits varied as follows: years 1–10: 4 percent, 11–20: 5.5 percent, 21–40: 7 percent.*

[16] *For example, age-weighted pay credits under the cash balance plans and early retirement provisions under the final-average plan.*

for the same 30-year period. However, if the hypothetical final-average plan were then converted to the hypothetical cash balance plan without the provision of any type of transition credit, the employee would not benefit from the rapid escalation in pension wealth from age 55 to 65 that is associated with the final average plan. Instead, during the final 10 years he or she would experience a slope of the accrual path similar[17] to that experienced by the participant who remains under the cash balance plan for the entire 30 years. As a result, barring any transition provisions, the cash balance participant at age 65 would experience a decrease in pension wealth of approximately 23 percent, compared with the final-average participant at age 65.

Another significant difference between a traditional defined benefit plan and a cash balance plan concerns the inherent uncertainty involved in estimating the nominal amount of retirement income. Traditional defined benefit plans are not typically thought of in this regard, since the amount is specified in a formula and (with the exception of certain integrated plans) can be directly computed once the average compensation and years of participation are known. However, it appears that an increasing percentage of defined benefit participants are now receiving their distributions in the form of lump-sum distributions (LSDs)—a form that can provide great uncertainty to employees with respect to the amount that they will receive, due to fluctuations in the relevant discount rates used in the benefit calculation.[18] In contrast, cash balance plans provide LSDs that are stabilized. Annuity values under cash balance arrangements may be subject to fluctuations in annuity purchase prices although it appears some employers are willing to hold annuity purchase rates constant in the plan.[19]

Potential Advantages of Cash Balance Over Final-Average Plans

There are number of reasons why an employer that sponsors a final-average defined benefit plan may be interested in converting to a cash balance plan:[20]

Ease of Communication vs. the "Invisible Plan" Syndrome

Sponsors of traditional defined benefit plans often bemoan the lack of recognition they receive from their employees, even though substantial sums of money are contributed and/or accrued annually on behalf of workers. When the quality of workers' information regarding traditional pension offerings was evaluated,[21] about one-third of workers queried were unable to answer any questions about early retirement requirements, and about two-thirds of those who offered answers about early retirement were wrong.[22] In contrast to explaining the complex benefit formulas used by traditional defined benefit plans, conveying information through theoretical account balances under cash balance plans facilitates employee appreciation of both current pension wealth and the annual pay and interest credits that increase pension value over time.

---

[17] *Note that they will not be exactly equal given that the pay credit differs from the assumed interest credited to the cash balance plan (5.6 percent).*

[18] *See Christopher M. Bone, "Statement before the ERISA Advisory Council Working Group on Hybrid Plans," ERISA Advisory Council (U.S. Department of Labor, Sept. 9, 1999).*

[19] *See Ron Gebhardtsbauer, "Testimony on Cash Balance Plans, Conversions and Disclosure," for ERISA Advisory Council (U.S. Department of Labor, May 6 and June 9, 1999).*

[20] *In addition to these retirement plan-specific reasons, there may also be overall compensation or administrative concerns that are specifically addressed through a conversion. Two of the more common reasons include supporting a total compensation philosophy in the context of a new performance-based arrangement with employees, and providing a platform for merging disparate pension plans as a result of merger and acquisitions activity (Towers Perrin, 1999).*

[21] *Using both administrative records and worker reports of pension provisions.*

[22] *See Olivia S. Mitchell, "Worker Knowledge of Pension Provisions,"* Journal of Labor Economics, *Vol. 6, no. 1 (January 1988): 21–40.*

Chart 5.3

HYPOTHETICAL PERCENTAGE INCREASES IN ANNUAL BENEFITS AT NRA CASH BALANCE VS. FINAL AVERAGE PLAN: IMPACT OF JOB TENURE

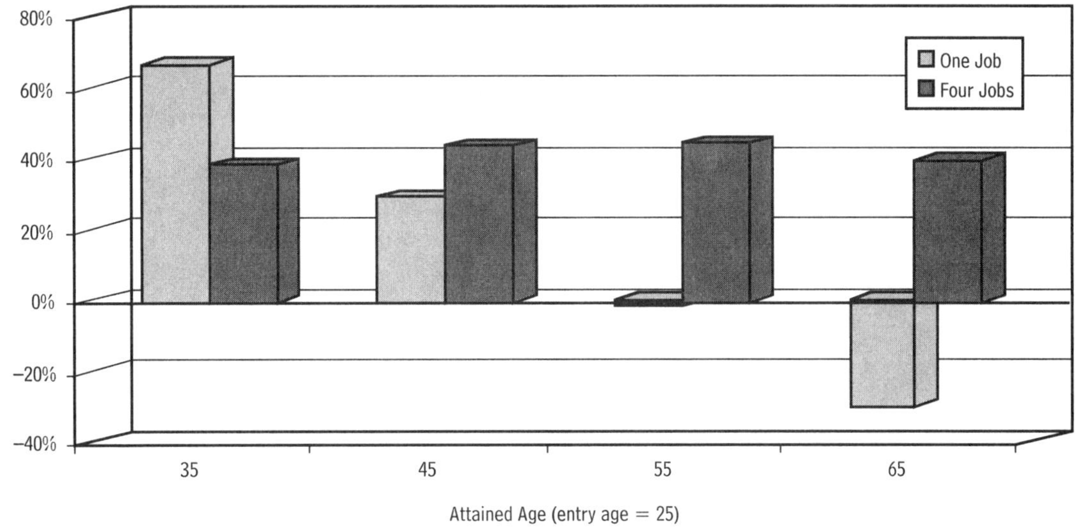

Source: Employee Benefit Research Institute tabulations based on tables from Patrick Purcell, Pension Issues: Cash-Balance Plans, CRS Report for Congress, May 24, 1999.

No Magic Numbers of Age and Service

Final-average defined benefit plans often require employees to satisfy some combination of age and service before they are entitled to retire with an early retirement subsidy. The magnitude of the dollar loss from leaving prior to that time can be substantial.[23] In contrast, the accrual pattern under a cash balance plan typically does not have a sudden, rapid increase after attainment of specific age and service criteria. As a result, cash balance plans are easier for employees to understand, provide a greater benefit to shorter-term workers, and are more attractive to a mobile work force.

Higher Benefits to Employees Who Do Not Stay With One Employer for Their Entire Career

Chart 5.3 shows the percentage increases in annual retirement benefits at normal retirement age for an employee in a hypothetical cash balance plan versus a hypothetical final-average defined benefit plan. The figures in this chart are tabulated from a Congressional Research Service (CRS) report to Congress that includes calculations for two types of employees: (a) one who enters the employer's plan at age 25 and remains in that plan for 40 years, and (b) one who changes jobs every 10 years.[24]

Comparing the two sets of bar graphs, one can see that for a hypothetical individual staying at the same job for his or her entire career, the cash balance plan provides a larger benefit after the first 10 and 20 years of service. But, by age 55, the final-average plan is slightly more valuable, and by normal retirement age (65) the benefit derived from the final-average plan would be 30 percent larger than the cash balance benefit.

However, this "one-job-for-life" scenario applies only to a small percentage of the work force.[25] Employees today are more likely to have four (if not more) jobs during their careers. The second set of bar graphs shows that for these more mobile workers, the series of cash balance plan

---

[23] *Richard A. Ippolito,* Pension Plans and Employee Performance: Evidence, Analysis and Policy, *(Chicago: University of Chicago Press, 1998).*

[24] *See Patrick Purcell, "Pension Issues: Cash-Balance Plans,"* CRS Report for Congress *(Washington, DC: Congressional Research Service, May 24, 1999).*

[25] *See Paul Yakoboski,. "Male and Female Tenure Continues to Move in Opposite Directions."* EBRI Notes *no. 2 (Employee Benefit Research Institute, February 1999): 1–4.*

benefits exceed those accrued under the final-average plans at every age, with the final retirement benefit approximately 40 percent larger than under a final-average type of plan.[26]

Potential Advantages of Cash Balance Over Defined Contribution Plans

Of course, an employer that sponsors a final-average defined *benefit* plan has the option of terminating the plan (assuming it is adequately funded) and setting up instead a defined *contribution* plan (such as a 401(k) plan) to provide the retirement benefit. However, there are several reasons why this may be problematic:

Ease of Conversion vs. New Plan Establishment

Whereas a conversion from a final-average defined benefit plan to a cash balance plan only requires a plan amendment,[27] terminating the same plan and setting up a successor defined contribution plan may trigger a reversion excise tax of either 20 percent or 50 percent.[28] If the defined benefit plan was overfunded, the surplus in a conversion to a cash balance plan would be used to reduce future contributions (as it would under the traditional plan); if it was underfunded, the unfunded liability is amortized in the normal fashion.[29]

Guarantee of Employee Participation

The noncontributory nature of most (if not all) cash balance plans eliminates the need to worry about employees who choose not to participate or make minimal contributions in a 401(k) arrangement.[30] As a result, employees are guaranteed a benefit under a cash balance plan without needing to actively choose to participate in the plan, and the plan is protected from possible disqualification due insufficient participation among lower-paid workers.

In contrast, research by Clark, Goodfellow, Schieber, and Warwick found that less than half of all workers ages 20–29 earning less than $15,000 per year contributed to their 401(k) plan.[31] This has led some to speculate that 401(k) plans are being adopted as a supplemental (as opposed to replacement) plan for a traditional defined benefit plan, and that the additional cost of the supplemental plan is being offset by reductions in the cost of the original plan. One way this could be accomplished is by the substitution of a cash balance plan for a traditional final-average defined benefit plan.

Retirement Pattern Predictability

In a defined benefit plan (including cash balance plans), investment risk is directly borne by the employer. In a defined contribution plan (such as a 401(k) plan), investment risk is borne by the individual worker. As a result, the employer is

---

[26] *In the case of the job-changer, it is assumed that the full amount of any cash balance proceeds would be reinvested in a tax-deferred retirement savings account and earn an average annual rate of return of 8.65 percent, while the employee covered by a final-average plan would remain in a terminated vested status and not receive lump-sum distributions.*

[27] *See Anna M. Rappaport, Michael L. Young, Christopher A. Levell, and Brad A. Blalock, "Cash Balance Pension Plans," in Michael Gordon, Olivia S. Mitchell, and Marc Twinney, eds.,* Positioning Pensions for the Twenty-First Century *(Philadelphia: University of Pennsylvania Press, 1997).*

[28] *See Michael J. Alderson and Jack L. VanDerhei, "Disturbing the Balance in Corporate Pension Policy: The Case of Excess Asset Reversion Legislation,"* Benefits Quarterly *(Third Quarter, 1991): 38–51.*

[29] *See Mark J. Warshawsky, "Funding of Defined Benefit Pension Plans," in MichaelGordon, Olivia S. Mitchell, and Marc Twinney, eds.,* Positioning Pensions for the Twenty-First Century *(Philadelphia: University of Pennsylvania Press, 1997).*

[30] *See Paul Yakoboski, "Salary Reduction Plans and Individual Saving for Retirement,"* EBRI Issue Brief *no. 155 (Employee Benefit Research Institute, November 1994), and Deborah A. Milne, Jack L. VanDerhei, and Paul J. Yakoboski, "Can We Save Enough to Retire? Participant Education in Defined Contribution Plans?"* EBRI Issue Brief *no. 160 (Employee Benefit Research Institute, April 1995).*

[31] *See Robert Clark, Gordon Goodfellow, Sylvester Schieber, and Drew Warwick, "Making the Most of 401(k) Plans: Who's Choosing What and Why?"* Working Paper *98-12 (Philadelphia: Pension Research Council, October 1998).*

better able to predict retirement patterns under a cash balance plan, since retirement income will not be susceptible to market fluctuations. Under a defined contribution plan, employers may face unexpected increases in early retirements during a strong bull market and unexpected delays of retirement during a market downturn (especially if it is prolonged).

Retirement Benefit Predictability

Since employers directly bear the investment risk under cash balance plans, they need not worry about overly conservative investments by their workers, as can occur in a 401(k) plan. Although approximately one-half of 401(k) participants have some equity market exposure through company stock and/or balanced funds, a significant percentage of them may be subjecting themselves to expected rates of return too low to generate sufficient retirement income at normal retirement age.[32]

Funding Flexibility

Finally, a cash balance plan may have more funding flexibility than a defined contribution plan, depending on the type of commitment made to employees. Although some profit-sharing plans provide for annual contributions that are entirely discretionary for the plan sponsor,[33] a defined benefit plan is the only vehicle that will allow employees to continue their normal benefit accruals while employer contributions are reduced or even temporarily curtailed.

■ Potential Limitations of a Cash Balance Conversion

Whatever the benefits of converting to a cash balance plan, there also are a number of tradeoffs:

Smaller Accruals for Older Workers

As mentioned earlier, unless some type of transition benefits are provided, older employees are likely to receive smaller accruals for their remaining years of service, regardless of whether a "wearaway" provision exists.

Preretirement Income Replacement

Although their understanding of current retirement wealth and future additions to that wealth will no doubt improve relative to the previous final average plan, employees actually may be more uncertain about how their future benefits will relate to their future earnings after conversion to a cash balance plan. For example, a final-average plan that pays 2 percent of an employee's average earnings during his or her last three years of service, by definition, replaces 50 percent of preretirement earnings after 25 years of service.[34] However, to understand the extent to which cash balance benefits will replace preretirement earnings is far more difficult, since cash balance plans are a type of a career-average formula that provides interest credits that are likely tied to some external financial market vehicle and/or index.

Lump-Sum Distributions

Due to the increased likelihood that participants in a cash balance plan will end up with a LSD as opposed to a lifetime annuity, it is more likely that they will face a longevity risk in addition to a post-retirement investment risk. It should be noted, however, that with some exceptions, cash balance plans are required to offer annuities as an option to their participants, and it appears that there is an increasing propensity for traditional final-average defined benefit plans to offer LSDs and for participants to choose them when offered.[35] Also, even though cash balance plans communicate benefits in terms of a lump-sum account balance, at least some

---

[32] *See Jack VanDerhei, Russell Galer, Carol Quick, and John Rea, "401(k) Plan Asset Allocation, Account Balances, and Loan Activity,"* EBRI Issue Brief *no. 205 (Employee Benefit Research Institute, January 1999).*

[33] *See Everett T., Allen, Jr., Joseph J. Melone, Jerry S. Rosenbloom and Jack L. VanDerhei,* Pension Planning: Pensions, Profit Sharing, and Other Deferred Compensation Plans, *Eighth edition (Homewood, IL: Richard D. Irwin, Inc., 1997).*

[34] *The calculation is obviously more complicated in an integrated plan.*

[35] *See Watson-Wyatt, "Choosy Employees Choose Lump Sums!"* Watson Wyatt Insider, *Vol. 8, no. 4 (April 1998).*

limit the ability of employees to cash out their accounts.[36]

Key Issues in Cash Balance Conversions

In recent months, there has been a flurry of press accounts, court cases, and legal and regulatory activities with respect to cash balance conversions. This section attempts to clarify some of the more complex and controversial concepts.

Do Cash Balance Plans Result in Cost Savings to the Sponsor?

It is certainly possible for conversion to a cash balance plan to result in lower long-term pension expense, depending on the generosity of the new plan relative to the existing plan. In essence, this is no different than switching from a defined benefit to a defined contribution plan, and similar projections would need to be applied to determine if this were the case.[37] However, even if such a calculation were performed on two retirement plans, it would not necessarily indicate the extent of cash balance savings, if any, since any savings due to cash balance plan conversion may be offset by other increases in benefits or compensation.[38]

Assuming such a calculation was performed, the cash balance plan may also prove to be more expensive than originally calculated if turnover is higher than assumed. This would result from plan assets being reduced below expected levels, and the spread between the accrual in the plan and the actual fund performance may be a factor in increased costs.[39] Turnover could increase due to future labor patterns that impact all employers, but it might also increase as a direct consequence of providing a more level benefit accrual over time that decreases the "job lock" attributes of the existing plan.

However, there may also be short-term abnormalities in the pension cost and/or expense structure resulting from the conversion. In essence, the claims of cost savings from a conversion to a cash balance plan may be at least partially due to a timing issue under the accounting and/or funding rules required for all defined benefit plans (including cash balance plans). Although the calculations are complex, one of the driving forces behind this short-term cost reduction involves the computation of the cost of accruing a benefit based on career-average pay (the cash balance plan) for one based on final-average pay under the previous plan.[40, 41]

Transition/Grandfathering

Several transition methods are available to a sponsor that chooses to mitigate the financial impact that may result in a switch from a traditional final-average plan to a cash balance plan:[42]

---

36 *For example, at AT&T employees can receive a cash payment for the entire amount in their accounts if the difference between the account balance and the highest year of eligible pay is $30,000 or less. Otherwise, employees are limited to a cash payment equal to one year's worth of their highest eligible pay, with the rest paid as a monthly annuity (Burlingame and Gulotta, 1998).*

37 *See Jack VanDerhei, "The Recapture of Excess Pension Assets,"* Benefits Quarterly, *Vol. 1, no. 3 (Third Quarter 1985): 1–13.*

38 *For example, Eastman Kodak reportedly will introduce a first-time match to its 401(k) plan to counterbalance losses from its conversion from a final-average plan to a cash balance plan (Morrow, 1999).*

39 *In addition to the potential cash flow problems arising from increased LSDs under cash balance plans, the liability durations of cash balance plans appear to be between seven to eight years as opposed to the 12- to 20-year durations typically calculated for traditional final average plans. Although the eventual impact (once the various transition provisions allow more of the liabilities to be generated via the new cash balance component) of the decreasing liability durations on the plan sponsor's asset allocation is debatable (Williamson, 1999), it would appear that the expected rate of return on cash balance portfolios will remain significantly greater than the expected interest rate credited to the employees.*

40 *See Elayne Robertson Demby, "Cash Balance Converts,"* Plan Sponsor *(June 1999): 22-30.*

41 *See Bone (1999) for a more complete description of the calculations required under FASB Statement No. 87.*

42 *See Anna M. Rappaport, Michael L. Young, Christopher A. Levell, and Brad A. Blalock, "Cash Balance Pension Plans," in Michael Gordon, Olivia S. Mitchell, and Marc Twinney, eds.,* Positioning Pensions for the Twenty-First Century *(Philadelphia: University of Pennsylvania Press, 1997).*

- Pay the greater of the benefit that would have been paid under the old plan and the benefit due under the new formula for a subset of the employees (either for a limited time period or until termination or retirement).
- Provide extra account balances at transition to make up for the greater benefit which would have been available at early retirement.
- Provide extra account balances to make up for the fact that final average earnings will not be directly used in the formula.
- Provide a supplemental additional benefit.

A PricewaterhouseCoopers survey of about 75 cash balance conversions reveals that in almost all cases the employer provided transition provisions beyond the legally required minimums.[43]

Wear-Away

If a final-average plan is converted to a cash balance plan, the initial value of a participant's cash balance account may be set at less than the value of benefits accrued under the previous plan. However, it is important to note that this may not reduce or take away previously earned benefits. It may mean, though, that initially some workers won't accrue any new benefits until the pay and interest credits to their hypothetical accounts bring the account balances up to the value of the old protected benefits.

Employers have flexibility in how they credit workers for the value of their benefits, and this result could be obtained by computing the opening balance of a participant's cash balance plan by using a discount rate that is higher than the current 30-year Treasury bond rate.[44]

As pointed out in recent testimony to the ERISA Advisory Council Working Group studying hybrid plans, benefit formulae that end up resulting in periods with no new accruals for some employees have been a practice approved by the Internal Revenue Service for many years.[45] Often plan changes, such as updating plan mortality assumptions, the resultant standardization of disparate pension plans as a result of mergers and acquisitions, or even revising a plan to meet new statutory requirements (such as legislative changes to the Sec. 401(a)(17) limits earlier this decade) can result in periods without new accruals.

Disclosure Requirements

Under current law, plans are required to notify participants of any amendment that will result in a significant reduction in the rate of future benefit accruals at least 15 days before the amendment takes effect.[46] However, present law does not require individual notices for each plan participant and does not require disclosure as to the effect the plan amendments will have on individual participants.

Recently, some have argued for the need to disclose to each employee the differences in his or her accrued benefits under the previous plan formula and his or her initial account balance under the cash balance plan. Moreover, they have argued that the wear-away period (if any) during a conversion should be explained, and a meaningful comparison should be provided to each worker of projected benefits under the amended plan compared with benefits that would have been earned

---

[43] *See Larry Sher, "A Workable Alternative to Defined Benefit Plans,"* Contingencies *(September/October 1999): 20–26.*

[44] *Sher (1999, p. 22) reports that more than two-thirds of the plans included in the PricewaterhouseCoopers survey used an interest rate that was approximately equal to or less than 30-year Treasury bond rate at the time of the conversion. However, some employers may desire to use a higher discount rate because the current 30-year Treasury bond rates are low relative to historical levels. The wear-away period actually experienced by a participant will be a function of the differential between the opening cash balance account and the present value of the accrued benefits under the previous defined benefit plan, as well as the future changes in discount rates. If the discount rate falls after the conversion, the present value of the previous benefits will increase, and the wear-away period experienced by the participant will increase (especially if the interest rate credited to the cash balance account is pegged to the 30-year Treasury bond rate). However, if the discount rate increases, the present value of the previous benefit will decrease, thereby reducing the wear-away period.*

[45] *Robert Chambers, testimony on behalf of Association of Private Pension and Welfare Plans.*

[46] *Previously accrued benefits are protected by IRC Sec. 411.*

under the previous plan formula. This appears to be based on a belief that it is critical for plan participants to have an appropriate opportunity to (a) voice their concerns regarding plan amendments so that employers are fully aware of them, and (b) alert regulators to issues surrounding cash balance conversions that they deem important.[47]

However, others in the pension policy community have questioned the logic in providing estimates under a benefit plan that no longer exists and have warned that Congress should proceed very cautiously in adding to the already substantial burdens of administering a cash balance or other defined benefit plan.[48] Employers may be unreceptive to projecting future benefits due to the extremely sensitive nature of the estimates.[49]

Conclusion

After a period where the number of defined benefit plans declined dramatically (mostly among small plans), traditional final-average defined benefit plans appear to have entered a new phase of evolution dating to 1985—the "hybrid plan evolution" (most publicized with the "cash balance" approach). This change reflects the overall movement of the employment-based retirement income system in the direction of "individual account" and "lump sum" arrangements, both defined benefit and defined contribution.

Certain populations of workers stand to benefit from such changes, in particular those who change jobs throughout their careers or those who leave the work force for periods of time. Certain classes of workers stand to potentially lose from the decline of traditional final-average defined benefit plans, depending on how the transition is managed. Potential losses can be mitigated through grandfathering and transition provisions.

"Individual account" and "lump sum" arrangements, both defined benefit and defined contribution, can offer tangible benefits for both plans sponsors and a majority of their workers, and as such may represent the next big wave of change in the employment-based plan system. Whether the "tangible benefits" of more capital accumulation for more individuals ultimately translates into more retirement income remains to be seen.

[47] *See Elizabeth A. White, "Cash Balance Plans Attorney Urges IRS Rules to Clarify Age-Discrimination Issues in Conversions," [[publication??]] Vol. 26, No. 32 (August 16, 1999): 2407.*

[48] *See Rita D. Metras, "Testimony for the Hearing on Pension Reform Legislation," Committee on Finance (U.S. Senate, June 30, 1999).*

[49] *See Sher, op. cit., p. 22) for an illustration of how increasing or decreasing the current 30-year Treasury bond rate by 1 percent can impact the relative comparisons between an existing traditional defined benefit plan and a new cash balance plan.*

References

Burlingame, Harold W., and Michael J. Gulotta. "Casestudy: Cash Balance Pension Plan Facilitates Restructuring the Workforce at AT&T." *Compensation and Benefits Review* (November/December 1998).

Demby, Elayne Robertson. "Cash Balance Converts." *Plan Sponsor* (June 1999): 22–30.

____. "Cash Balance 'Whipsaw.'" *Plan Sponsor* (May 1999): 74–76.

Morrow, Rebecca. "Conversions To Cash Balance Plans Highlight Importance of Defined Contribution/401(k) Approach." *IOMA's Defined Contribution Plan Investing*. September 1999.

Purcell, Patrick. "Pension Issues: Cash-Balance Plans." *CRS Report for Congress*. (May 24, 1999).

Towers Perin. "The Controversy Over Cash Balance Plans." *Hot Topics*. 1999.

White, Elizabeth A. "Cash Balance Plans: Attorney Urges IRS Rules to Clarify Age-Discrimination Issues in Conversions," *BNA Pension & Benefits Reporter*, Vol. 26, No. 32 (August 16, 1999): 2407–2049.

Williamson, Christine. "Stock Allocation Hikes Predicted as Defined Benefit Plans Shift to Cash Balance." *Pensions & Investments* (September 6, 1999): 1ff.

6

The New Pension Economics: Defined Contribution Plans and Sorting

by Richard A. Ippolito, George Mason University School of Law

Introduction

Over the 25 years since the enactment of ERISA there has been a dramatic change in the structure of pension plans in the private sector. Defined benefit plans gradually have ceded their dominant position to the defined contribution variety. In the early 1980s, defined benefit plans covered 80 percent of all workers with a pension; by 1999, this share had fallen to about 40 percent. Not only is this trend showing no signs of abatement, it understates actual shifts because many defined benefit plans have been amended to the cash balance variety, which are defined contribution plans in all but name.

Some of this shift is attributable to changing industrial employment patterns, but the decline in demand for the defined benefit product is widespread, suggesting causes that are more fundamental. Primary candidates include changing tax and regulatory policy and the introduction of 401(k) plans (effective in 1981). After introducing this pension product, which provided new competition in the pension market, Congress enacted laws that increased both the regulatory and tax costs on the dominant and existing product, notably defined benefit plans. The effects were both predictable and profound.

These developments have potentially large implications for companies that have relied on defined benefit plans to influence their productivity—they are subjects that have defined pension economics over the past several decades. The "new pension economics" undoubtedly will shift focus toward understanding how 401(k)s and other defined contribution plans can in part substitute for defined benefit plans to help firms attain higher productivity at the same time that they provide workers the opportunity to save for retirement. In addition, the "old" emphasis on "optimal" corporate funding and asset allocation decisions will shift to a consideration of individuals' willingness to contribute to 401(k) plans and their investment habits.

This discussion presents data that describe trends in pension plan types; discusses the most likely reasons for these trends; and considers their implication for productivity in firms. There are two other important issues that are related to these trends, which are ignored. One is related to the consideration of the financial implications for the firm of operating a defined contribution plan versus a defined benefit plan. The other is the implication of the new composition of pension plan coverage for the level and distribution of retirement income for future cohorts of retirees.

Market Developments in Pension Plan Type

The Trend in Number of Plans

Chart 6.1 shows the number of single-employer pension plans insured by the Pension Benefit Guaranty Corporation (PBGC) from 1980 to 1998. It shows that this number peaked in 1985 at about 112,000 and declined sharply to about 42,000 plans in 1998.[1] The reduction was not proportional across all plan sizes. Panel a of chart 6.2 shows

[1] *To describe pension trends, I rely on data from the PBGC (1999), U. S. Department of Labor (1999), and my own calculations from the Annual Form 5500 Annual Pension Plan Tapes.*

Chart 6.1

Number of Single-Employer Insured Plans

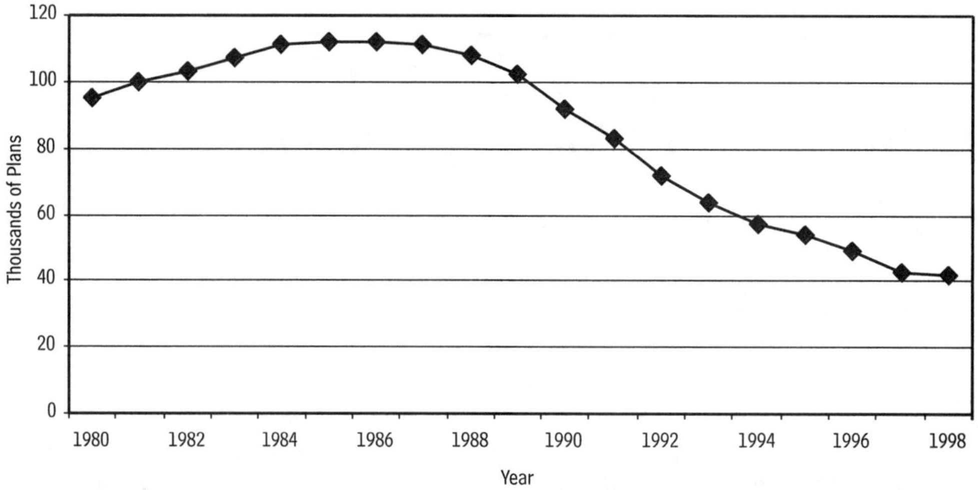

Source: Pension Benefit Guaranty Corporation, *Pension Insurance Data Book, 1998* (Washington, DC: Pension Benefit Guaranty Corporation, 1999), table S-17.

that the number of plans with fewer than 100 participants declined from about 90,000 in 1985 to 27,000 in 1998. There also was a sharp decline in plans with between 100 and 999 participants. In 1985, there were more than 18,000 plans in this size range but, by 1998, only about 11,000 were operating, a reduction of about 40 percent.

Panel b of chart 6.2 shows the number of large plans over time (using a different scale). In marked contrast to the trends for smaller plans, the number of plans with between 1,000 and 9,999 participants grew by about 15 percent, from 3,223 in 1980 to 3,713 in 1998. The number of plans with at least 10,000 plans has grown from 354 in 1985 to 544 in 1998, an increase of over 50 percent; and most of this growth has occurred since 1985.

The growth in the number of large plans is attributable to three factors. First, the decision to terminate a defined benefit plan in favor of a defined contribution plans has been more frequently observed in the small-to-medium plan size universe. Second, the rapid growth of inactive participants (retirees and separated vested participants) has pushed some plans into higher size

Chart 6.2

Number of Single-Employer Insured Plans by Size, Selected Years

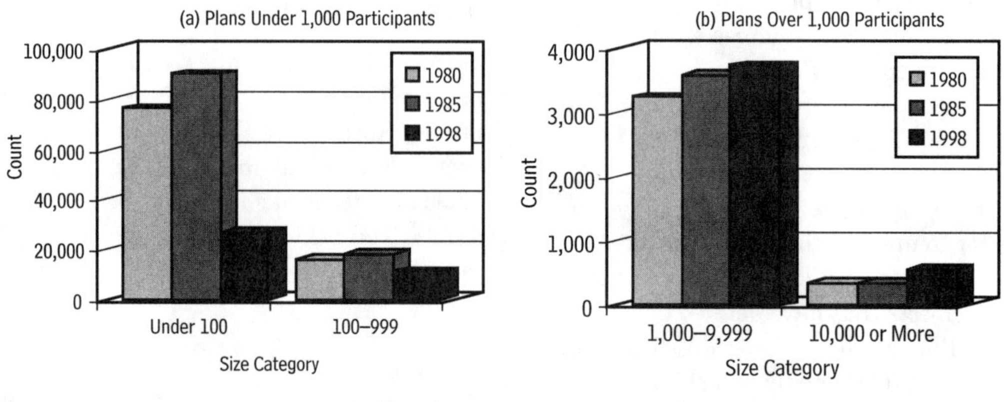

Source: Pension Benefit Guaranty Corporation, *Pension Insurance Data Book, 1998* (Washington, DC: Pension Benefit Guaranty Corporation, 1999), table S-17.

categories (see below). Third, and finally, there has been considerable plan merger activity over the period.[2]

The Trend in Number of Participants

In contrast to the dramatic reduction in the number of plans, the number of participants in single-employer defined benefit plans has shown modest growth. In 1980 there were 27.5 million participants in defined benefit plans. By 1998, this number had increased to over 33 million.

These numbers, however, are not indicative of the future of the defined benefit system, because total participants include retirees (or their surviving spouses) and separated vested participants. These categories of participants are reflective of past coverage patterns in defined benefit plans. A better forward-looking measure is the trend in the number of active participants: these are workers earning pension accruals currently.

Chart 6.3 shows modest growth in the number of total participants from 1980 to 1998 (solid line schedule with diamonds). Trends in the composition of participant types, however, are markedly different. In contrast to the rapid growth in the number of retirees and separated vesteds (line schedule with asterisks), the number of active participants has been declining since the late 1980s (line schedule with square markers). In 1988, there were 22.4 million active participants in single-employer defined benefit plans; by 1998, this number had fallen to 18.1 million, a decrease of almost 20 percent. These trends mean that the maturity level of the defined benefit system has been increasing.

For example, in 1980, inactive participants accounted for only 22 percent of total participants in defined benefit plans; by 1988, this number had increased to 29 percent. By 1998, almost 45 percent of the participants in defined benefit plans were inactive participants. It is likely that in the next few years, the number of active workers in these plans will represent the minority of participants.

Chart 6.4 shows this trend in a somewhat different way. It portrays the portion of pension *liabilities* attributable to inactive participants over the period. The figure shows two series, one for all defined benefit plans that filed a form-5500 annual report, and another for a longitudinal sample of 1,900 defined benefit plans that survived the entire period (Ippolito, 1999a). Either series shows similar

[2] *A study of a longitudinal sample of plans confirms that plan mergers and growth in inactive participants each explained a substantial portion of the increase in the number of large plans (Ippolito and Thompson, forthcoming).*

Chart 6.3

Pension Plan Participants, Single-Employer Plans, 1980–1998

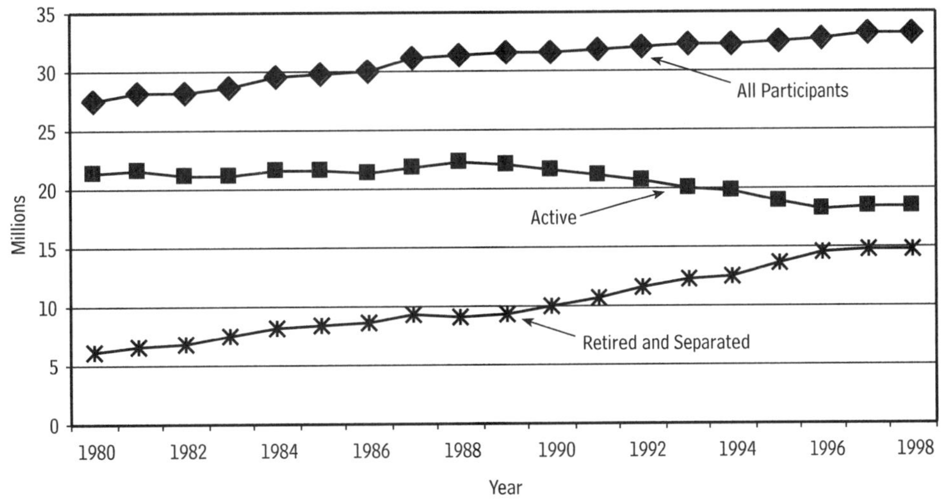

Source: Pension Benefit Guaranty Corporation, *Pension Insurance Data Book, 1998* (Washington, DC: Pension Benefit Guaranty Corporation, 1999), tables s-16 and s-19.

Chart 6.4
PENSION PLAN MATURITY, 1980–1995

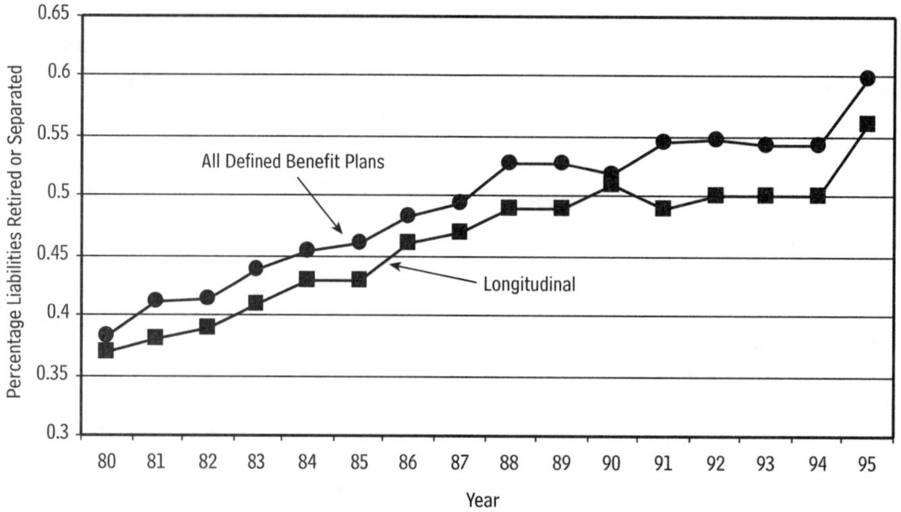

Source: Calculations from the Form 5500 Annual Report Tapes for either all single-employer defined benefit plans with at least 100 participants, or exclusively for the 1,900 longitudinal plan sample comprised only of single-employer plans that survived from 1980–1995. All liability calculations are standardized to a 6.5 percent interest rate and GAM mortality.

results, namely, that in 1980, roughly three in every eight dollars in liabilities were attributable to retirees and separated vesteds. By 1995, this ratio had increased to almost three in every five dollars of liabilities.

Percentage of Covered Workers

The reduction in absolute numbers of workers covered by defined benefit plans takes on even more significance when consideration is given to the overall growth in the labor market. Since 1980, the private labor force and has grown at the rate of about 1.5 percent per year, and the overall pension coverage rate remained about the same (45 percent),[3] the absolute reduction in defined benefit coverage of workers means that its share of coverage has been falling rapidly. Defined contribution plans are covering an ever-increasing portion of the private work force that has a pension.

Chart 6.5 shows primary coverage rates by pension plan type over the period 1980 to 1999. It depicts the overall pension coverage rate in the private sector, which was roughly constant from 1980 to 1999; the share of workers covered by a defined benefit plan; and the share of workers covered exclusively by a defined contribution plan.[4]

It is apparent that the share of workers with a defined benefit plan fell dramatically over the period. Indeed, by the mid-1990s, defined benefit plans no longer covered the majority of covered workers in the private sector, a substantial decline from their 80 percent-plus share in the early 1980s. As of 1999, the estimated market share of defined benefit plans is 42 percent, and reasonable extrapolations suggest that defined benefit plans will attain clear minority status over the next decade.[5]

Employment Shifts and Preference Changes

Part of the shift away from defined benefit plans reflects employment shifts from traditional defined

---

[3] *See U.S. Department of Labor (1999). If only full-time workers are counted, the coverage rate is approximately 50 percent.*

[4] *Using the methodology of the U. S. Department of Labor (1999), if a worker has two plans, and one is a defined benefit, then the worker is automatically classified as covered primarily by a defined benefit plan. Only when workers have only a defined contribution plan are they classified as covered by a primary defined contribution plan.*

[5] *Shares after 1996 assume that the overall coverage rate remains at 46 percent; pension type shares of this amount are based on information about labor market growth on the assumption that the absolute number of active participants does not decline further.*

Chart 6.5

PERCENTAGE OF PRIVATE LABOR FORCE COVERED BY TYPE OF PENSION, 1980–1999

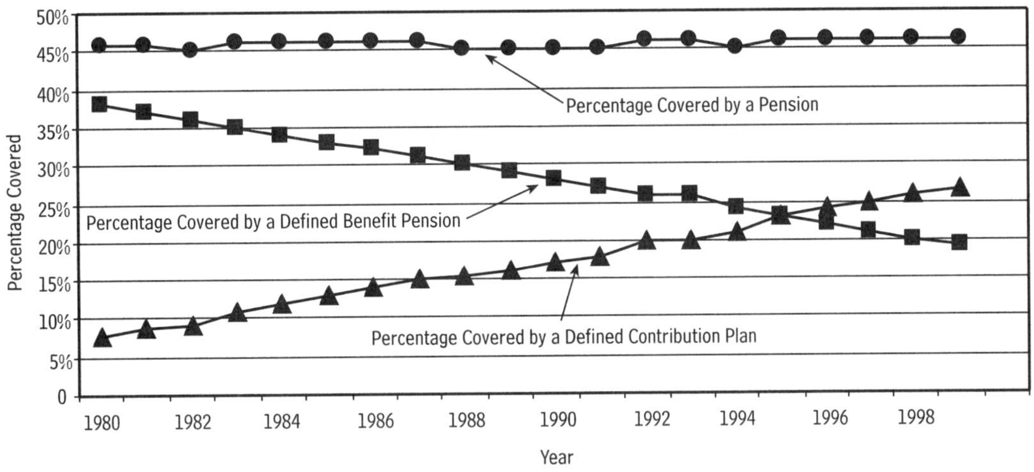

Source: U.S. Department of Labor, Pension and Welfare Benefits Administration, *Private Pension Plan Bulletin: Abstract of 1995 Form 5500 Annual Reports*, no. 8 (Spring 1999). Participants in 401(k) plans who do not contribute are not included as pension covered in these data.

benefit firms and industries (e.g., large, unionized firms in the manufacturing sector), to firms and industries that traditionally favored defined contribution plans (e.g., smaller, nonunion firms in the service sector). Several studies have estimated that upward of 50 percent of the lost defined benefit share may be attributable to employment shifts. But these studies also reveal a sharp decline in employer preferences for defined benefit plans across all portions of the private sector.[6]

The latter point is illustrated in chart 6.6, which shows the percentage of pension workers in the private sector covered by a defined benefit plan in 1979 and 1995 by manufacturing versus nonmanufacturing sectors, union versus nonunion workers, and size of plan. The data, which by construction are independent of employment shifts, evince two important features.[7] First, preferences for defined benefit plans have fallen significantly in every category, inclusive of the union sector, the manufacturing sector, and the largest plan-size categories. Second, preferences have shifted more in those sectors that previously had less marked preferences for defined benefit plans.

Moreover, all of the measures understate the trend toward defined contribution plans. During the mid-1980s, an innovative amendment to a defined benefit plan was introduced that effectively converts a defined benefit plan to a defined contribution plan without triggering the reversion tax (see below). These "cash balance" plans assign individual account balances to workers, and the rates of return on these accounts are guaranteed (usually equal to a Treasury rate). This guarantee is sufficient to retain the defined benefit label, but for all intents and purposes, these plans are defined contribution plans disguised as defined benefit plans.

The empirical problem is that there is no way to distinguish a cash balance plan from a traditional defined benefit plan without actual inspection of the attachments to the annual pen-

---

[6] *Several studies have used standard statistical methods to disentangle the portion of the reduction in defined benefit market share over time (Clark and McDermed 1993[1990 in refs.], Kruse (1995), Ippolito (1998), Gustman and Steinmeier (1992). Generally, these studies conclude that about half of the reduction in defined benefit share is explained by employment shifts, and the remaining half by preference changes away from these types of plans.*

[7] *The calculations are made directly from the form 5500 tapes in either year.*

Chart 6.6

PREFERENCES FOR DEFINED BENEFIT PLANS, BY CATEGORY, 1979 VS. 1995

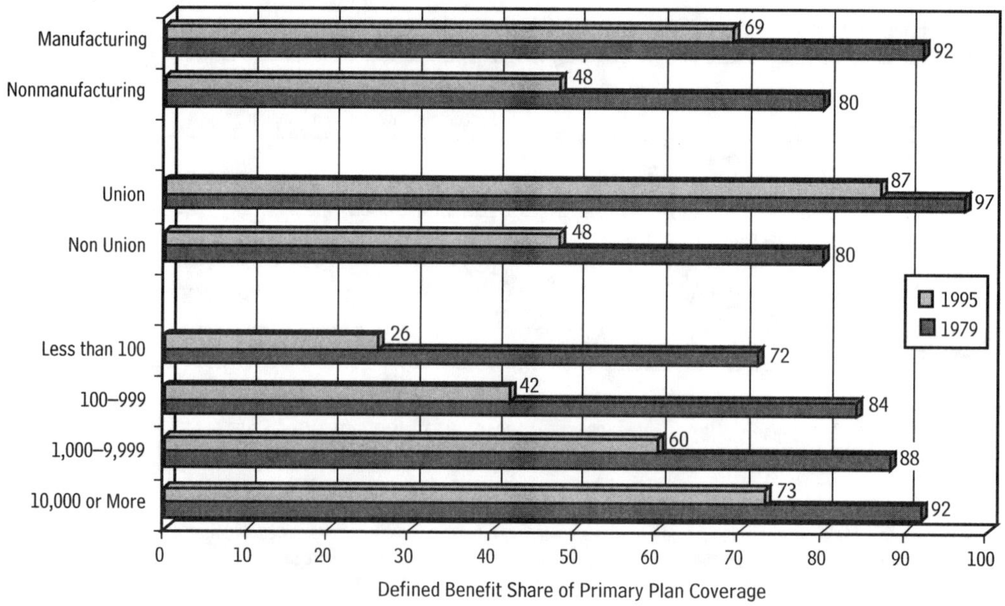

sion plan reports.[8] Available data suggest that over the nine-year period 1986–1995, approximately 10 percent of overfunded large defined benefit plans with at least $25 million in assets have made the conversion.[9]

■ Analyzing the Problem

While it is apparent that the trend is distinctly favorable to defined contribution plans, the question remains: Independent of employment shifts, what explains the reduction in preferences for defined benefit plans? Assuming the defined benefit plans continue to add value to the firm, then it is logical to assume that either the cost of using these plans has increased or new substitute pension products have reduced demand for the defined benefit variety. There is ample evidence that both of these phenomena have occurred.

---

[8] *When the amendment is made, the sponsor calculates the present value of legal pension liabilities and creates individual account balances usually in these amounts. Assets beyond these amounts ("excess assets") are retained in the plan. The firm awards future contributions to each worker's account on the basis of some formula (often a percentage of pay). The key feature of the cash balance plan is that it requires only an amendment to the plan, not termination, and thus, does not trigger the reversion tax on excess assets in the plan. The firm can make future contributions to employees' accounts from excess assets.*

[9] *The basis for this estimate comes from a special sample of annual pension reports sent in hard copy to the PBGC from the Internal Revenue Service Centers. The sample is principally designed to capture reports for large underfunded plans, but since the IRS sends all annual reports for all sponsored pension plans in those firms, a sample of large salary plans is collected (these are the kinds of plans expected to have excess assets). In the 1995 collection year, 264 salary plans with at least $25 million in pension liabilities were evaluated by hand, inclusive of all attachments. Fully 28, or 10.6 percent, were cash balance plans. These figures are similar to those reported in Ippolito and Thompson (forthcoming) for a longitudinal sample of defined benefit plans. Starting in the 1999 plan year, the form 5500 annual pension plan reports will contain a question asking about cash balance status. These new data ought to provide the basis for a more definitive evaluation of the spread of cash balance plans.*

Regulatory Costs

One price-related hypothesis points to higher regulatory costs for defined benefit plans. To help evaluate this hypothesis, the Hay/Huggins Company developed administrative cost indices for defined benefit plans from 1981 through 1991. For comparison, they calculated the administrative costs of operating a 401(k) plan with employer matching contributions.

The results showed that the differential cost of operating a defined benefit plan increased for all size classes over the period, but that the increases were largest for smaller plans. For example, the differential cost of operating the largest defined benefit plan increased by $16 per participant. The increase in differential cost for a 500-participant plan was $32. For small plans the increases in cost was dramatic. In 1981, the differential cost of operating a defined benefit plan with 15 participants was $45 per participant. By 1991, the difference had increased to $227.

Moreover, owing to one-time adjustments to comply with new legislation, costs in some intervening years during the 1980s were even higher. These increases are sufficiently high to explain the substantial reduction in defined benefit plan preference for small plans (see above), but they do not plausibly explain the shift to larger plans.

Tax Issues

A related cost hypotheses is that the tax advantage of using defined benefit plans was reduced through a series of changes in the tax code. Since these tax changes predominantly affected defined benefit plans, the implied increase in tax liability to the plan sponsor tilted the plan-type decision in favor of defined contribution.

One example of these changes was the imposition of the so-called 150 percent full-funding limit in 1987 legislation, which affected many defined benefit plans, but numerous other tax alterations also affected these plans.[10] The changes were particularly effective for firms with relatively young work forces, presumably the kinds of firms that are making new pension decisions.[11] Unlike the regulatory cost explanation, the tax hypothesis is not specific to firm or plan size.

One empirical fact is certain. Funding ratios clearly have declined markedly over time, and these reductions are independent of terminations. The solid line in chart 6.7 shows the average standardized funding ratio in each year from a longitudinal sample over the period 1980–1995 from a recent study of funding (Ippolito, 1999a).[12] During the early 1980s, funding ratios generally increased, reflecting a rebounding from poor investment returns during the 1970s. Beginning in the mid-1980s, however, this growth noticeably flattened, and it began falling after 1990. In 1986, in the typical defined benefit plan, for every $100 in liabilities, there were $125 in pension assets. By 1995, there was only $107 in assets for every $100 liabilities.

The reduction is not explained by changing interest rates used to discount pension annuities. The funding ratios in the figure are calculated using the same 6.5 interest rate in all years. Nor is it explained by poor investment performance. The *excess* return for a balanced portfolio over the 1986–1995 period was 5.4 percent per annum (the cumulative value of excess returns is shown by the dashed-line schedule with closed boxes in chart 6.7).[13] The pattern of funding ratios is not

---

[10] The new funding limit was part of the Omnibus Budget Reconciliation Act of 1987 and was closely related to the Pension Protection Act enacted in the same year. Other changes, however, also were made to constrain funding. For example, the Tax Reform Act of 1986 prohibited the value of projected wages (that is, the value of w exp(g(R-a)) in expression 1) from exceeding $200,000 in nominal terms. In 1992, this limit was further reduced to $150,000. For most plans, these constraints are redundant to the full-funding limit imposed in 1988. For a compilation of all the tax and cost issues, see ERISA Industry Committee (1996). Also see American Academy of Actuaries (1993). Hay Huggins (1989) and Ippolito (1998).

[11] The younger the work force the more important the projection feature of old funding rules, and therefore the more likely it is that the new funding rules constrained funding compared with prior periods.

[12] All liabilities are converted to a 6.5 percent interest rate and GAM 83 mortality.

[13] I use a 50-50 mix of S&P returns and the Solomon bond index returns for the years 1986 through 1994. The excess return is $r = 2r_s + 2r_b - r_t$, where r_s is the nominal returns on S&P stocks, r_b is the nominal return on long-term corporate bonds, and r_t is the one-year Treasury bill rate. All data are from Ibbotson (1998). Since pension data reflect beginning-year values, the returns I use are lagged one year to correspond with the observations on pension funding.

Chart 6.7

FUNDING RATIOS, 1980–1995

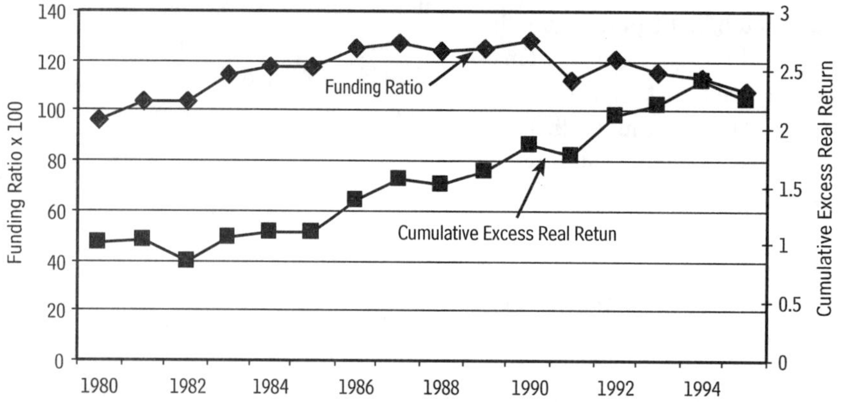

Source: Funding ratios: Longitudinal database, form 5500 annual pension reports. All liabilities are adjusted to a 6.5 percent interest rate and GAM 83 mortality table. Numbers reflect beginning-year values. Excess returns are equal to the return on a 50-50 portfolio of stocks and bonds minus the one-year Treasury bill rate from Ibbotson Associates, Stocks, Bonds, Bills and Inflation 1926–1998.

Chart 6.8

FUNDING RATIOS, 1986 VERSUS 1995

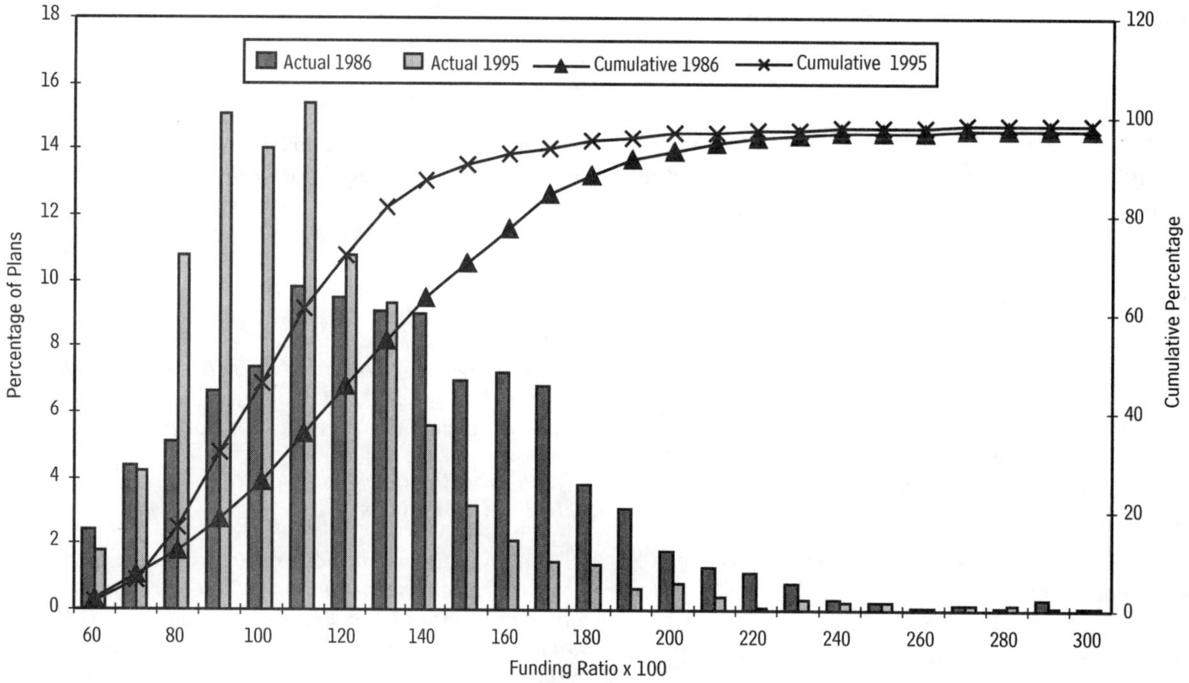

Source: Longitudinal data base, form 5500 annual pension reports. All liabilities are adjusted to a 6.5 percent interest rate and GAM 83 mortality table. Numbers reflect beginning-year values Longitudinal data base.

Chart 6.9
PRIMARY COVERAGE 1979 AND 1995

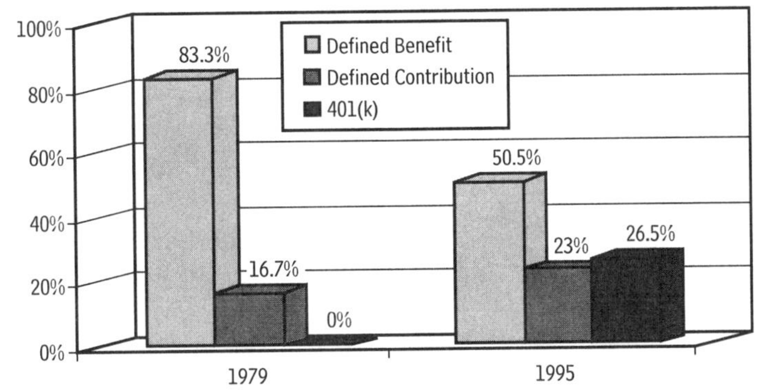

Denotes the percentage of pension-covered workers in their primary pension plan; secondary coverage is excluded. Includes only participation in plans with more than 100 participants; and excludes workers who do not participate in their 401(k) plan.

Source: U.S. Department of Labor, Private Pension Plan Bulletin: Abstract of 1995 Form 5500 Annual Reports, Pension and Welfare Benefits Administration, Number 8, Spring 1999.

suggestive of gradual changes in the retirement market, say owing to increasing maturity of pensions, but of some stimulus that plausibly explains rapid and systematic change throughout the industry over a relatively short period. Tax policy is an obvious candidate.

Chart 6.8 shows the distributions of (standardized) funding ratios for a longitudinal sample of 1,900 pension plans that existed over the period 1986–1995. The standardized interest rate and mortality table are chosen to be consistent with the 150 percent full-funding limit in 1995 on the assumption that sponsors chose the lowest permissible current liability interest rate to meet the test. It is apparent that plan funding fell dramatically over the period, and that the distribution has fallen far lower than the level enforced by the introduction of a new full-funding limit.[14]

The evidence shows that sponsors have voluntarily reduced pension plan funding, and that most plans now have reduced their funding status well below those affected by the new funding limits. I have argued elsewhere that the most likely underlying reason for this change is the introduction of a sequence of reversion taxes starting at 10 percent in 1986 and reaching 50 percent in 1990. These taxes effectively increased the sponsor's legal pension liability beyond termination values, if and only if, it maintained overfunding in the plan. The financial implications of this change are apparent, and have led most firms to shed a large portion of excess assets in the defined benefit plans that they sponsor (Ippolito, 1999a).

Introduction of 401(k) Plans

An alternative (but not mutually exclusive) explanation for the observed switches in plan preferences away from defined benefit plans is the introduction of 401(k) plans. In effect, a new competing product was introduced to the market, which worked to reduce demand for defined benefit plans.

Arguably, 401(k) plans are a superior variety of defined contribution plans. Like traditional defined contribution plans, the 401(k) permits an unconditional employer contribution (either a fixed dollar amount or a percentage of pay, or profits) to all employees. Beyond this, however, the 401(k) is unique. First, workers can make voluntary pre-tax contributions to the plan, affording them more freedom to attain desired savings rates beyond the employer's contribution. Second,

14 *I chose the 6.5 percent interest rate because it was the lowest allowed for purposes of calculating the limit in the 1995 plan year.*

the firm can match part or all of worker contributions. The matching feature of the 401(k) plan permits the firm to selectively pay higher wages to workers who reveal themselves as savers.

In some sense, the growth of 401(k) plans is at odds with the increasing-cost hypothesis. Compared with a straightforward money purchase or profit-sharing plan, the 401(k) plan is more costly to administer because the voluntary contribution rates must be monitored to ensure compliance with Internal Revenue Code discrimination requirements. These laws restrict the amount that higher-paid workers can contribute compared with lower-paid workers.

The market penetration of 401(k) plans has been substantial. For example, consider that over the period 1981–1995, while traditional defined contribution plans (i.e., those without a 401(k) component) increased their share in the primary pension market from 17 percent to 24 percent, 401(k) plans captured 26 percent of the primary pension market. That is, in 1995, one in every four covered workers in the single-employer universe was covered exclusively by a 401(k) plan (chart 6.9).[15]

Impact on Defined Benefit Plans

The introduction of 401(k) plans had two effects on the demand for defined benefit plans. First, it reduced the demand for defined benefit plans. Second, it made the demand more sensitive to price. The higher price elasticity reflects the existence of viable substitutes, namely 401(k) plans, making defined benefit plans more vulnerable to increases in their after-tax operational costs. The system might have tolerated either the introduction of the new substitute or higher regulatory and tax costs. The combination of these factors at a time when employment growth was not favorable to these sectors overwhelmed the industry.

■ Lessons from the Trends

Looking forward over the next 25 years, the evidence is not favorable for a viable defined benefit pension system in the private sector. The defined benefit share of covered workers has fallen in half from 1983 to 1999, and further, the absolute number of active workers in these plans is falling. The plans that remain are substantially more mature and less well funded than in the 1980s. And there is a decisive trend in favor of cash balance amendments, meaning that the trend toward defined contribution plans is more pronounced than suggested by the estimates reported above and elsewhere. For all intents and purposes, the future of defined benefit plans in the private sector may be limited to a small portion of covered workers.[16]

In addition, since employment shifts have dramatically favored firms and industries that traditionally had the lowest demand for defined benefit plans, it follows that, to have appeal in this market, the defined benefit vehicle likely needs to be reconsidered to allow more of the features of defined contribution plans. This may be one reason for the growing popularity of cash balance plans and the higher frequency of lump-sum options in defined benefit plans, which again emphasizes the drift toward plans with defined-contribution plan characteristics.

■ The New Pension Economics: The Power of Sorting

An important question from the perspective of efficiency is whether the trend toward defined contribution plans has important implications for employers who previously relied on defined benefit plans to help them manage the overall productivity of their work forces, notably by helping reduce the quit rate and by providing a way to control the distribution of retirement ages in the firm. Clearly, these "behavior-modifying" characteristics of defined benefit plans have dominated pension economics over the past two decades.

In thinking about this problem, it is useful first to recall that employment patterns have

---

[15] *This number excludes workers who had a 401(k) plan but chose not to contribute. The U. S. Department of Labor does not include noncontributors to the 401(k) plan. See U.S. Department of Labor (1999).*

[16] *Defined benefit plans continue to dominate in the public sector (Employee Benefit Research Institute, 1997). Even here, however, there are some signs of change. For example, for all hires after 1983, the federal government defined benefit plan is about half as generous as the old plan. It now is supplemented by a matching 401(k) plan.*

shifted away from the kinds of employers that previously attached highest value to these kinds of plans (chart 6.6); thus, the marketplace is now dominated by the kinds of employers that historically were less enthusiastic users of defined benefit plans in the past. Second, the rapid spread of defined contribution plans, especially the 401(k) variety, has caused a rethinking about the dismissive idea that these plans are mostly tax-favored savings accounts with few implications for employers.

The genesis of the new thinking, or perhaps the rethinking of an old idea, is that the most important impact of pensions may not be in their power to affect the behavior of employees but rather to help the firm select and retain high-quality workers. The idea is that worker attributes are more or less a given, and thus it is difficult for employers to alter the behavior associated with these characteristics. In this approach, it is more profitable for firms to find ways to select the kinds of workers that the firm wants in their employ, and to encourage those that are not suited to the firm to either not enter in the first place or, if they do enter, to make a quick departure. The interesting question is how pensions can help the firm attain these goals.

An important paper that introduced "selection effects" to labor market literature is Salop and Salop (1976). They argued that there are two kinds of workers, "quitters" and "stayers." In this model, any deferred wage scheme naturally attracts stayers because quitters tend to attach a lower probability of obtaining the deferred portion of the wage. Viewed in this way, a defined benefit plan does not so much sway workers' decisions whether to quit or stay with the firm, but rather acts to select a disproportionate number of stayers to the firm's employ. The very act of setting up such a scheme accomplishes lower quitting. Evidence reported in Allen et al. (1993) and Ippolito (1998) find evidence using quit rate data that are consistent with this idea.

More recently, findings reported by Gustman and Steinmeier (1993, 1994) show that, compared with the quit rates of uncovered workers, quit rates of workers in *defined contribution* plans also are abnormally low (although not as low as rates in defined benefit plans). This is a somewhat peculiar finding because the existing pension economics literature explains lower pension quitting by appealing to the pension capital losses imposed on workers who prematurely leave firms that use defined benefit plans. But defined contribution plans do not impose a substantial cost on those who quit.[17] This finding raises the question whether pensions in general provide a kind of sorting function for stayers, and, if so, how and why this sorting works.

One idea I have advanced is this: the attribute that makes some workers "savers" also makes them "high-quality" workers (Ippolito, 1999b). Thus, any compensation package that emphasizes pensions will naturally attract savers. Assuming that firms will expend more effort to retain their best workers (by paying them more, among other things), then it follows that high-quality workers will more often attain long tenure. We now have the connection we want: pensions attract savers, who also are high-quality workers. Since the firms will work harder to retain their better workers, it follows that savers will tend to exhibit the characteristic of being a "stayer." Elsewhere, I have reported substantial empirical evidence supporting the hypothesis that 401(k) savers have higher performance ratings, higher rates of and future promotions, less absenteeism, a lower likelihood of being fired or laid off, and so on (Ippolito, 1998).

These findings imply that the use of ordinary pension plans can encourage desirable sorting at a lower cost than defined benefit plans. If firms use defined benefit plans, they must pay a premium to workers because they sacrifice their opportunities to leave the firm for a higher wage elsewhere,[18] that is, workers will not indenture themselves for zero compensation (Ippolito, 1998). In addition, as shown above, firms are not permitted to fully fund defined benefit plans, particularly if they have an 'immature"age-service structure in

[17] *Apart from a short vesting period, the value of pension accounts belong to workers, and thus, is not affected by their decision to leave.*

[18] *That is, defined benefit plans award full value only to workers who stay until retirement age; those who leave early absorb substantial pension capital losses. This means that looking ahead, workers who enter these contracts know that they will find it uneconomical to take some higher-paying jobs that might arise over their tenure with this firm (Ippolito, 1998).*

the firm, and thus are at a tax disadvantage compared with equally generous defined contribution plans. They also incur more regulatory costs and are less flexible than defined contribution plans; and firms cannot terminate the plan without incurring confiscatory reversion taxes. Sponsors also are required to participate in a pension insurance system that poses the possibility of catastrophic risk on sponsors of defined benefit plans.[19] Thus, if defined contribution plans can accomplish important sorting effects, it follows that it may be economical to use these plans in place of their more expensive counterparts.

■ An Underlying Theory of the Sorting Principle

Why are savers better workers than nonsavers? I have advanced the notion that an important component of the explanation may lie in the worker's discount rate (Ippolito, 1998). It is natural to think that the quality of being a low discounter enhances productivity. Low discounters are less likely to take a day off on a whim, instead valuing the long-term implications of absenteeism on their reputation for reliability. They are less likely to mistreat machines and equipment because they recognize the long-term benefit of being labeled a "low-cost" employee. And they are motivated to work hard to gain the benefits of more promotions. In short, the self-motivation of low discounters economizes on firms' monitoring costs.[20]

High discounters are influenced disproportionately by benefits realized over a short horizon, and thus the firm either must expend resources to encourage them to act as though they have a lower discount rate, or accept the implications of myopic behavior. I do not propose that high quality is defined exclusively by workers' discount rates, but rather that, for some firms, the dominant traits of a high-quality worker are highly correlated with this attribute.

Sorting of High and Low Discounters

All other things the same, it is natural to think that firms that offer pensions tend to attract low discounters. Low discounters attach a high value to a pension plan, whereas high discounters attach a disproportionate value to cash compensation only. Thus, the first-order effect of pensions is to attract savers. In a perfect world, no high discounters would enter a pension firm. But information is not perfect in the job market, and job choices may be limited to those that do not offer the worker's ideal mix of compensation components.[21]

A natural outcome of this process is that firms set up to employ low discounters must contend with the entry of some high discounters. The firm's problem is to minimize the costs of these hires either by encouraging their early exit or by inducing them to pay themselves a lower wage. A shortcoming of defined benefit plans is that, once high discounters enter, there is no obvious way to find them and encourage them to leave. Defined contribution pensions plans are natural vehicles to effect these outcomes.

---

[19] *Defined benefit plans are covered by mandatory federal insurance in the event of underfunding at the time of bankruptcy (administered by PBGC). The fees bear only a vague resemblance to market pricing, and more importantly, the insurance is not hedged. Thus, the bankruptcy of a few large firms can create dramatic deficits that pose the risk of substantial premium assessments on those who remain viable. The problem can become particularly acute in periods of poor stock market performance and low interest rates. While taxpayers as a whole presumably hold some portion of this implicit government guarantee, sponsors of defined benefit plans presumably are the first line of financing for catastrophic insurance events that befall the system.*

[20] *Low discounters are also natural candidates for production functions that emphasize the development of firm-specific capital. But the focus of the paper is limited to the self-discipline aspects of low discounters. Thus, the efficiency of sorting arises from the simple proposition that low discounters require less monitoring.*

[21] *It is natural to think that low discounters will more often be successful in their search for a job that is a good match. Job shopping is inherently an investment activity. Shopping costs incurred early in the career result in the long-term benefits of finding the "right" job. Low discounters should thus invest more in the search process and have a greater likelihood of selecting a firm that values their long-term outlook. High discounters presumably are less-careful job shoppers, and thus more frequently take jobs at firms with production functions designed for low discounters.*

The Economics of Quitting a Defined Contribution Firm

I now consider the efficacy of a defined contribution pension in correcting hiring errors. Suppose that a firm offers a simple defined contribution plan where it contributes some amount, S, of workers' pay to their pension accounts. Vesting is immediate. Borrowing is not permitted. While this compensation component seems naively simple, it provides a valuable sorting function for the firm. A key feature of defined contribution plans from this perspective is the condition attached to the pension: in order to obtain the balance in the account, the worker must quit. In effect, the contribution to the worker's account is a form of forced savings. Low discounters attach value to having savings for consumption in future periods and therefore see the account balance as just another form of compensation. In contrast, high discounters attach little value to future periods, and want to spend their income immediately. To them, monies in a deferred account are less valuable than cash in hand. The desired incentive is attained: high discounters are more likely to quit the firm in order to obtain access to the monies in their pension accounts.

We now have an economic function for defined contribution plans: The lump sum provided by defined contribution plans upon quitting encourages high discounters to select themselves for early departure from the firm. In effect, the plan continually sifts the work force for high discounters, thereby improving the composition of the firm's work force over time. Workers who are the highest discounters are most likely to quit with the shortest tenure: They are anxious to obtain access to the amount S in their accounts. Those with the next-highest discount rates are most likely to leave next. That is, at the end of the second period of tenure, the available lump sum is 2S, and after the third period, 3S, and so on. Gradually, all the high discounters find it economic to depart the firm. Workers who demonstrate that they can resist the lump sum reveal their low discount rates. The firm accomplishes the desired effect without expending any resources.

The Economics of 401(k) Plans

I have thus far considered only defined contribution plans to which the firm contributes a fixed percentage of pay. I now consider a more flexible defined contribution plan, the so-called 401(k). Such a plan can be characterized by fixed contributions like a plain defined contribution plan. But it also permits workers to make voluntary tax-deductible contributions, often with employer matching contributions. Since 401(k) plans permit workers to choose their savings rate, they are more efficient savings vehicles than plain defined contribution plans. This proposition is apparent. But 401(k) plans also can play a sorting role in the firm. In contrast to ordinary defined contribution plans that rely entirely on the sorting out feature of plain defined contribution plans, 401(k) plans encourage workers to align their pay and productivity.

The economics of the matching provision in 401(k) plans is simply put: Among otherwise identical workers, firms pay savers more than nonsavers. In a plain defined contribution plan, the firm can, and presumably does, reduce the cash wage in exchange for the pension contribution. But 401(k) contribution decisions are voluntary. Presumably, the firm does not *ex post* selectively reduce cash wages of particular workers who receive matching amounts. It also is reasonable to assume that profit-maximizing firms do not award "extra" wages to workers unrelated to their value of marginal product. These facts suggest that firms that pay matching amounts in the 401(k) plan attach special value to workers who are inclined to save.

I advance the idea that firms employing matching formulas are effecting a valuable sort, albeit a more sophisticated one than the lump-sum effects in plain defined contribution plans described above (Ippolito, 1998). By relying more on voluntary savings decisions, the employer sacrifices some of the benefits of forced savings that characterize plain defined contribution plans and thus loses some of the sorting-out effects of available lump sums. In return, without expending monitoring costs, the firm encourages workers to align their pay and value of marginal product across discount rates.

■ Conclusion

It is apparent that, after dominating the private sector for almost 100 years, defined benefit plans no longer are the plan of choice. Defined contribution plans now have almost 60 percent of this market, and projections seem favorable for their further expansion of market share until they have attained dominance during the next decade. Part of this trend is attributable to shifts in employment patterns that favor firms and industries that traditionally had a lower preference for defined benefit plans. But the increasing regulatory burden and unfavorable developments in the tax treatment of defined benefit plans also contributed to their demise. These cost issues were particularly detrimental in the face of a new competing pension, the 401(k) plan, that itself enjoyed the full benefits of favorable pension tax treatment and less regulatory burden, particularly in the sense that workers are not required to save in these plans, nor are employers required to contribute if workers choose not to participate.

The rise of defined contribution plans does not imply a lesser role for pension economics. It merely shifts the emphasis toward different ways in which pensions can help firms improve their productivity. The new pension economics recognizes the importance of defined contribution plans in effecting desirable sorting functions. Savers are better workers than nonsavers, and thus any compensation scheme that emphasizes pensions will tend to sort in a disproportionate number of higher-quality workers. At the same time, these plans encourage nonsavers who enter pension firms either to self select themselves out of the firm after a short tenure or to choose to pay themselves lower compensation by eschewing the matching 401(k) plan offered by the employer. The future of the new pension economics lies in further evaluating the impact of various defined contribution configurations on selection and in helping devise new approaches to accomplish the desired combination of skills in the firm.

In addition, new ways will have to be discovered to encourage the timely departure of older workers without violating discrimination laws that have been enacted. I have shown elsewhere that older workers clearly become less productive in firms while in their 50s mostly because of deteriorating heath (Ippolito, 1999c), and thus, ruling out age-based wage reductions that are fraught with litigation potential, firms will need to figure out how to "sort out" older workers in a timely fashion without the time-honored incentives in defined benefit plans.

Finally, the trend toward defined contribution plans also has clear implications for the retirement income of future generations of retirees. Clearly, employees have more control over their own savings rates in the new plan environment and have more say in their choice of portfolios in their plans. It is not obvious that these changes necessarily mean an alteration in the distribution of income over older ages in the future. But much empirical work will need to be done to study the long-term impact of these changes on the elderly's living standards. I have not addressed these issues in this discussion. Clearly these efforts will comprise the public policy segment of the new pension economics literature.

References

Allen, Steven, Robert Clark and Ann A. McDermed. "Job Mobility, Older Workers and the Role of Pensions." *Journal of Human Resources* 28 (Summer 1993): 463–481.

American Academy of Actuaries. *The Impact of Government Regulation on Defined Benefit Pension Plan Terminations*. Special Report. Washington, DC: American Society of Actuaries, March 1993.

Clark, Robert, and Ann McDermed. *The Choice of Pension Plans in a Changing Environment.* Washington, DC: American Enterprise Institute, 1990.

Employee Benefit Research Institute. *Databook on Employee Benefits*. Washington, DC: Employee Benefit Research Institute , 1997.

ERISA Industry Committee. "Getting the Job Done: A White Paper on Emerging Pension Issues." Washington, DC: ERISA Industry Committee, July 1996.

Gustman, Alan, and Thomas Steinmeier. "Pension Portability and Labor Mobility: Evidence from the SIPP." *Journal of Public Economics* 50 (March 1993): 299–323.

_______, *Pension Incentives and Job Mobility*. Kalamazoo, MI: Upjohn Institute, 1994.

________. "The Stampede Towards Defined Contribution Plans." *Industrial Relations*, 31 (Spring 1992): 361–369.

Gustman, Alan, Olivia Mitchell, and Thomas

Steinmeier. "The Role of Pensions in the Labor Market: A Survey of the Literature." *Industrial Labor Relations Review* 47 (April 1994), 417–438.

Hay Huggins Co. *Pension Plan Expense Study for the PBGC*. Washington, DC: Hay Huggins Co., 1990.

_______. *OBRA 1987: The Impact of Limiting Contributions to Defined Benefit Plans*. Washington, DC: Hay Huggins Co., September 1989.

Ippolito, Richard A. *Pension Plans and Employee Performance*. Chicago: University of Chicago Press, 1998.

_______. " Reversion Taxes, Contingent Benefits and The Decline in Pension Funding." Mimeo. George Mason University School of Law, 1999a.

_______. "Stayers as Workers and Savers: Towards Reconciling the Pension-Quit Literature." Mimeo. George Mason University School of Law, 1999b.

_______. "Age, Failure Rates and Retirement: New Evidence on an Old Idea." Mimeo. George Mason University School of Law, 1999c.

_______ and John Thompson. "The Survival Rate of Defined Benefit Plans, 1987-1995." *Industrial Relations* (forthcoming).

Jovanovic, Boyan. "Job Matching and the Theory of Turnover." *Journal of Political Economy* 87 (October 1979): 972–990.

Kruse, Douglas. "Pension Substitution in the 1980s: Why the Shift Towards Defined Contribution Plans?" *Industrial Relations* 34 (April 1995): 218–241.

Latimar, Murray. *Industrial Pension Systems*. New York: Industrial Relations Counselors, 1932.

Parnes, Herbert. *The Pre-Retirement Years*. Washington, DC: U.S. Government Printing Office, 1974.

Pension Benefit Guaranty Corporation. *Pension Insurance Data Book, 1998*. Washington, DC: Pension Benefit Guaranty Corporation, 1999.

Quinn, Joseph, Richard Burkhauser, and Daniel Myers. *Passing the Torch: The Influence of Economic Incentives on Work and Retirement*. Kalamazoo, MI: Upjohn Institute, 1990.

Salop, Joanne, and Steven Salop. "Self Selection and Turnover in the Labor Market." *Quarterly Journal of Economics* 90 (November 1976), 620–627.

U.S. Department of Labor. Pension and Welfare Benefits Administration. *Private Pension Plan Bulletin: Abstract of 1995 Form 5500 Annual Reports*. No. 8 (Spring 1999).

Williamson, Samuel. "Pensions in the U.S. and Canada before 1930: An Historical Perspective." In *Trends in Pensions*. Washington, DC: U.S. Department of Labor, 1992.

7

Organized Labor's Perspective on the Future of Defined Benefit Pension Plans

by David S. Blitzstein, United Food and Commercial Workers International Union

Introduction

Historically, the labor movement played a major role in creating the modern private pension system in America. The first pensions negotiated in coal, auto, and steel in the late 1940s and early 1950s set the pattern for pension benefits in union and nonunion firms that eventually spread to 40 percent of the work force by the 1960s.

The defined benefit pension model is quite compatible with basic union principles. Zvi Bodie's description of "pensions as retirement income insurance" is something that unions and workers understand. The five risks to retirement income security that Bodie described—replacement rate, Social Security retrenchment, longevity, investment risk, and inflation—have traditionally been pension bargaining objectives that Labor has tried to mitigate and protect workers from.[1]

The labor movement also espouses an institutional system of economics in which the role of unions is to ensure that the human and social costs of work do not fall totally on workers. This system of trade union economics is based on the believe that benefits like pensions are a fixed social overhead cost that has equal status with the fixed costs of capital of the corporation. The following statement from the fact-finding board in the 1949 steel industry labor dispute is consistent with this concept of fixed social overhead cost: "...we think that all industry, in the absence of adequate government programs, owes an obligation to workers to provide for the maintenance of the human body in the form of medical and similar benefits and full depreciation in the form of old-age retirement—the same way it does now for plant and equipment.[2] This historic government decision is the very essence of the post-World War II social contract understanding among labor, management, and government. A critical corollary of this trade union theory is that social costs should not be shifted elsewhere and that firms that fail to pay the full-cost social wage to their workers should not be subsidized by government or other firms.

I mention this history and economic theory to put Labor's view of private pensions in proper perspective. Labor embraced defined benefit plans because they are a natural outcome of our political and economic philosophy as a social institution. Unfortunately, economic and social trends have turned against both organized labor and the defined benefit pension plan system. In fact, there is reason to believe that the survival of the $3.0 plus trillion defined benefit pension system is at risk.

The stagnation and decline of the traditional defined benefit plans cannot be analyzed as an isolated event within the limited context of employee benefits or the American retirement system. The decline of defined benefit plans is symptomatic of greater social change and possibly a portent of future social and economic conflict in America. In the greater scheme of things, from the perspective of political economy, the defined benefit vs. defined contribution debate reflects a series of critical policy dilemmas in our country, including the role of the corporation.

---

[1] *Zvi Bodie, "Pensions as Retirement Income Insurance,"* Journal of Economic Literature, *Vol. 28 (March 1990): 28–49.*

[2] *Steel Industry Board,* Report to the President of the United States on the Labor Dispute in the Basic Steel Industry, *September 10, 1949, p. 55.*

■ The New Economy

The backdrop to these policy dilemmas is the emergence of the so-called "new economy" with its low unemployment, job growth and wage moderation, and growing prosperity gap. But according to MIT labor economist Paul Osterman, what is fundamentally new are the rules that govern the labor market. "The ties binding workers and companies have frayed". In Osterman's words, "In the new era, profitable companies lay off employees ... various forms of temporary and contingent employment are on the rise ... (the resulting) lack of loyalty (between employer and employee) works both ways ... and pay for performance is the norm and the rhetoric of the market has penetrated deeply within the firm ... resulting in a explosion of inequality."[3] What Osterman describes has obviously resulted in a dramatic weakening of the labor movement. The balance of power between labor and management has moved against workers. We are in a period where employers are all-powerful and they know it.

The new economy manifests itself in the private pension system with the displacement of the social contract model by a model that promotes "individual responsibility," employee empowerment and firm flexibility at the expense of risk sharing and the breakdown of group insurance. This transition to the individual responsibility model has been greatly accommodated by one of the longest periods of economic growth and stock market boom in U.S. history. Many commentators, including myself, question whether the individual responsibility model can survive the test of a prolonged market downturn or a recession. Only time will tell.

But have the individual responsibility model and its tool—the defined contribution plan—really been accepted? Recent surveys raise serious questions. This past summer Fidelity Investments surveyed 401(k) participants and found that only 8 percent were confidant that they will have enough money to retire.[4] The Fidelity survey also discovered that 50 percent of those surveyed had taken loans from their 401(k) accounts. Another recent survey sponsored by Consumer Federation of Primerica found that Americans were in no mood to save despite eight consecutive years of prosperity. Of those participating in the survey, one-half of the households had accumulated less than $1,000 in net financial assets, and 40 percent of those earning less than $35,000 believe they are more likely to accumulate wealth by winning a lottery than by careful saving and investing.[5] It would seem that in the current environment, the quiz show "Who Wants to be a Millionaire?" resounds more with the public than the lofty ideals of individual responsibility.

Hugh Heclo, who has written on political risk and Social Security reform, has highlighted a serious flaw in the defined contribution model that is worth noting. Heclo argues, quite logically I believe, that the foundation of individual account plans, namely, that "its your own money," will make it more difficult in the long run to sustain such nest eggs for retirement.[6] This would suggest that politicians will never have the courage to resolve the defined contribution leakage problem, converting defined contribution plans into real retirement systems.

Management theorists are also thinking about the implications of shattering the social contract and whether the individual responsibility model is wearing out its welcome. In a recent forum, Sanford Jacoby of UCLA described the real change occurring in the employer-employee relationship as a shift in the "risk burden." "It's the logic of managed care, it's the logic of larger deductibles, it's the logic behind the shift from defined benefit to defined contribution plans, it's the logic of the open-ended yet continuing employment relationship." In the same policy forum, Peter Cappelli, director of the Wharton School's Center for Human Resources, talked about "management without commitment" and how this new environment raises serious problems for employers in

---

[3] *Paul Osterman, "Comment and Analysis,"* Financial Times, *Sept. 17, 1999.*

[4] *Arleen Jacobuis, "Few 104(k) participants confident their retirement savings are adequate,"* Pensions & Investments, *July 26, 1999, p. 51.*

[5] Financial Times, *"Americans in no mood to save despite eight years of prosperity," October 29, 1999.*

[6] *Hugh Heclo, "Political Risk and Social Security Reform,"* National Academy of Social Insurance Social Security Brief, *no. 1 (September 1998).*

terms of retention of valuable employees.[7]

Margaret Blair, a senior fellow at Brookings, in her book *Ownership and Control*, posits that if human resources are critical to the success of the firm, then firms will experience increasing pressure (1) to improve their ability to attract and retain these resources; (2) modify their investment practices to ensure these human resources are fully developed, utilized, and do not depreciate; (3) and, modify their compensation and governance structures to better align the interests of employees and shareholders.[8] If this human resource primacy model of management really takes hold, firms might have no choice but to accommodate an aging work force with real pension plans. This presents the possibility that employers may have reason to re-think the utility of defined benefit plans.

Cost and competition are primary drivers in an employer's decisions not to sponsor defined benefit plans or to terminate plans altogether. I'm sure this is the driving force behind many employer efforts to convert traditional defined benefit plans into cash balance plans. A recent article by Barry Riley in *the Financial Times of London* captured the point so well.[9] In that perfect British understatement, Riley reminded us that "in the long run, pensions do cost a lot of money." The pressures of globalization, disinflation, and cut-throat domestic competition have further influenced employers to limit or eliminate their pension obligations. The fact that 50 percent of the work force has no retirement program and that less than 25 percent of the work force participates in a defined benefit plan accentuates these competitive pressures. Moreover, the Financial Accounting Standards Board's FASB 87 accounting rules lay another liability and risk factor on defined benefit plans that most employers would prefer not to contend with. FASB's treatment of defined benefit plans on a termination/settlement basis, ignores the fact that they are ongoing entities. My own opinion is that FASB 87 in its current form greatly weakens employer support for defined benefit plans.

What I find interesting about the current environment is that employers are dropping their commitment to defined benefit plans when many of these plans have been overfunded for long periods of time and have provided employers with extended contribution holidays. In effect, defined benefit plans with prolonged contribution holidays were more than cost competitive with defined contribution plans that were making matching contributions upwards of 5 percent of payroll.

This is where I believe Sylvester Schieber, of Watson Wyatt, has offered some exceptional insights. In a recent report he prepared called *Stretching the Pension Dollar*, Schieber suggests that "the contribution holidays created by OBRA '87 ultimately may prove to be a narcotic that will be the death knell for some defined benefit plans."[10] Schieber demonstrates that the pension liabilities incurred by the increasing age and tenure of the work force will catch up with the overfunding of the early 1990s. When it does, the shock for some employers of having to re-institute a pension contribution of 7 percent to 8 percent of payroll after paying nothing for so many years will prompt employers to abandon their defined benefit plans en mass.

Whether it's Social Security reform or private pension reform, citizens and policymakers invariably reject the notion that "there is no free lunch." Unfortunately, our half-broken retirement system is about to give us a reality check on the subject of the real cost of providing adequate retirements. Again, Sylvester Schieber, in an article titled *Retirement Income Adequacy at Risk*, estimates that workers who start saving at age 32, at various salary levels between $12,500 and $80,000, would have to save between 11.1 percent and

---

[7] *Bureau of National Affairs Pension Benefits, "Labor Relations Scholars Analyze Shift in Employer-Employee Relationships," Vol. 26, no. 17 (April 26, 1999): 1180.*

[8] *Thomas A. Kochan and Margaret M. Blair, "Human Capital and the American Corporation: Perspectives from Industry,"* Perspectives on Work *(The Magazine of the IRRA), Vol. 2, no. 1 (1998).*

[9] *Barry Riley, "The Trouble with Pensions,"* Financial Times, *Nov. 13–14, 1999.*

[10] *Sylvester J. Schieber, Richard Joss, Marjorie M. Kulash,* Stretching the Pension Dollar: Improving U.S. Retirement Security and National Savings by Enhancing Employer-based Pension Plans. *Prepared for the American Council for Capital Formation and the Association of Private Pension and Welfare Plans, Aug. 1999, p. 7.*

23.5 percent of salary each year to meet acceptable replacement income rates.[11] These are not small numbers, and they are significantly higher than what most workers are actually saving through their defined contribution plans. The message is not an easy sell politically because it is harsh and real. There is no free lunch, and if we want to avoid a return to the future where 50 percent of the retired population is living in poverty, private pensions will have to play a major role. The only other option is to expand Social Security into a national retirement program with much higher levels of replacement income, requiring a sizable increase in taxes.

Bottom-line, defined benefit plans are in trouble and facing serious issues of survival, ironically at time when they should be actively promoted and defended by public policymakers. A dismantling of the defined benefit pension system would be a generational tragedy that would greatly exacerbate the retirement savings/demographic crisis that is a constant theme throughout the developed world. In some strange Orwellian way, defined benefit plans have become a victim of their own success. Their overfunded status and surplus assets are seen as a liability and a tax revenue drain by corporations and government. A viable pension system is in the process of being dismantled at a time when it has reached its financial zenith, for lack of outspoken advocates and strong constituents.

A Possible Future for Defined Benefit Plans

Is there another "future" for defined benefit plans? I will describe a few "what if" scenarios:

1. The "market-collapse" scenario could greatly discredit the individual responsibility model, and refocus attention on the strong attributes of defined benefit plans. Of course, the market-collapse scenario is a two-edged sword that would also hurt defined benefit plans. Yet, because of their actuarial funding structure, the financial pain will not be as immediately felt in defined benefit plans. In contrast, the psychological pain of shrinking defined contribution accounts would be something akin to the bank failures of the Great Depression.

2. The rethinking of the social contract between employer and employee might offer another opportunity for a defined benefit plan rebirth. The acceptance of emerging management theories and their new emphasis on the critical competitive nature of human resources could change corporate governance structures and accounting decision-making systems. Social cost accounting might gain credibility as firms find it necessary to measure the extent of their human capital investment. Under such a scenario, defined benefit pensions might be measured as a capital investment rather than as a total liability. Employers would also see that defined benefit plans can be an effective tool for retaining older workers, which could become a serious competitive advantage as the work force ages. In the meantime, defined benefit plans need to experiment with pension benefits and employment arrangements that phase in retirement in a cost-effective way to avoid unnecessary turnover and training costs for sponsoring firms. Robert Paul's ideas about reconsidering voluntary employee contributions in defined benefit plans should also be explored.[12]

3. A third scenario involves the White House and Congress. At some point government will have to tackle the pension coverage problem in our system. So far Congress has avoided this critical issue by tinkering with tax regulation and creating fiscally dangerous front-loaded individual account solutions to promote savings. This too will fail. A movement will grow, similar to the Townsend movement or the railroad workers pension campaign in the 1930s, or maybe modeled off the popular "living wage movement," which has had success in over 40 locations nationwide, to pressure politicians to fix the coverage crisis. One possibility is that

---

[11] *Dan M. McGill, Kyle N. Brown, John j. Haley, Sylvester J. Schieber,* Fundamentals of Private Pensions, *7th Edition (Philadelphia: Pension Research Council, The Wharton School of the University of Pennsylvania, 1996).*

[12] *Robert D. Paul, "Is the Time Right for Allowing Pretax Employee Contributions to Pension Plans?"* Compensation & Benefits Management *(Winter 1996): 14–19.*

Congress will mandate a "minimum pension contribution" for employers similar to the minimum wage. Existing private plans would be allowed to compete for newly covered workers and their minimum pension contributions in similar industries. Instead of creating thousands of new plans, employees could elect into existing employer plans based on benefit design, in effect creating a series of industry multiemployer plans. The existing rules and regulations for multiemployer plans could be modified for this new model. Also, the Australian superannuation pension model might provide insights.

Another option is that Congress might adopt a "responsible corporation" legislation similar to that proposed by a Democratic Congressional task force chaired by Sen. Jeff Bingaman (D-NM) that creates a new category of corporation that would receive a variety of benefits from government in exchange for maintaining a more reliable social compact with its employees, including defined benefit pension plans. The corporation would receive favorable tax treatment, selective regulatory relief, and certain training and technology subsidies in return for rebuilding a social contract with its workers.

Hopefully, the future of defined benefit plans will receive the attention it deserves in the upcoming presidential and congressional campaigns.

8

Small Business Defined Benefit Plans

by Kathleen Havey, Chamber of Commerce of the United States

Introduction

Every other year, the U.S. Chamber of Commerce does a study of businesses of every size, sector, and region of the country on their employee benefits policies. And to take two years for comparison sake, since we are at the 25th anniversary of the Employee Retirement Income Security Act (ERISA), looking between the years 1975 and 1998, we see that spending on retirement benefits as a percentage of payroll has actually increased by more than 25 percent in the last 25 years or so. Yet, in relative terms, it should come as no surprise to you that the proportion of retirement dollars being spent on defined benefit pension plans has decreased substantially, while the most significant increase was, of course, in the 401(k) arena, a category that didn't even exist when we were asking the questions back in the early 1970's.

Overcoming the Barriers

Where are we now? Dallas Salisbury's discussion[1] and the Small Employer Retirement Survey do a good job of laying out some of the barriers to retirement plan formation. I would like to discuss three of the major reasons employers cited more than half of the time by respondents for not offering a retirement plan. Number one, employees prefer wages and/or other benefits. Number two, required company contributions are too excessive. And number three, revenue is too uncertain to commit to a plan.

What can be done to counter these barriers to plan formation? I would like to take a slightly more optimistic look at how we can develop plan coverage in the small business market. Clearly businesses feel the need to be on somewhat of a secure footing before they are interested and willing to take a look at starting a retirement plan of any sort. I don't think there is anything we can do to convince the brand new start-up business to set up a plan for their workers right off the bat. And in fact, according to the data from EBRI, almost every company that has a retirement plan also has paid vacation time and health care coverage; those two benefits generally are offered by employers before retirement benefits.

However, since small businesses are really driving the economy in terms of job creation and formation, we cannot ignore this particular sector of the labor force. The U.S. Chamber is forming a partnership with the Department of Labor and the Small Business Administration to launch a Web site that will be geared toward small business owners to help them decide which type of pension plan is best for them.

The whole process of figuring out, "Is it a 401(k) or is it a savings incentive match plan for employees (SIMPLE) or would I want to go with a defined benefit plan?" can be very intimidating to small business owners, for whom retirement plans are far afield from their core line of business. The Web site that we are putting together will walk employers through some very basic questions about whether they want to have an employee match or not, what type of vesting criteria they would have, and so on. At the end, the site outlines which retirement plan best meets the employer's criteria. We hope to have this Web site launched in the first quarter of next year. And we are very optimistic that it will help educate employers on some of their options.

Second, employees prefer wages and/or other benefits. Now this is a common refrain that I

---

[1] *See Dallas L. Salisbury, "Development of Private Retirement Programs," in this volume.*

hear from a lot of plan sponsors, and certainly it is common among those who do not sponsor a plan. Here again, education is the key to showing employees why it is in their best interest to have a retirement plan at work and to participate in it. We have seen in the last couple of years that the media are paying closer attention to this issue as the baby boomers get a little bit closer to their retirement.

We need to have the infrastructure in place so that, as more and more people and businesses become concerned about retirement, the tools are there with the least amount of obstacles possible for as many people to be covered as possible.

Third, required company contributions are too expensive. Now as I have alluded to earlier, the notion of diving into the complex regulations and statutes governing pensions and retirement plans is very intimidating to many small business owners. However, on the legislative front there are a number of things we can do to help incentivize small business plan formation.

One issue that is addressed by Jack VanDerhei[2] is the Secure Assets For Employees (SAFE) and the Secure Money Annuity or Retirement Trust (SMART) plans. I won't go into the details of those plans since he has covered it, but I will point out that according to Paul Yakoboski,[3] 81 percent of the net loss of defined benefit plans are in companies with fewer than 25 workers. And so here again I think offering as many viable retirement options to this segment of the work force as we can is really essential.

SAFE and SMART are important proposals currently pending before Congress. However, because SAFE and SMART are a type of cash balance plan, I think that passing any new legislation right now encouraging the formation of cash balance plans is treading on risky ground. Attempting to move SAFE or SMART through the legislative process would immediately tie the bills into the larger controversies, regardless of whether the issues were directly related or not. We cannot expect to pass SAFE or SMART or a compromise before the larger cash balance issues are addressed. However, I believe that these bills are worth trying. We cannot know if they are going to be successful or not unless we do pass them into law. And I hope that next year the climate will be right for us to be able to move ahead on that issue.

■ Legislation

Finally, I want to briefly mention a few of the provisions in more comprehensive bills that are currently pending before Congress: H.R. 1102, introduced by Reps. Rob Portman (R-OH) and Benjamin Cardin (D-MD); S. 741, introduced by Sens. Bob Graham (D-FL) and Charles Grassley (R-IA) and S. 646, introduced by Sens. William Roth (R-DE) and Max Baucus (D-MT). The provisions I will mention are included in some or all of these bills.

First of all, modifications to top-heavy requirements. Currently, small businesses, in addition to whatever match or nonelective contribution they make into a retirement plan, also are often considered to be top-heavy plans and therefore have to make additional contributions above and beyond what they already were planning on contributing. These bills would modify top-heavy requirements, narrowing them somewhat so that, for example, 401(k) matching contributions would be able to count toward a top-heavy employer requirement.

Restoration of Limits

Some of the limits that were scaled back in the 1980s decrease the incentives for small business owners to offer a plan. The Chamber is a very strong supporter of restoring those limits in order to increase the incentives for small companies to offer retirement plans.

Allowing Plan Loans for Small Businesses

This is something of a symbolic issue and it is one that irks a lot of small business owners. Why shouldn't a small business owner be able to take a loan out of the plan, just like the other employees, when he or she is the one who established it in the first place?

---

[2] See Jack VanDerhei and Ken McDonnell, "Current Provisions and Recent Trends in Qualified Single-Employer Defined Contribution Plans in the Private Sector," in this volume.

[3] See Paul Yakoboski, "Overview of the Defined Benefit System," in this volume.

Finally, a Small Business Tax Credit

This is an interesting issue, because when it was proposed about a year or so ago, it was viewed by a lot of inside-the-Beltway types as more of a political issue—one that resonated with politicians—rather than one that could actually help plan formation. And yet when I was looking through some of the EBRI background data, it stated that, according to their survey, a tax credit for starting a retirement plan was one of the two items most likely to lead business owners to seriously consider sponsoring a retirement plan. Here again, we can point to a fairly straightforward tax policy change that might actually have a discernible impact on the sponsorship of plans in the small business sector. Certainly we already, through the tax code, try to encourage other behavior that the government considers positive, like owning a home (through the mortgage interest deduction) or offering employee education assistance (through employer tax deductibility). Creating a start-up small business tax credit to offset some of the initial expenses of starting a retirement plan might provide small business owners the incentive they need to start a plan.

9

Defined Benefit Plans From a Small Employer's Perspective

by Jack Stewart, Principal Financial Group

Introduction

In 1975, before the Employee Retirement Income Security Act of 1974 (ERISA) started, there were around 103,000 defined benefit plans, and most of those—in fact, about 83,000—were for smaller employers (with fewer than 100 employees). Bigger employers had 20,000 defined benefit plans.

In 1995, the latest year for which statistics are available, there were approximately 69,000 defined benefit plans; 52,000 were smaller plans and 17,000 were large plans, with the numbers holding steady, at least for the larger employers.

But if you look at plan participants, you can see there are more plan members under defined benefit plans today than under ERISA days, and I find that interesting. The sad part of it is that the growth has all been in the over-100-employee category. There are today more than 38 million employees in defined benefit plans sponsored by larger employers (with more than 100 employees) and fewer than one million, about 890,000 in small plans. So a big change has occurred in 20 years in terms of defined benefit plan membership.

There has been much discussion of why fewer small employers have plans. ERISA may have had something to do with it. Employers face increased government regulation, required funding, and Pension Benefit Guaranty Corporation (PBGC) premiums. I don't need to repeat what has been said before. It is just more difficult for smaller employers to have that commitment and to make that contribution to a defined benefit plan.

SAFE AND SMART Plans

The Secure Assets for Employees (SAFE) and Secure Money Annuity or Retirement Trust (SMART) options have been discussed before Congress during the last few years. The basic question for us at Principal and nationally would be: can either of these features, if they become law—which I think they will eventually—reverse the trend away from defined benefit plans? I think the short answer is we don't think so.

Certainly there are a lot of highlights in SAFE and SMART. These plans establish individual accounts for each employee. They are more portable. They provide a certain base benefit of 1 percent, 2 percent, or 3 percent of pay times years of service. There are simplified filing requirements. No or lower PBGC premiums. The benefits are much more portable. And obviously the accounts are built at the plan member level.

Marketing is an issue. To illustrate, a word about our own defined benefit marketing experience. We sell around 2,500 401(k) plans per year, so we have an experienced sales force. About three years ago, we undertook an extensive effort to train our same sales force on defined benefit plans, hoping to generate more business for us and more coverage under defined benefit plans.

The results after three years of this training have been so-so at best. We were able to increase the number of defined benefit sales, meaning double, but double is from 50 to 100 per year, and that is a lot different from 2,000 to 2,500 401(k)s. And the other part of this is that the majority of the sales that we did have for defined benefit plans were either takeover plans that were already established someplace else or they were for a city or governmental agency.

Very few—maybe 15 to 20 of these—were for brand new plans. So you can see there is not the demand out there from employers.

The reason why the SAFE and SMART features won't help, at least in our opinion, can be found in the Employee Benefit Research Institute small employer retirement survey. Revenue uncertainty is one consideration. There are just so many things that the smaller employers have to worry about, and one of them is just making sure bills are paid, that the employees' payrolls are met, and the business is still running. The last thing they have to think about is a plan, let alone a defined benefit plan. They have to worry more about being in business in five to 10 years.

The other thing that has been hit on as well is that potential plan members, employees, don't really demand a defined benefit plan. They know somebody who has a 401(k), and they want a 401(k) as well. So the employee awareness and appreciation for the defined benefit plan is certainly lacking.

Most employees want to see their accounts via the Internet. They want to dial up a voice response system and know what is in their account and they want to be able to control it. Certainly they don't plan on being long-term employees. Most of them will have jobs with six, seven, or eight employers over the years. They want to have a portable benefit. So a traditional defined benefit plan really won't work there, either.

■ Other Options

Are there other ideas? Contributors to this book have discussed hybrid plans and cash balance. I think certainly those are coming. Will they be embraced by smaller employers? At this time I would sort of doubt it. One approach that we have been trying to discuss with certain members of Congress and within the PBGC is perhaps to find a way to combine the best of the defined benefit plan with a 401(k) plan under one plan, one document, one 5500.

There would be, of course, separate asset pools for the defined benefit side and for the deferral side. But we think it is important for employers and employees and their advisors to look at a single source for the replacement ratio. It makes a little more sense for it to come from one plan, that is, to put all retirement income under one umbrella.

In other words, there could be a defined benefit of, say, a percent of pay times years of service and then employees would be allowed to put in their deferrals and build on top of the base of the defined benefit.

■ Conclusion

We conclude that certainly defined benefit plans can be designed to meet the smaller employers' needs, especially those who have been in business for 10 or 15 years. They've got the business stable and now it is time to think about a benefit. They can reward past service. They can design the plan to hopefully provide a good benefit for most, if not all, of their employees.

But the problem is not that many smaller businesses survive into the 15th and 20th year to get to that stable point. What do you do in the meantime? I think it is clear that the demand by smaller employers for defined benefit plans by their employees will continue to decrease, and the obvious conclusion is that in five or 10 years from now, there will be many fewer defined benefit plans for employers with fewer than 100 employees than there are now.

10

A Realistic Appraisal of Increasing Pension Coverage by Small Business

by William J. Dennis, National Federation of Independent Business

Introduction

Reading Paul Yakoboski's discussion,[1] I came to table 2, which presents plan trends by plan size. Immediately, I got out my calculator. As soon as I see tables, I tend to do that. I recalculated the table in terms of percentage change in defined benefit and defined contribution plans and then on the net.

What we see is almost a linear decline in defined benefit plans by plan size over time. In other words, the most frequent plan losses occurred among the very smallest. The percentage decline fell as plans got larger. The defined contribution plan pattern was a bit more complex. Nonetheless, the percentage of those plans grew by size category up to the 200–499 employee size and then declined again.

For the total plans, we saw a roof-top type pattern. We saw that the larger firms grew, the more likely they were to add a pension plan until they reached the 50–99 employee group. Then, the number began to decline again. These data force us to ask why the shift among small firms in particular. Why do so relatively few have pension plans?

Small Business Owners' Perspective

The obvious way to answer these questions is to ask the owners. Indeed, they have been asked on many occasions. The first time I asked was back in 1985 and their response was very simple. We can't afford one. Lewin did some work for the Small Business Administration in the early 1990s, and got an answer that the income of the owner was too unstable. Greenwald and Associates asked the question somewhat differently for the Employee Benefit Research Institute (EBRI) a couple of years ago. The wording, in effect, was what would encourage you to adopt a pension plan? The answer was an increase in profits or business tax credits. And just this year, EBRI asked again and its researchers received an answer that revenue is too uncertain.

The Cost of Pensions

These data raise a further question. Are small businesses telling the truth or are these just socially desirable answers? Recently, I undertook some empirical work to answer that question. In fact, the operating hypothesis was that business income is related to the provision of a pension plan and also the level of compensation and provision of health insurance. The latter are for a different discussion. Indeed, I found that there was a very strong relationship between owner income from the business and the provision of a pension plan. I also found that firm size was highly related to pension provision, suggesting economies of scale.

None of this is really great news. Emily Andrews wrote a book on small businesses and pensions for EBRI a decade ago. The book's title said it all: *Pension Policy and Small Employers: At What Price Coverage?*

After reviewing various types of pension proposals, Andrews concluded that, yes, you can increase the participation of small firms. You can successfully encourage them to offer pensions more

[1] *See Paul Yakoboski, "Overview of the U.S. Employment-Based Retirement Income System," in this volume.*

frequently. But at what cost? How much in tax revenues would have to be foregone to impact coverage?

There are also other costs than revenues foregone, or at least trade-offs. For example, health insurance. Many of the firms that do not provide pension plans also don't provide health insurance. In fact, in the mid-1980s, when I was looking at the issue carefully. I found that almost always a firm had health insurance if they had a pension plan. Today that isn't necessarily true. A trade-off is occurring in some firms.

Encouraging Pension Plan Provision

This discussion was supposed to focus on defined benefit plans. However, the relevant issue is not how to encourage small business owners to provide a defined benefit plan. The issue is how to encourage them to provide any plan.

The answer is simple. You can raise their earnings, indirectly through tax subsidies or other ways. Perhaps you can even get at the issue of income stabilization. But it is important to recognize and remember that self-employed people and small business owners as a group are not wealthy people.

The median income of a self-employed person is just above the median income of the typical working American. The average income is much greater, but the median income is just about on average. In the early part of this decade, it was below median income. You are not talking about a group of wealthy people with lots of disposable cash. So, to the extent that you can raise their earnings, you raise their ability to provide pensions.

The second point that you should understand when dealing with small firms is that the median life expectancy of a firm at birth is five years or a little less. One in 20 firms will last 20 years. So when discussing both return, which is highly associated with how long you have been in business, and risk, the ability to absorb risk in a defined benefit program, we must keep business life expectancy tables in mind.

Other than raising earnings, what can you do? You can cut costs. Cut administrative hassles. That is the free alternative. To some extent, that has been done by moving to defined contribution plans.

The third point revolves around the question: does the benefit that you are offering get somebody in the front door? That result has become increasingly critical. I have been working with small business owners for almost a quarter of a century now. One thing I have learned is that at this particular juncture they are facing labor problems in terms of shortages as they have never faced them before.

Therefore, it becomes a critical issue that we know what attracts and keeps employees. In this regard, it is important to understand that small business employs disproportionately young and old workers, disproportionately secondary workers. And from earlier discussions, I guess they employ disproportionately nonsavers, though I have not seen a firm size tabulation before.

There are exceptions. You will find very sophisticated high-tech firms that will design special programs. Often these programs are designed around the most valuable employee, not employees in general. You will also find highly successful small businesses that provide their employees a full range of benefits.

Plan Choice

Why would a small employer, assuming that he has a pension plan or the desire to have a pension plan, choose a cash balance, hybrid defined benefit, or some other plan in this particular genre? The answer is he probably wouldn't.

Forgetting the questionable legislative status that would make any tax advisor cringe, look at the critical questions. What type of plan is the easiest to finance? What plan minimizes the hassles and the complexities for the owner and is the easiest one for him to understand? What brings people in the front door? There are always exceptions to this general observation. There are peculiarities of the work force. That is one of the reasons a flexible system is very nice.

But I think that there is no doubt for the majority: Defined benefit programs just aren't in the cards.

11

The Future of Defined Contribution Plans: Participation and Contribution Behavior

by E. Scott Peterson, Hewitt Associates LLC

Background

Defined contribution plans are widely popular and successful programs. Overall, employees understand them, appreciate them, and use them effectively. They are a favorite topic for the press—not merely in benefit and investment publications, but in the popular press as well. Yet for all the popularity of 401(k) plans, many employees must be persuaded to join them. Whether it is lack of available funds for saving or the perception that these plans only serve the need of meeting far-off retirement needs, one-fifth or more of eligible employees often do not take advantage of the these programs. Plan sponsors constantly feel challenged to increase participation in their plans, to ensure that all employees are adequately prepared for retirement and that highly compensated employees are able to maximize the amounts they can defer.

Given these circumstances, what are the most effective tools for promoting involvement among participants? This discussion examines five factors that influence plan participation, and discusses the impact of each in determining employee behavior. These factors are:

- Company match
- Effective communication and education campaigns
- Flexible plan provisions and administrative procedures
- Passive ("automatic") enrollment
- Competing company initiatives

Company Match

The most common structure for employer contributions in 401(k) plans is a company match. Amounts contributed by employees are matched by their employer. Fifty percent is the most prevalent rate, though some plans match as high as 100 percent or more and others match as little as 15 cents per dollar. Intuitively, it is reasonable to expect that the presence of a company match would have a strong positive influence on employee contribution behavior. In fact, while the expected correlation is present, the impact on actual behavior is not what might be expected. Consider the following examples.

Professors David Laibson of Harvard University and Andrew Metrick of The Wharton School of Business have undertaken a study in collaboration with Hewitt Associates to examine participant behavior. The initial step in the study was to examine a single plan population. This group, which is comprised of over 28,000 employees, is spread across 50 business units of the company. Each business unit determines the matching formula; match rates vary from 25 percent to 100 percent across location. Other aspects of plan design and operation are the same for the entire population, so this situation provided a unique opportunity to examine the correlation between match rate and various aspects of participation.

The study captured demographic data such as age, gender, tenure with the company, and hourly versus salaried pay status in addition to work location. It allowed Laibson and Metrick to correlate the likelihood of participating with each of these variables in addition to the level of match that the employee would earn. The findings suggest two key points:

The rate of match is *not* a strong influence in employees' decisions about whether or not to join a 401(k) plan. Specifically, varying the match rate for a participant is less likely to influence an

Chart 11.1

PERCENTAGE POINT INCREASE IN PROBABILITY OF PARTICIPATION

45-Year-Old male Salaried Employee Earning $35,000/Year With 10 Years at Company and a 50 Percent Match Rate)

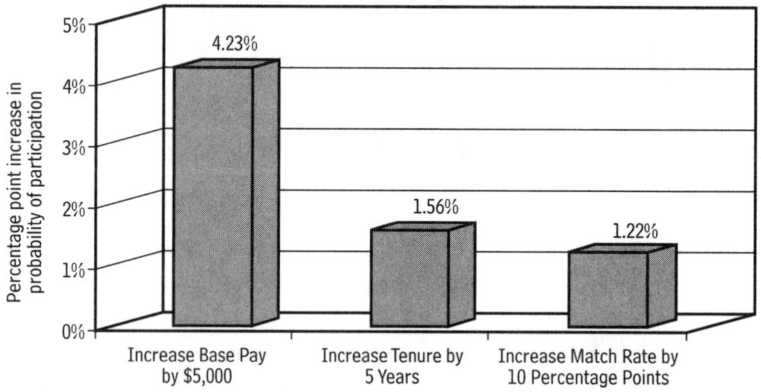

Baseline probability = 59.7%

Source: Hewitt Associates.

employee's decision to join a plan than are changes in the individual's circumstances such as increases in pay or tenure with the company. As a baseline, the study used a 45-year-old male earning $35,000 per year with 10 years of service and eligible for a 50 percent match. Overall, the likelihood of such an individual participating in the plan was 59.7 percent. As shown in chart 11.1, increasing the match rate by 10 percentage points was less likely to positively influence the employees' likelihood of participating than either changes in base pay or in length of service with the company.

This premise—that changing the rate of match does not have a significant influence on employees' likelihood of participating—is also borne out by the results of Hewitt Associates' latest survey of 401(k) plan practices—1999 Trends and Experience in 401(k) Plans. This survey, as illustrated by table 11.1, confirms that, while the absolute presence or absence of a match impacts employees' decisions to participate, the rate of match offered is not particularly significant.

For employees electing to join a plan, the rate of match offered does influence the level of contribution elected. The Laibson and Metrick study looked at the same baseline employee (pay of $35,000, 10 years of service, and 50 percent match) and correlated the same variables to rate of contribution among plan participants. This time, the results were different. As shown in chart 11.2, increasing the rate of match by 10 percentage points was more likely to positively influence participants' rates of contributions than increasing pay or service.

While this evidence suggests that increasing the rate of match in a plan will encourage employees who are already motivated to save to increase their levels of participation, it is less clear that this same practice will entice nonsavers to join a 401(k) plan initially.

Table 11.1

PARTICIPATION RATES

Plan Design Features	Average Participation Rate
Level of Employer Contribution ($) (on Employee Contributions)	
No employer contribution	65%
Any employer contribution	79
$0.25 match	76
$0.26–$0.49 match	77
$0.50 match	77
$0.51–$0.99 match	81
$1.00 match	81
Other contributions (e.g., discretionary profit sharing contribution)	79
Graded match	79
Based on length of service	81
Based on company performance	79

Source: Hewitt Associates.

Chart 11.2
EXPECTED PERCENTAGE POINT INCREASE IN TOTAL CONTRIBUTION RATES
(45-Year-Old Male Salaried Employee Earning $35,000/Year With 10 Years at Company and a 50 Percent Match Rate

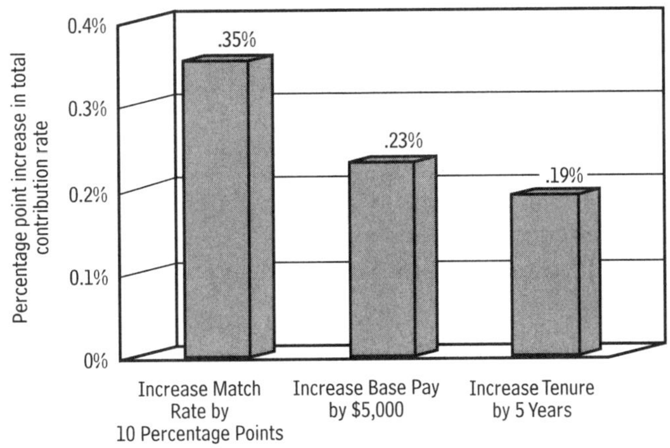

Baseline expected contribution rate = 3.90%

Souarce: Hewitt Associates.

Effective Communication and Education Campaigns

Communication campaigns are neither new nor unique to 401(k) plans. Employers have recognized the need to sell the benefits of these programs since as long as savings plans have existed. As the number and variety of savings and investment alternatives has grown, however, the need for sales-oriented communication and education materials has grown. Plan sponsors have found the need to compete for scarce savings dollars with other company plans (e.g., stock purchase plans), other tax-favored individual programs (such as individual retirement accounts), and a plethora of retail investment alternatives. In addition, 401(k) plans themselves have become more complicated in general and offer greater choices in particular. Employees need more information to make informed decisions about the levels and forms of savings and investment options to select.

Specifically, in helping employees make decisions about the right investment options, it has become increasingly important to ensure that they choose to join a 401(k) plan. The Hewitt 401(k) survey shows how the average number of investment options in 401(k) plans has grown over time (table 11.2):

While the increase in number of funds has largely come in response to requests from employees themselves for specific additional alternatives, the resulting range of funds has frequently resulted in confusion and uncertainty about the right investment choices for individual participants. Plan sponsors have responded by expanding their communication efforts. More space in plan materials is devoted to describing specific investment alternatives in the plan. Increasingly, many employers have come to view broader investment education as a critical part of basic plan communication. More recently, plan sponsors have begun providing employees access to specific investment advice—a practice that was unheard of only two years ago.

Table 11.2
INVESTMENT FUNDS

Year	Average Number of Investment Funds
1999	11
1997	8
1995	6
1993	4.5
1991	3.7

Source: Hewitt Associates.

Flexible Plan Provisions and Administrative Procedures

Today, rank-and-file employees can take advantage of a wide variety of financial services in the retail market. Service and flexibility have become watchwords of the industry. Consumers' expectations for products that are responsive and easy to use carry over to the 401(k) world as well. Even within the highly regulated 401(k) plan environment, participants have come to expect plans that offer as much access and flexibility as can be allowed as well as quick, accurate execution of all plan activity. Access to plan balances by telephone and over the Internet has moved from an appealing "extra" to the minimum expectation voiced by employees. Employers must continue to improve service in order to meet participant demands. It is clear that ease of use and access influence consumers' decisions to use any product, and 401(k) plans are no exception to this reality.

Passive ("Automatic") Enrollment

Employee inertia can be an unintentional detriment to participation in any voluntary benefit program. To combat this, some employers have introduced the concept of passive enrollment in their 401(k) plans. Such a provision provides for employees to be automatically enrolled in their savings plans when they become eligible unless they specifically elect otherwise. Enrollment is at a minimum level of participation (e.g., 2 percent or 3 percent), and contributions are typically invested in the most conservative investment election (some plans also use the company stock fund as the default investment election).

The result of this practice on overall plan participation is clear. Plans with a passive enrollment feature commonly experience participation rates of 95 percent of eligible employees—15 percent above that of similar plans requiring active enrollment. It is less clear, however, what impact these provisions have on the levels of contributions and investment decisions of people who are defaulted into the plan (e.g., whether employees who might be inclined to contribute at higher levels will accept the basic default election). The intention is that getting employees into a plan when initially eligible will get them accustomed to saving and engaged in the program; that once in, they will realize the benefits of the plan and participate more actively. As more employers get experience with enrollment practices of this nature, it will be interesting to monitor overall trends in participation to ensure that "defaulted" employees do, in fact, make the transition to more active participation in the plan over time.

Competing Company Initiatives

As previously stated, plan sponsors are faced with the prospect of competing with other financial services for scarce employee savings dollars. Sometimes, in fact, the competition comes from other company programs. Programs that encourage company ownership, such as employee stock purchase plans, are a good example of this. Given the need to demonstrate that 401(k) plans do not discriminate in operation (i.e., through the ADP and ACP tests), it is important that competing initiatives not steal an inordinate amount of participation from the plans.

The point here is not to suggest that 401(k) plans should always be favored or promoted over other programs. Instead, it is to acknowledge that employees need assistance in understanding the alternatives they are offered, and help in determining the right way to use such vehicles to meet their capital accumulation goals. Traditionally, most employers who offer multiple plans have tended to have separate communication and delivery of each program. As employees seek more information about the implications and trade-offs of various alternatives, consolidated campaigns that describe how such programs fit together and complement one another prove to be the most effective.

Summary

Though nearly 20 years old, 401(k) plans continue to be exciting, engaging benefits for employees. They are a good vehicle for promoting individuals' sense of responsibility for retirement as well as employees' appreciation of amounts provided by their employers. Yet, realizing these benefits requires constant work by plan sponsors to promote wise behavior by employees. Through the right mix of plan provisions and effective, efficient delivery practices (covering both communication and administration), curious—or even wary—employees can be easily converted to savvy plan participants.

12

Defined Contribution Plan Distribution Trends

by John DeStefano, Fidelity Investments

Introduction

At Fidelity, we have also analyzed participant behavior at the end of the spectrum that indicates what happens when they leave their employer and are eligible to take their money out of their defined contribution plan.

Clearly, the intention of defined contribution plans is for participants to contribute over their employment, for the assets to grow tax deferred until retirement, and then for them to withdraw funds as needed to live off of in retirement.

Is that how it's working? For the most part, yes. But a number of trends are beginning to emerge that are cause at least for greater study and attention, if not concern. These trends pertain to:

- participants and assets that are eligible for distribution and are in fact distributed from plans;
- where those assets are going and what that means to the retirement savings of the participants;
- what participants are telling us they need in terms of information and education; and
- and the implications of this data for the industry.

Changes in demographics and the economic climate are increasing the number of terminated employees—those eligible to take a distribution from their defined contribution plan.

These employees fall into two categories, both of which are experiencing tremendous growth for different reasons:

- retirees (chart 12.1) and
- job changers (chart 12.2).

As the baby boomers age, we are seeing people retire in record numbers. In 1950, only 12 million people in this country were over age 65;

Chart 12.1
GROWTH OF THE POPULATION AGES 65 AND OVER

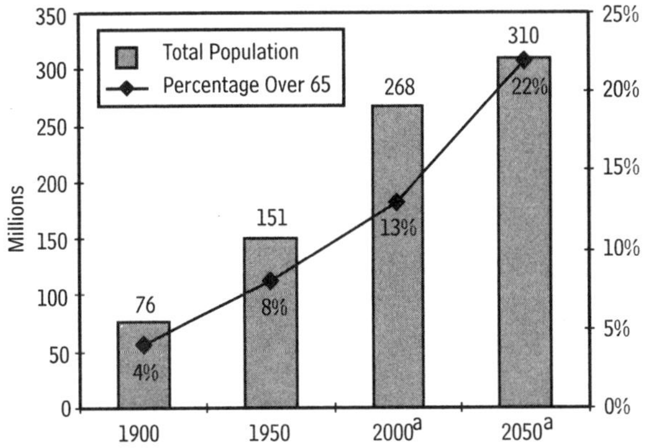

Source: U.S. Census Bureau.
[a]Projected.

Chart 12.2
JOB TENURE: WORKERS AGES 20 AND OVER

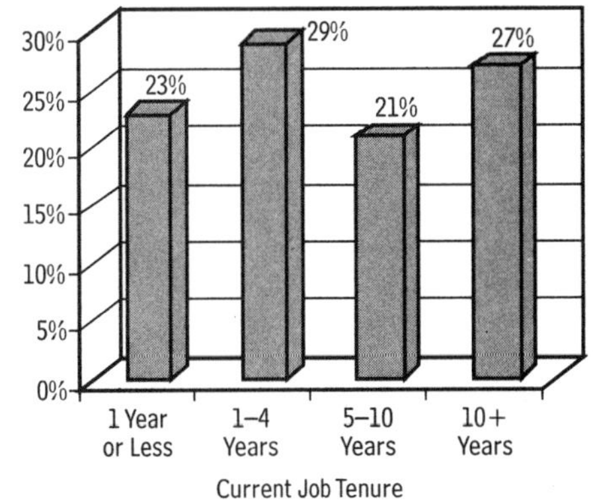

Source: Employee Benefit Research Institute compilation of U.S. Bureau of Labor Statistics, 1996.

Chart 12.3
Distribution Options for Terminated Participants

- Keep Assets in Original DC Plan
- Roll Assets Over
    - —Rollover IRA
    - —Annuity
- Move Assets to New DC Plan
- Take Cash Distribution

Source: Fidelity Investments.

next year it will be 35 million, and in 2050, 68 million!

In addition, these retirees are expected to live longer, and therefore will have even more significant financial needs in retirement.

Finally, as we see the traditional model of retirement (work for one company for 30 years, then retire on a pension) shifting, and more retirees are working part time, going back to school, etc., retirees need to examine a much broader array of options for what to do with their defined contribution money than they used to.

Distribution Options

There are basically four options for a defined contribution participant who has left his employer (chart 12.3):

- Leave the assets in the plan. If a participant has been employed with one employer for a long time, and has a plan with a broad array of investment and withdrawal options, this can be a very attractive option. It is also an option that many participants are unaware of (more data later).
- Roll the assets over.
- A rollover individual retirement account (IRA) is often an attractive option for a participant who has multiple small accounts and wants to consolidate, or who has limited choices in his or her defined contribution plan.
- An annuity can sometimes also be appropriate for retiring participants.
- Move assets to the new plan. For job changers, sometimes the best option is to consolidate in their new employers plan.

All three options above preserve the tax-deferred status of the assets. Therefore, we should encourage all three, depending on the individual's specific financial situation.

- However, the fourth option is very popular—to take a cash distribution.

This behavior unfortunately results not only in the participant losing tax-deferred status if the proceeds are not rolled over to a qualified plan within 60 days, but may also result taxes being withheld by the record keeper.

Which Options Are People Choosing?

It's difficult to get good data on how many participants are leaving their assets in the plan, but we estimate it's about one-half. Much of this is due to inertia, on their part, but this has a net positive effect on their retirement savings.

- For those taking distributions, you can see that the majority are rolling over to a rollover IRA. Spectrem found in a study earlier this year that almost two-thirds of assets distributed from 401(k) plans were rolled over to an IRA (chart 12.4).
- Another 10 percent or so was transferred into another qualified vehicle.

Chart 12.4
Annual Distributions

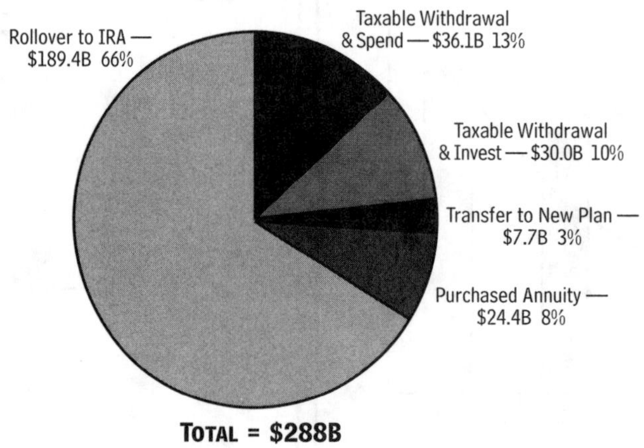

Total = $288B

Source: Spectrum Group, *Lump Sum Distributions from Retirement Plans, 1999.*

Chart 12.5

Distribution Behavior: 57 Percent of 401(k) Participants Took Their Plan Assets in Cash

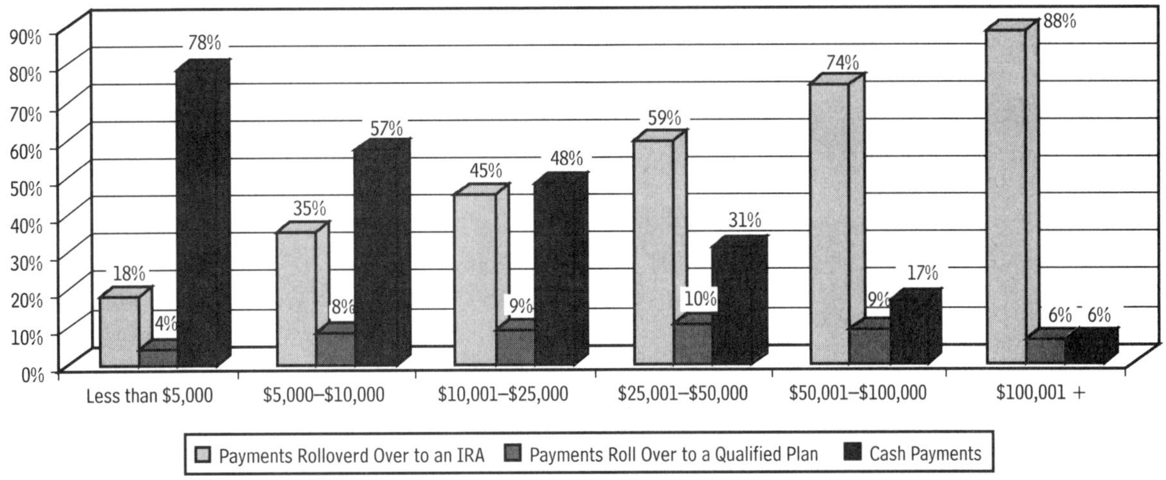

Source: Hewitt Associates LLC, Lincolnshire, IL, 1998.

However, alarmingly, almost 25 percent of assets were taken in cash:

- Just over one-half of participants spent the money—losing their accrued retirement savings altogether.
- The rest invested it. However, due to the penalties and loss of tax-favored status, these participants may have significantly decreased their long-term savings potential by choosing to take their assets in cash.

This trend is confirmed by some research that Hewitt did earlier this year (chart 12.5). The study concludes that 57 percent of all participants taking distributions take them in cash. A large percentage of these people have very small balances (<$5,000), and in some cases are forced out of their plans by their former employer.

However, there are significant numbers of participants with higher balances who are taking distributions in cash:

- 31 percent of those with balances $25,000–$50,000.
- 16 percent of those with balances of $50,000–$100,000.

Chart 12.6

Do Participants Have the Information They Need?

- 35 percent report receiving no information on distribution options/tax implications from the employer they left.
- 15 percent did not know they had the option to leave the assets in their previous employer's plan.
- 69% sought advice or information from another source.

Source: Fidelity Investments, Terminated Participant Survey, 1999.

What Is Driving Participants to Sub-optimize Their Retirement Savings?

Certainly some can be attributed to people who need the money. However, at Fidelity, we have found that this trend is in large part due to ignorance.

We asked terminated participants in our 401(k) plans about their distribution behavior (chart 12.6):

- Over one-third said they had not received any information from their former employer about their distribution options or the tax consequences associated with those options.
- In fact, 15 percent did not know that they had the option to remain in the plan.
- And participants are clearly looking for help—69 percent looked elsewhere for advice on where to put their money.

Both we and our clients are concerned about this trend, and therefore over the past

Chart 12.7
FIRSCo[a] PARTICIPANT EDUCATION AND SUPPORT

- Phone Retirement Specialists
- Internet Tools
- Workshops and Seminars
- Distribution Kits

Source: Fidelity Investments.
[a]Fidelity Institutional Retirement Services.

several years have undertaken a number of efforts to increase employees' education and knowledge about their distribution options and the tax consequences associated with them (chart 12.7):

- Every participant who calls to take a distribution is informed of his distribution options and the tax implications.
- Our NetBenefits participant service site has a host of income planning and asset allocation tools, as well as content on distribution options and tax issues.
- We offer a several workshops and seminars for employees to help walk them through step by step the best approach for handling their defined contribution assets.
- And we have distribution kits available to terminated employees which review all of the same issues, as well as (in many cases) any issues specific to their plans.

We have done some in-depth analysis of participant behavior, and have found that with each of these tools, we see a significant increase in the percentage of assets that are staying in a tax-deferred vehicle.

Chart 12.8
SUMMARY

- Assets eligible for distribution from defined contribution plans are increasing.
- Participants are not always aware of their options, and the impact on their retirement savings.
- As a result, many are taking action that does not maximize their long term savings potential.
- Increased information and education from employers and plan providers is required.

Source: Fidelity Investments.

Conclusion

To summarize (chart 12.8):

Demographic and economic changes are increasing the amount of defined contribution money eligible for distribution. *The bad news:* Uninformed participants often make decisions about those assets that are detrimental to their long-term retirement security. *The good news:*

- A significant number of employees are informed and are making the right decisions.
- Employees are eager for more information and education around these issues.
- When employees are educated, they change their behavior.

13

Technology and Retirement Plans

by Byron D. Oliver, CIGNA Retirement
& Investment Services

Introduction

Let me begin my comments by saying the thing that is important to know about me and my organization is that we are totally marketing based; with all of our experience focused on the investment money management business and the administration of all forms of defined contribution, defined benefit, and nonqualified plans.

It is out of this background that we have developed our views about the primary forces that are having a major impact on the retirement business today, and in the future. I want to make this point in the beginning, because although my assigned topic is technology, from my point of view, it is very hard to separate marketing from technology.

For example, the most significant innovation in our business over the last six or seven years has been to provide customers with the ability to call their 401(k) plan and make fund changes 24 hours a day, seven days a week. This innovation is "marketing," but it is clearly driven by technology—which is a combination that we will continue to find as we go forward.

Administration and Technology Issues

Earlier this year, we conducted a study in cooperation with Yankelovich to better understand what employees and employer sponsors value about their retirement plans.

The key points are things that you might anticipate: people want lots of value for their plans; they want plans that are easy to deal with; they want them delivered quickly and efficiently; and, of course, employers are looking for the opportunity to lower costs.

Beneath that data, however, we a see huge need for support and understanding regarding the administration and technology issues that are driving our business today. For example, five or six years ago when we met with a plan sponsor, we would spend 75 percent of our time talking about investments—efficient frontiers, betas, and all of those things. About 25 percent of our time would be spent discussing some of the administrative aspects of the program.

Today, that experience is reversed: 75 percent of our discussion is focused on administrative issues and 25 percent on investments.

Recently, I had the opportunity to meet with a very large plan sponsor. During the course of a two-hour meeting, we spent one hour discussing the pros and cons of unit-based accounting versus share-based accounting on company stock. We spent the second hour mostly talking about same-day closing of outside funds, Window Sweep, and all of those various technical things that are driving our business. We spent only about 15 or 20 minutes talking about the investments.

This wasn't our agenda; it was the client's. It marks a very fundamental difference in what is important to clients today, how technology can fill this need, and how it is in fact driving this need.

Let's turn now to how these forces will impact our business going forward. There are plenty of important issues in our environment, but there are two that I think are really worth talking about: one is the concept of "retailization" and the other is the integration of the benefits business.

Retailization

My first comment on retailization is, that while I am not sure that there is such a word, the underlying concept is important as anything in our business today. The essence of it is the power of the individual and its combination with the development of technology.

If we examine the past five years, there has been absolutely nothing that has had more impact in our business than the power of choice, and what has happened with technology to support that choice. I believe that this trend will continue.

Let's go down history's lane about six years and consider what a typical 401(k) plan looked like. It used to be that plans had three or four investment options and statements mailed once a quarter. If you were lucky, you got them by the end of the quarter. And if you were really lucky, they may have been correct.

At the time, communication was thought of as basically doing enrollments—getting through the enrollments—and that was it.

Now, let's consider products today. In the average plan that we install today, we have 12 different investment choices. We have self-directed capability. If plan sponsors want 3,000 choices—I have no idea why they would want that, but some do choose it—participants can make changes through call centers, voice response systems, or Internet, 24 hours a day, seven days a week.

The enrollment aspect has become a very minor piece. Today's communications emphasis includes ongoing education, ongoing support, ongoing financial planning and so forth.

All of this change has been driven by the power of the individual combined with the power of technology. A huge impact, and I believe it will be one of the sustaining impacts as we go forward.

There are two areas where we will see it the most: in individual financial planning and in e-commerce. First, we are going to see it in financial planning for participants. The various programs that are currently out there offer basic modeling that I call "near" financial planning. But looking ahead we are going to see *total* financial planning as providers partner with different investment consultants.

Total financial planning will not be just for the wealthy, but for the typical 401(k) investor. It is coming and it is going to be available—as early as next year. It certainly will be available from our company next year.

The other area is e-commerce, which is going to have a phenomenal impact as we continue to develop the technological applications. Two years ago, when we introduced e-commerce in a substantial way, we had a huge debate on whether there would be much of an impact.

It turned out that from a base of zero, today 33 percent of all of our 401(k) transactions are driven over the Internet. Think about that—fully one-third of our transactions in just two years.

By this time next year we expect more than 50 percent will be driven over the Internet. From our standpoint it offers a remarkable opportunity to provide information, education, and training in ways that we have never done before, as well as open different sites around the country.

My point is that over the past five years the defining force driving retirement plans, and particularly 401(k) plans, has been the consumer's demand for choice combined with our ability to develop technology to support their needs. We expect the retailization of retirement will continue into the future.

Integration of Benefits

Let's examine a second key issue: integration of benefits. This has been around a while, and you might ask the question, "What is different? Can we integrate administration, and why would we want to move in this direction?"

What is going to make this benefit integration work is technology that we are all developing and the ability to make this a Web-based technology.

The challenge that we have today is that the current systems are neither cost-effective nor service-attentive.

Think about the typical corporation: it may have a different provider for a defined benefit plan, 401(k) plan, nonqualified plan, and health care—which may be sliced three or four ways—dental, and so forth. In this environment, the simplest things—such as an address change—has to be fed 10 or 12 times. If it is fed 10 or 12 times, there will be errors that lead to additional cost and service dissatisfaction.

My view is that we are going to a more integrated environment, and with the technology we are developing, it is going to work. In the case of my organization, we will take out at least 25 percent of the cost of administering the business and we'll improve the service quotient by a significant margin.

In the competitive world that we live in today, anytime you can bring anything to market for 25 percent less *and* improve service you are going to have an impact.

I will go out on a limb: I believe that the integrators—the ones that can do it successfully and have the resources to build the Web-based technology to support it—will have the same impact in this business as the mutual funds had in the late 1980s and the early 1990s.

Conclusion

By bringing both their retail communications capability and their retail technology into the retirement arena, the mutual funds literally changed the rules of the game, and with it, the whole face of competition throughout the decade.

That same landscape change can be accomplished over the next five years through the combination of marketing and technology to integrate benefits on behalf of the "retail" benefit plan customer.

I could discuss a lot of other forces in our business, but none would have the impact that the combination of these two defining forces—marketing and technology—have had, and will have, on our business.

14

Web Sourcing and Retirement Plans

by William Arnone, Ernst & Young

Introduction

What I will try to do is complement some of the things Byron Oliver[1] said and point out some other things that I think are key to the Websourcing of retirement plans and their supportive functions, and ultimately the impact on retirement income of the end-users, the participants in the plans, whom all of us are theoretically in the business of serving.

What I would like to do is cover the following issues:

- What is the value proposition for Websourcing? This will provide a broader context and a broader framework.
- How is Websourcing changing the provision of retirement income?
- And what will employee retirement planning look like in the year 2005, 2004, 2003, 2002, 2001, 2000—who knows, it could be much sooner than we think or much later.

I happen to believe that the pace of change will be accelerating even more, but I view with trepidation trying to make any type of predictions about the short- or long-term future. I read some time ago that, after the telephone was invented, one of the leading futurists of the time was quoted as saying the following: "The invention of the telephone is a revolutionary development. I can see the day in the not too distant future when every town in America will have one of these."

It is very easy to really miss the impact of something. So I will try not to portray this as being too far reaching. But a year from now we may look at the discussions in this book and say, boy, how far off were we in terms of the acceleration of change.

Websourcing

Let's take a look at the Websourcing value proposition. It is not something new. Just to put this in context, outsourcing in general enables human resources (HR) and benefits professionals to focus on strategic issues and contribute more as business partners and consultants to the enterprise by doing three basic things: 1) reducing administrivia; 2) diverting routine questions to external sources that can handle them more efficiently; and 3) focusing on the employee, the customer.

To echo what Byron Oliver said, it really is a customer-focused approach where the marketplace is your employee population. And the two key concepts that are emerging here—and these are similar to the whole electronic commerce revolution—are the notions of self-service and customer intimacy. I think we have to be careful to keep our ears close to the customer to make sure that the customer, in this case the employee, is not immediately labeling things negatively. I have already seen that and I guess others have also.

The word "empowerment" now in many employee populations is not perceived well. It already is a tainted concept on the part of the end user. I think, unfortunately, the words "cash balance" have gotten off to that same type of start, where immediately people associate a cash balance plan as "something being done to me" as opposed to "something being done for me." And I would submit that the term "self-service" also runs the risk of having that same type of negative connotation. And a good sign of it is if an employee says to you, "Self-service, is that a noun or is that a verb?"

If any of you are involved in farming, when one animal services another, I think you understand what that connotation can mean. I guess there aren't enough farmers who belong to EBRI. Of course, when you then juxtapose "customer

---

[1] *See Byron Oliver, "Technology and Retirement Plans," in this volume.*

intimacy" with that concept, this also could have a very backfiring effect.

Drivers for Web Sourcing

I would like to look at two of the big drivers for Websourcing. There are many, but the two I would like to look at are the benefits drivers and cultural drivers.

One benefits driver is being able to translate plan features—dry, technical plan features—into value from the perspective of the employee, again, as the customer. Then you have to market that value to the employee.

A second benefit driver is to facilitate benefit plan changes that require both attitudinal change and, more importantly, behavioral change on the part of the employee. We need to help employees take more responsibility for making critical decisions in and among their benefit plans.

Some other benefit drivers: generate greater employee appreciation for the employer's investment in total compensation and benefits. The Web has the amazing ability to do instant quantification, which, if it is done right, can show people what the employer is paying for something and what the employee is paying for something and do it in a total, comprehensive and personalized way. This can be a very powerful ad message to the employee, again as the customer.

This can be especially important to the extent you are trying to shift your role from the guarantor of benefits to the facilitator of benefits, to make more attractive this whole notion of the work site as the marketplace, with flexible and voluntary benefit offerings being an increasing part of the picture, and less of it being employer-guaranteed or employer-paid-for and employer-provided.

Perhaps as important are the cultural drivers. One driver is the notion that you want to promote a self-reliant mindset, that it is in our interest for people to take more control. You want to engage employees as active partners in the unified enterprise of your company or organization. The Web, because of its ubiquity and its uniformity, guaranteeing consistency if it is done the right way, and its power, can have an enormous impact on the perception of the individual employee.

And then a final cultural driver is to transmit and instill the core values of the company or organization in all aspects of the enterprise. More and more companies are trying to articulate what they stand for. And, to the extent the Web can be an effective medium to instill values and reinforce them on a regular basis, Websourcing becomes critical.

To me, one of the major issues is what really is advice. And I would like to come back to that whole question, because I don't think we have been focusing enough on what it really is and what is it not.

The Changing Fundamentals

Let's look at the changing fundamentals of the employee benefits industry. All of us, no matter what our perspective is, are affected by two major changes in the fundamentals of doing business today. In the old days, when I would meet with a client, I would pretty much say, look, there are three key elements you are looking for when you hire any outside provider: quality, speed, and cost. And in the old days, the rule was two out of three.

If you want something that is good and something that is fast, it won't be cheap. If you want something that is good and cheap, you can't get it quickly. And if you want something that is fast and cheap, it will not be good. Those days are gone. I am learning that every day. People are saying, I want it all. I want all three.

The second fundamental change is the notion of connectivity. Plan sponsors are saying to plan providers: we want all of you to get together and integrate your offerings to serve the plan participant. And this notion of connectivity among the three entities—plan participant, sponsor, and provider—is getting more and more attention, with dramatic impacts on how we do business.

Web Stages

Let's look at three Web stages when it comes to HR and benefits. What stage is the human resource benefit function in? Most companies, if they are in any stage, it is the first stage, the lowest. They haven't even begun to use the Web for anything more than providing on-line brochures. They are still taking traditional ways of doing business and just using another medium to do it. The next stage is an intermediate stage where front-end applications are being done online—enrollments online. But then, after the front stage, the back stage becomes the traditional way. After applications are done online, there are still some other things that are happening that are not automated and therefore not comprehensive.

The advanced stage would be integrated transactions, where all data bases are linked and integrated, so that in effect you've got a consistent and coherent approach to the benefits for the end user.

Employee Decision Making

When it comes to Websourcing and retirement income, clearly we are changing the nature of employee decision making. All of this means, number one, employees will now expect to have the most current data at their fingertips.

Employees now with access to automated tools don't like to think that the automated tool has data on it that are even a week old. They expect the data to be current, right to the point. They'll want instant access, 24 by 7 by 365, to highly personalized information. They're saying, "I don't want you to give me generic information. I want it to be mine. I want it to reflect my situation." They'll want dynamic modeling, where they can do "what-ifs" in a much more sophisticated and much more powerful way than they ever could do before. Also, the Web—because it offers access any place, any time—enables more involvement with family and others in the overall planning process.

So when it comes to employee retirement planning of the future, here is what I suggest we are going to see. First of all, most things will go online. The human element will shrink dramatically. This means group learning can be online, individual counseling online, personal advice online. We'll see much more proactive intervention—instead of waiting for the employee to say, "Here is what is happening in my life," you anticipate that and bring resources and solutions to the attention of the employee in advance.

And then finally we'll see total life cycle management, where the employee in effect relies on the Web to run his or her life. And it may not even be run from a desktop. It may be that, in the future, we will all be wearing the Web. Maybe on our wrists or maybe around our heads. But it may be that it really is with us at all times and we are relying on it as an ongoing management mechanism.

On the subject of personal advice, I just want to make one point. It seems to me there is a very big distinction between an employee who says, "The provider recommended a course of action for me and I then made the decision" and where the employee says, "The provider made the decision for me."

To me, that is the key distinction. To what extent do plan sponsors want any employee who says, "I didn't really decide that, the firm you hired decided it for me." So I think discussions about investment advice have to go beyond the term "advice" and really look at this question. Where is the locus of decision making? Is it still with the participant, or has it been transferred to a third party?

A couple of other issues. What does "personalized" mean? It really means different things to different people. Where is the employee in the life cycle? For some employees it is "what is my learning style? How do I like to receive data?" For others, it is based on their level of financial savvy.

For some, it might be any other parameters they can think of. Websourcing also gives "contributory" a new meaning. It is the employee collaborating with the provider in developing tools that the employee can relate to. In many cases, it means self-diagnostic tools. Let the employee take a test that will categorize the employee among these different frameworks.

The Big Picture

One last item, transactional issues. The focus here is on data linkage, data integration, and data mining. From the big picture perspective, imagine being able, as a plan sponsor, to take a snapshot of your entire population and analyze how people are positioned for retirement security. You can then slice and dice that data by age of employee, tenure with the company, level of pay, gender, ethnicity and other diversity issues, location, and position.

Can you imagine the power of being able to look at your employee population at any point in time and slice and dice the data in the most meaningful ways? It gives whole new meaning to the notion of fiduciary liability and fiduciary responsibility, but it seems to me this is the likely outcome of the Websourcing revolution.

Policy and What Lies Ahead

15

The Future Planning for Retirement Security

by Donald H. Sauvigné, IBM

Introduction

I would agree with many of the contributors to this book. I would agree with John Rother's[1] point about the have's and have not's and bifricating the work force if we are not careful going forward. I would agree with all of those elements. I would disagree with his comments that the cash balance debate indicates some failure on the part of the Employee Retirement Income Security Act of 1974 (ERISA). I do not agree with that, or with his implications regarding IBM's cash balance plan.

The Future

Some of the comments I would like to make in view of the discussions in this book concern the future of private retirement plans.

First, I think the outcome of the future, whether it is the future of 25 years or five years, is not the issue. Rather, I think that there is a great probability that the outcome of the future is going to be laid in the year 2000. It can be laid positively or it can be laid negatively. But I think the outcome is going to be driven by actions in 2000. And I don't think we should underestimate the power, or the consequences, of what those actions might be. And I direct that at the cash balance debates that occupy the collective focus of some of the discussions in this book.

I think the problem that we have at the moment is that the debates that we are having are very much piece-parts. They are defined benefit, they are defined contribution, they are Social Security, they are the have's and the have not's.

And we still do not have any substance of a national, formal retirement policy underlining the debate. So some actions that might be be taken imprudently and too quickly, because they may be politically driven or politically influenced, could seriously damage the have's, to use John Rother's point.

I personally am very much an advocate for the have not's and the process of doing more for those who are not covered by an employer's pension plan. But if we act congressionally or regulatorily in a way that mandates or creates environments in which those businesses that have elected to provide retirement security elect not to do so in the future, we will do serious damage to the entirety of the financial security of our work force.

So I think that we need to be careful that we don't think, design, legislate, or regulate next year or in 2005, as we did in 1974 or 1986 or literally in the early part of this decade. Things have changed so fundamentally and so fast that the financial security of the work force is very much dependent upon the flexibility that the employer has in managing the outcomes and the success, perhaps survival, of the firm. And I don't think we can lose sight of that. If we do, I think we can make some real, real bad mistakes.

Retirement Security

It is in business' interest to have attractive and retentive benefit plans...but not to the point of "handcuffin" the business in a way that puts its competitiveness at risk.

You would think someone from IBM, a

---

[1] *See John Rother, "The Politics of Change," in this volume.*

nonunionized organization, and David Blitzstein,[2] a spokesperson for the United Food and Commercial Workers International Union, would not have much in common. But I think a lot of his comments are right on point and absolutely accurate—for instance, what he says about the social commitment or the concept of that social commitment.

I think the current pension plan debate is focusing on a piece-part called the cash balance plan. It is not focusing on retirement security. It is not focusing on adaptive flexibility. It is focusing on "a" design and categorizing companies that embrace change as good or bad as opposed to focusing on the entirety of the employment relationship. And I think that is what David Blitzstein is talking about.

There is an "entirety" that has to be looked at here from the total employment relationship. And we have got to make sure that concept has a basis. That goes to the heart of benefit adequacy, not just replacement income adequacy but benefit adequacy, of which replacement income is a part. The rest includes medical coverage/access, savings vehicles, education, cash compensation, skill enhancement, etc.

Some of the contributors to this book speak of changing attitude and changing behavior and changing the responsiveness of the individual to us in terms of individual responsibilities. I certainly agree with all of that. I think that all of us who make these things work—regulators, legislators, and employers—need to work collaboratively and find solutions that are conducive to positive outcomes for all our constituents.

---

[2] *See David Blitzstein, "Organized Labor's Perspective on the Future of Defined Benefit Pension Plans," in this volume.*

16

The Politics of Change

by John Rother, AARP

Introduction

The discussions in this book make a timely transition from technology to politics. Why did Congress in 1999 focus on pension issues? It was courtesy of the employees at IBM, who used the Web not only to calculate their own circumstances but also to organize themselves vis-a-vis pension changes that they opposed. The use of technology, I believe, will be successful not only in changing IBM policies but also in changing the rules for the broader society. So I think that the power of information and technology has political as well as personal relevance.

Looking back 25 years, I worked for Sen. Jacob Javits, so I have a feeling of pride that the Employee Retirement Income Security Act of 1974 (ERISA) really did accomplish its fundamental purpose, which was to secure the promise. Today, we are not talking about problems of people who are not receiving promised benefits. But what ERISA didn't address is everything beyond securing the promise, and I think these issues are going to define the agenda going forward. And in particular, it seems to me there are three issues that will be dominant.

Three Future Issues

One issue is the fact that whether it is defined benefit or defined contribution, we are stuck on overall rates of pension coverage in this country. We still have half the population in the work force who don't have a payroll deduction mechanism for contributing to their own future. We can't expect the population to prepare for that future if they don't have some regular mechanism that encourages them to save and if we don't have supportive structures for them.

The debate between defined benefit and defined contribution is interesting and significant as far as it goes, but it really misses the larger point—the fact that so many people, particularly so many people who need it, are outside either one of these structures. In this regard, it was significant that the administration's major pension proposal, building on earlier proposals from Sen. William Roth (R-DE) and Rep. John Kasich, (R-OH) was to establish in effect a national 401(k) as an alternative for people who had no private plan of their own. I certainly think that is one idea that we ought to keep in front of us.

A second issue is inherent in shifting risk from the firm to the individual. We do have to recognize the fundamental fact that not everybody is economically prudent with regard to their own future. In fact, there are an alarming number of grasshoppers in our society, people who are basically in a live-for-today mode. This is true whether or not they are making good incomes or inadequate incomes. They are going to spend the money today. Maybe we are prepared to say, okay, that is their problem and they will have to live with it in the future.

But I do think it is going to have political ramifications if we don't do something fairly assertive to help them think longer term. If we just let them go, then we are creating a very, very powerful constituency to expand Social Security in the future. We are creating a very powerful constituency to raise taxes on employers in the future. In my judgment, the rhetoric of defined contribution and shifting the risk to the individual can only be successful if it is accompanied by enough of a context and structure to support individuals making prudent choices. And for too large a part of the population, we are not seeing that behavior today. Unless we act in time for the boomer generation, this lack of long-term foresight will have serious political implications.

The third issue is risk. Today we have a situation where everyone is a winner because of the stock market. Regardless of whether you are an employer with a defined benefit plan or you are an employee with a defined contribution, everyone has won. That is not going to continue. And when that market comes down—and it is only a question of when—that is going to change the politics of this whole debate. Then there will be some losers as well as some winners. I think that we should be thinking now about what we can do to minimize that risk. What kinds of structures would help people feel that if they did take a risk, they were appropriately warned, if you will, about that risk? I worry about what the implications might be if millions of Americans woke up to losses and felt they had been misled, or felt that they had been put at risk without understanding what could happen. In this regard, it seems to me that the cash balance debate this year was a case study in the failure of ERISA.

ERISA failed because the employees who were affected by cash balance transitions did not know or understand what was happening to them. That may have been intended by the employers, but nonetheless ERISA was supposed to be there to protect employees and help them understand their rights with pensions, and that did not happen with cash balance transitions. So whether you favor them or not, I think it is an example of where ERISA did not anticipate the employees' need to be informed, and so did not work.

■ The Role of Demographics

Finally, the political debate will be increasingly shaped by demographics—the aging of the baby boom. We find that as boomers reach their 50s they are increasingly focused on retirement—their own retirement, the retirement of their peers, and the circumstances of their parents.

What this means is that we are in for another 10 or 20 years of political debate focused on retirement issues, because that is where the majority of our population is. To the extent that we can take the opportunity that we have today—as a consequence of a very prosperous economy—to think longer term, we can change some of the retirement policies in this country to more inclusive solutions.

But if we fail to do this, what we are left with is an hourglass economy of have's and have not's that is going to turn into an even more dramatic hourglass shaped retirement population. We will have a minority, maybe one-third to 40 percent, who are economically secure and who have pensions and savings and health coverage, and then we will have a larger group who feel very vulnerable and will only have Social Security and Medicare standing between them and complete loss of dignity. I think that prospect is something that we should, in the name of political prudence, try to avoid. We only have a few years to act on it.

17

Pensions on the A List

by Brian Graff, American Society of Pension Actuaries

Introduction

As recently as 1993, when I would go to Capitol Hill and desperately try to talk to a member of Congress about pensions, I can assure you that this was the last thing he or she wanted to talk about. Since then, the climate has dramatically changed. Today, you are getting invited to come and talk to members of Congress because they want to hear about cash balance plans. The reason all of this is happening is appropriately described in this book. I think, clearly, that what is driving this is the fact that our population is significantly more concerned about retirement. One thing we know is that members of Congress and politicians generally are very good at reading polls.

Pension issues are now on the A list. Unfortunately, there is a price that goes along with this. That price is that the issues that we care about on a regular basis are now very much a concern of the average member of Congress. Consequently, these members are delving into things and issues that before we would have to try to get them to pay attention to. The most prominent example of this is the cash balance plan debate.

Certainly, cash balance plans are going to be a focus of significant attention in 2000. In a speech the just before last Thanksgiving, Vice President Gore spoke about the cash balance plan issue. So a presidential nominee is talking about wearaway. Now is that scary or what?

Pension Issues Become Political

The point is that these issues are becoming increasingly political. Again, this is a function of the fact that average Americans now cares more about these issues. And when issues become increasingly political, there is a natural connection and a natural result of mischief that can occur that is not necessarily based entirely on policy.

Pension issues are now, I think for the first time, becoming a significantly part of the political discussion. At a meeting of the Democratic Policy Committee (the group that sets the political agenda for the Democrats in Congress) in the fall of 1999 they discussed the possibility of using pensions to their advantage as a political issue going into presidential elections. What they meant was using the issue of pensions similarly to the way they use the issue of health. And those who work in the health area know how well that is going.

What they are now talking about is focusing on pensions, i.e., on issues that will show them as defending the interest of participants and perhaps portraying Republicans as protecting the interest of employers and using that to their advantage. This would include reexamining a lot of the core retirement security issues that, frankly, have not been examined since the Employee Retirement Income Security Act of 1974 (ERISA) was under discussion. I am referring to basic concepts of vesting, participation, coverage, spousal protection, and nondiscrimination rules.

I think all of these core subjects are going to be up for grabs in the upcoming years, because this has now risen to the political level. Like it or not, that is the reality.

What does this mean for the discussion about defined benefit plans versus defined contribution plans? What it means is, congratulations, defined contribution wins. You know what the prize is? The prize is that all of those issues that Congress considered as important for the primary retirement vehicle during the discussion of ERISA and during the 1980s, namely defined benefit plans, are now open for discussion for what is now the primary retirement vehicle, defined contribution plans.

What this means is that concepts such as spousal consent, joint and survivor annuity requirements, and other similar requirements that apply to defined benefit plans are all open discussion in the context of defined contribution plans. You will see, in upcoming years, all of these issues examined, just as they were examined in the 1980s for defined benefit plans. That is the prize, I am sorry to say—for better or for worse, depending on your point of view.

Conclusion

I think the next five to 10 years are going to be incredibly fascinating for retirement policy issues, and they are going to be very different from what they have ever been before because of the increasingly political nature of these issues.

All of us need to recognize that as we consider our policy positions and go forward with trying to shape and agendas. Because although it is important to recognize the interests of employers and sponsors, and that has usually been the main focus of retirement policy, henceforth the issues of participants are going to be increasingly more prominent as a result of demographics and also as a result of the technology, as John Rother[1] mentioned.

I think one of the most fascinating things about this cash balance debate has been the use of the Internet as a way to stimulate debate and discussion, and I imagine that it has not gone unnoticed by employee groups. I am sure we will be seeing more usage of these technologies as issues like these develop.

---

[1] *See John Rother, "The Politics of Change," in this volume.*

18

The Small Business Administration Perspective

by Kenneth D. Simonson, Small Business Administration

Introduction

Let me start with a disclaimer and a couple of advertisements. I am not speaking for an official government position here. The advertisements are for the Office of Advocacy and for yourselves. I work in the Office of Advocacy of the Small Business Administration, which is a unique government agency.

Role of the Office of Advocacy

Our role is to make sure that the rest of government does not impose disproportionate burdens on small entities, including small nonprofits and small local governments. And we also to do research on the role of small business and influences on it and provide data on that.

A lot of our work can be found at the Advocacy Web site, which is at www.sba.gov/advo. We have an Office of Economic Research that produces, in conjunction with the Census Bureau, the Statistics of Income Division of Internal Revenue Seervice, and the Federal Reserve, among others, data broken out by size of business, by gender of sole proprietorship, and by loans by size of loan, for instance.

Many of these data are also available on the Web site, but I would also encourage those who are interested to talk to our staff and learn what is available or to propose research. We are currently in a position to delve into some of the questions that I hope are burning in the minds of those in the pension field, and we would welcome research proposals.

Role of the Office of Interagency Affairs

The Office of Interagency Affairs' role is to enforce or encourage agencies to go along with the mandates of the Regulatory Flexibility Act of 1980 and its offspring, the Small Business Regulatory Enforcement Fairness Act of 1996 (SBREFA), which requires agencies, when they propose rules, to take into account whether there would be a significant economic impact on a substantial number of small entities.

These are all words laden with import that can be pretty hard to pin down, but it is a role that we find the agencies are taking increasingly seriously, and we hope that it is changing the culture within the rulemaking parts of agencies in order to make sure that they really are leveling the playing field and not tilting it against small entities.

We have been quite encouraged by the attitude of officials in Treasury, the Pension Welfare and Benefits Administration, and the Pension Benefit Guaranty Corporation to try to minimize the administrative burdens and the cost for small employers and to make good faith estimates of what those costs would be, and if possible to find ways of mitigating them.

Good Intentions vs. Actual Results

Despite these considerations, it is a long way between good intentions and actual results. And I think that the situation has been very well captured by the Employee Benefit Research Institute's small employer retirement survey. It shows that small employers are still worried primarily about their profitability and are very reluctant to get into a situation where they are going to be forced to pay out benefits or make contributions to a plan when they are not even sure that they will have any profits or how long they will be in business.

As William Dennis[1] points out, there is tremendous turnover among small businesses. Certainly there are plenty of them for sellers of plans to go after and try to encourage to establish a plan. I have been doing research on sole proprietorships, and have learned that there are more than 19 million of them. More than 19 million Schedule C's have been filed in the latest filing year, 1997. Most of these are extremely tiny, and they are not prospects for growing into corporations or even viable partnerships.

However, we do see a fair amount of graduation into employer firms. Typically, there are about 800,000 new employer firms a year. Several hundred thousand are also exiting the world of employer firms every year, either because they are being absorbed by other businesses or they are being dissolved for whatever reason. I don't want to characterize these occurrences as failures.

There are a lot of reasons that companies close up shop. But the moral is that for many businesses that look as if they would be prospects for setting up a pension plan, this turns out not to be the case. The owners don't really have the expectation that they will be keeping the business in that form for more than a brief number of years, and/or they are dealing with a pool of employees who don't expect to stay with the company long enough to be attracted by a pension plan based on longevity.

And finally, employees may be looking for compensation in a form that sets nothing aside, even in a way that they can access within a few years.

[1] *See William J. Dennis, "A Realistic Appraisal of Increasing Pension Coverage by Small Business," in this book.*

A Useful Approach

I think you have to look at what is it that will provide something useful to these firms. I was mildly surprised that none of the discussions in this book addresses the employee staffing side. I think this has become an increasingly attractive option in its various forms to small employers.

While contingent work has gotten a bad name in some quarters, it is also true that for many small employers turning to an outside source of labor handles a lot of problems that the firm experiences in terms of doing its own recruiting and training and in dealing with compensation and retention issues.

And small employers also see an outside source of labor as potentially providing a more stable labor force and certainly one more able to provide pensions and other kinds of benefits that would make their own company a more attractive place to stay and work while at the same time giving them, as the recipients of those labor services, more flexibility about the size of their work force and the skill set that they would be using over any period.

I think the increasing growth of the digital economy implies that there is going to be continued churning and very rapid growth of some firms but equally rapid turnaround in the direction that those firms pursue and in the business structure that they have as they merge with other firms or develop new lines of business. Then the prospect of trying to attract workers and keep the right set of workers through a long-lived pension plan is going to be increasingly dim.

Therefore, the future for providing compensation in a way that will keep workers around and keep the right set of workers around will increasingly be related to employee stock options and other forms that let the workers choose how they want to receive the compensation, while minimizing the lock-in effect on employers of having to guarantee a certain benefit and a certain amount of administrative cost going along with that.

Conclusion

In our role as advocates for small entities, we want to hear from organizations large and small concerning the administrative problems they are facing are so that we can bring them to the attention of other agencies, including Congress.

Our office does get to testify and provide comment on legislation independent of the general Administration position, and I think that it has been valuable both to small entity representatives and to Congress to hear an independent voice within the Executive Branch. And then let us hear from you as to what you believe are feasible and useful research proposals that would make at least marginal changes in the attractiveness of the retirement system for small entities and their employees.

19

Company-Sponsored Retirement Plans: The Political Horizon

by Peter J. McCauley, Pharmacia and Upjohn, Inc.

Introduction

The discussions in this book review the current and future role of plan sponsors and the pros and cons of many of the retirement income instruments available to plan sponsors large and small to help their employees provide for retirement. Although there is significant discussion of the various retirement instruments today, I would like to step back and review again the issues.

The Three Legged Stool

The first issue it seems to me is not which retirement income instrument to select or what to do with Social Security. The issue is not defined benefit plans vs. defined contribution plans vs. individual tax effective savings vs. Social Security—individual investment accounts vs. monthly income. The issue is the adequate delivery and availability of retirement income benefits—adequate inflation-adjusted income replacement at retirement

I have just completed a pension redesign project for my company. In my analysis I evaluated over 90 different defined benefit, defined contribution, and hybrid plan designs, including our existing plans. In addition, there were numerous variations of the 90 basic design structures, including the elimination of all company-sponsored retirement plans. At the end of the day we changed very little to our existing plan designs. We found that our savings plan and defined benefit plans, when combined with Social Security, were competitive and delivered adequate retirement income. What struck me about this analysis is that the folks that designed these plans 30, 40, or 50 years ago got it right. The same objectives and policies developed when these plans were implemented long ago are valid today. The three-legged stool of Social Security, company-sponsored plans, and personal savings is effective today in delivering adequate retirement income for those career employees who were lucky enough to benefit from these programs. Obviously, there are many approaching or in retirement today who did not have these programs available to them. The point is the three-legged stool is still a benchmark formula for adequate retirement income.

Longevity

The second issue is good news/ bad news. People are living longer. That is good news. The bad news from all of our perspectives is that existing plan structures are more expensive because benefits will have to be paid for longer periods of time. The increased expense resulting from increased mortality will make it difficult for the government and the private sector to support existing plan structures now and in the future.

Changing Demographics

The third issue is the changing demographics. The three-legged stool program previously described was designed to reward the career employee. Although career employees will continue to exist in the future, a smaller percentage of today's employees will remain with the same employer for their entire career. There is also an increase in the contingent work force and those who work for employers who do not provide company-sponsored retirement plans. Although we seem to hear about the number of Americans not covered by medical coverage, I am not sure I have seen similar data on those not covered by retirement plans. It seems employees will become increasingly more responsible for creating and maintaining their own retirement income programs as they move through their careers with different employers.

The Current Political State and the Ideal State

The current political state as it relates to Social Security and company-sponsored retirement plans seems to be reactive. Congress appears to be reacting to changes and modifications in private employer-sponsored retirement plans. Although we all know about the real Y2k of retirement issues, the aging of the baby boomers, there is no real champion in Congress owning the retirement income policy issue as there was in the days of Employee Retirement Income Security Act. There appears to be no national retirement income policy.

So what about the ideal state? I thought about a national retirement income policy that would embrace both retirement income replacement and retiree medical issues, including long term care. These are goals—a destination. For starters, the policy would include these seven simple guiding principles:

1. Encourage private employer sponsorship of retirement income replacement plans and programs. Imagine the pressure on governmental systems, including Social Security, if corporate America—large and small, public and private, for profit and nonprofit—eliminated plan sponsorship. One way to evaluate the value of a program is to eliminate it. What would be the financial and political impact of the elimination of employer-sponsored and individually supported retirement plans?

2. Define a basic government floor of protection income replacement benefit and retirement age from which employer or individual can build company or individually sponsored plans. Social Security may provide at best 38 percent of final pay. However, the Social Security benefit eligibility age is rising.

3. Support full disclosure and communication of government, company, and individual retirement benefits. Support and, if need be, subsidize programs and communication that help participants better understand the programs and benefits available to them and how these programs impact their personal financial objectives.

4. Develop and communicate retirement income adequacy standards. The 70 percent standard mentioned earlier is one guideline. What are some easy to understand adequate retirement income guidelines at various ages?

5. Encourage Total Retirement Income Communication earlier. What are the sources of retirement income replacement? What are the gaps? What actions are required to fill in these gaps?

6. Encourage regulatory streamlining. Current regulations are a barrier to ongoing plan sponsorship. Review the objective of the regulations to see if they still apply in today's environment and in view of the previously suggested guiding principles. Clean up the regulations as much as possible to make plans easier to operate. What is the return on investment for the government expense relating to the development and administration of qualified plan regulation?

7. Encourage portability of benefits: Encourage administration and programs that permit employees to take or have access to retirement benefits at retirement.

Conclusion

By no means do I suggest this is a complete policy. It is a start and basically a summary in some form or another of items mentioned in this book. Build on it and better it. What I hope the listing of these seven guiding principles does is help change the focus of the discussion to an overall umbrella national income replacement policy from a discussion of the individual merits of each individual part.

20

Perspectives on Retirement Policy

by Howard Fluhr, The Segal Company

Introduction

My task was described to me as one of commenting on the presentations made by my colleagues in this book. As a result, I have the observations that follow, but (here is my caveat) they should not be taken as gospel. In fact, 25 years ago, just after the passage of the Employee Retirement Income Security Act of 1974 (ERISA), I was asked to predict the future of employee benefits 25 years hence (in 1999). If I was graded on what I predicted then, I would certainly not even receive a middling mark. That is how much the environment has changed over this quarter-century. We can expect no less change over the next 25 years. That is as far as I will go with prognosticating. Here are my observations:

Observations

- **Increased longevity**. People are spending more years in retirement not only because of longer life spans but also because they are retiring earlier. In fact, they may outlive their defined contribution assets. There is a conflicting trend here because people are also working at older ages and undertaking serial careers. Understanding these conflicts is not simple. Because these and other conflicting patterns are occurring simultaneously, most of the pundits move either to the left side or the right side of the ledger and develop great theories. The degree to which my assignment is to predict future trends, my prediction is that *people will either work more or work less.*

- **Perpetual asset management**. The idea is that, as one gets closer to retirement age (whatever that is or will be), one shifts investments from instruments that provide variable returns (with more risk) to those that promise fixed income (with relatively little risk). If one is going to live for 30 or 40 years in retirement, that theory may not work out so well. In fact, there are many questions about this and, as I look forward, I am getting a little nervous about them for myself.

- **Equities are going to soar**. You know that. All you have to do is to look at what has been happening in the market. In fact, last year was quite unbelievable. In fact, equities will continue to soar. Or, their values will plunge. This is a given.

- **Full employment** is another circumstance we will need to consider. Will we have nearly full employment, as we have now? Or, will economic circumstances and immigration patterns change? Both could affect our labor supply and employment levels.

- **Workweeks will be shorter.** This has been discussed for years. However, all of the statistics show that, currently, most people are working longer hours. What happened to the shorter work week concept? Will Gen X'ers and those who come after react strongly to this and push for more family and more leisure time? There are those who say this is already happening.

- **Social Security will be weakened**. It is interesting to note that if the current best advice is to keep investing as if the last 10 years are a predictor of the future, as opposed to the last 20, 30, 40 or 100 years, then Social Security will get repaired. Obviously, there is a will to do that, and we actually have an idea about how to do it. However, if the last 10 years are not a good predictor of the future and investment markets change significantly, then Social Security may not be repaired. It will, however, again be a very necessary floor of protection for a large percentage of our population.

- **Private pension coverage as an employer's choice will disappear**. As time goes on, fewer employers will elect to provide employees with retirement coverage and an increasing percentage of working Americans will not have private pension coverage. However, they may have *mandated private coverage*. The idea has been raised before and it has been raised again in these discussions. Currently, there is tinkering going on.

  We have had very little discussion in these pages about the notion figured out by employers a long time ago that defined benefit and defined contribution plans, in conjunction with each other, provide the ideal coverage. That is, the concept of capital accumulation and of a floor of protection that is secure. The issues of older/younger, short service/long service, risk takers/non-risk takers are all included with the combination.

  If future financial security is the goal, we should not lose sight of this balancing act. In fact, because the last 10 years have been a boom time for many people, some question the need for employer plans. Employees should be on their own. It is a great idea. After all, with the technology and education available for defined contribution plans, everyone investing his or her own money is equivalent to a Wall Street expert who makes $2 million a year. Employees are empowered. They didn't ask for it, but they are. Let's get back to the idea of conflicting trends; in the face of this long-term economic boom and the creation of great individual wealth, how do we account for the fact that the income gap is widening?

- **Pension simplification will be enacted**. Everyone favors it—particularly for small employers. Simplification makes sense. Somebody ought to be paying attention to it. What is the argument against it? And, what is the current incentive to maintain plans? That is an issue that has to be addressed. But, we have been through this many times before, going back to pre- ERISA times.

  Are there incentives to legislate simplification? Unfortunately, there is not enough incentive to do it now. Why bother? Congress will not act just because some of the people in the employee benefits field are upset about unnecessary complexity. Even the fact that small employers would be better employers, in a sense, if regulations to introduce and maintain retirement plans were to be simpler, is not important enough so far.

- **Cash balance plans are the answer. Cash balance plans are not the answer**. There is much discussion of cash balance plans, but, of course, they are not perfect. If an employer has a given amount to spend, and there are different constituencies to take care of, then choices about where to spend available resources have to be made. This is not exactly a complex concept. But, what we have is legislation, regulation, and journalism by anecdote. My observation is that decisions are made by anecdote. People are interviewed on the street, "Did you realize when you got this cash balance plan...." How on earth could the average person know about such a complex subject?

  Actually cash balance is an antidote to certain circumstances. The issue concerns whether people will have short careers versus long careers, whether they are younger workers versus older workers, and whether they understand these accounts. The cash balance concept is not perfect, but we have not seen any perfect ideas.

- **There will be technological unemployment**. Apparently, e-commerce will lead to a slew of people sitting around with nothing to do because all of the stores will disappear and everything will be delivered to customers somehow. But, will consumers be able to experience the touch and feel they get from visiting brick and mortar establishments? Will we be able to get the same thing through cyber-visualization from TV monitors or hand held PC-like devices? My observation is that technology will continue to change.

- **The creation of employment will continue to move to a lot of small companies**. We all know that small businesses are currently accounting for most of the job creation in this country. However, the *Wall Street Journal* recently referred to an increase among huge companies—such as Exxon and Mobil. Will that mean the creation or elimination of jobs?

Conclusion

What is the future? There will be more federal legislation and regulation with unintended consequences. That is the one occurrence I am comfortable predicting. I have supreme confidence in that. And, it is just as predictable for the next 25 years as it was 25 years ago.

About five or six years ago, when I was Vice President of the Pension Council of the Academy of Actuaries, we had great hopes about getting some discussion in Washington on all of these issues, as opposed to the politics. We are reliving it today. I fervently hope that something will happen now.

Appendix

Small Business Retirement Plan Legislative Proposals

by Bill Pierron, EBRI

The following legislative proposals introduced during the first session of the 106th Congress (1999) were aimed, in whole or in part, at generating greater retirement plan sponsorship among small employers. These summaries are not meant to be comprehensive, and focus solely on the provisions of the bills that deal specifically with small-business retirement plans. In addition to the bills discussed below, a number of retirement-related provisions were lifted primarily from H.R. 1102 and included in H.R. 2488, the omnibus tax cut bill that was vetoed by President Clinton. These provisions, which focused primarily on raising the contribution limits, were also attached to minimum wage increase proposals at the end of this congressional session, but stood little chance of enactment at this writing.

The Secure Assets For Employees (SAFE) Plan Act (Simplified Defined Benefit Plan)

H.R. 2190, cosponsored by Reps. Nancy Johnson (R-CT) and Earl Pomeroy (D-ND), would create a simplified defined benefit plan with the same eligibility and participation requirements as the SIMPLE defined contribution plan for businesses with 100 or fewer employees. In essence, SAFE is a cash balance pension plan with mandatory annuitization upon retirement. Benefits would be fully vested and portable upon job termination.

An employer sponsoring a SAFE plan would provide all eligible employees a benefit equal to 1 percent, 2 percent, or 3 percent of compensation for each year of service. Companies that experience revenue fluctuations could choose to cut the minimum benefit to 1 percent or 2 percent in a given year. The bill would also allow employers to credit employees for up to 10 years of past service. SAFE plan sponsors would not be required to pay premiums to the Pension Benefit Guaranty Corporation (PBGC), as do sponsors of defined benefit pension plans. Assets would have to be held in the form of insurance company annuities or in trust in certain specified investment products.

SAFE previously had been introduced in the last Congress as H.R. 1656, but this year's version of the legislation contains different actuarial assumptions. As introduced in 1997, H.R. 1656 specified that SAFE plans would be required to use a specified conservative actuarial assumption of a fixed 5 percent, to ensure the minimum retirement benefit. Under the current legislation (H.R. 2190), SAFE plans would be required to use specified conservative actuarial assumptions of 3 percent to 5 percent to ensure the minimum retirement benefit. SAFE also has been included in S. 741 and S. 649 (see below). A similar proposal, the Secure Money Annuity or Retirement Trust (SMART) plan was supported by the Clinton administration, Pension Benefit Guaranty Corporation Executive Director David Strauss, and a number of Democratic lawmakers (see further description below).

The Pension Coverage and Portability Act

S. 741, cosponsored by Sens. Bob Graham (D-FL) and Charles Grassley (R-IA), contains a number of provisions designed to simplify plan administration and encourage plan sponsorship and participation among small employers. Similar legislation (H.R. 1102, see below) was introduced in the House by Reps. Rob Portman (R-OH) and Ben Cardin (D-MD).

The bill contains provisions aimed at providing relief to employers from the Sec. 416 "top-heavy" rules of the tax code. Under the rules, a plan is deemed top heavy if more than 60 percent of the accounts or accrued benefits under the plan are attributable to key employees. If so, the plan must satisfy tougher requirements for vesting and for contributions and benefits. The bill would modify how the 60 percent figure is calculated, to include only benefits accrued or contributions made in the prior year. The bill also would repeal the current requirement that the sponsor of a "frozen" defined benefit plan continue to make contributions on behalf of non-key employees.

The bill would reduce premiums for small employers whose defined benefit plans are insured by PBGC, cutting the premiums from $19 per participant to $5 during the first five years that a small-business defined benefit plan exists.

The bill also includes a start-up tax credit for small businesses that adopt plans; the SAFE defined benefit plan (see H.R. 2190); and elimination of Internal Revenue Service (IRS) user fees that new plan sponsors must pay when they apply for IRS approval.

Comprehensive Retirement Security and Pension Reform Act

H.R. 1102, cosponsored by Reps. Rob Portman (R-OH) and Ben Cardin (D-MD), includes numerous provisions designed to simplify plan administration and encourage more small employers to offer plans.

The bill would modify the tax code's "top-heavy" rules by simplifying the definition of a key employee; streamline the deduction and reporting rules for small businesses (those with 100 or fewer employees); and eliminate IRS user fees for information requests regarding small business pension plans.

The bill would provide incentives for employers to establish tax-deferred salary reduction plans that automatically enroll employees, and would grant relief from "excessive PBGC premiums" for new small-business defined benefit plans.

The bill also would establish a $2,000 tax credit for the establishment or administration of a new small-business pension plan, or the retirement-related education of employees. The credit would amount to $1,000 in the first year of plan operation and $500 per year in the subsequent two years.

The bill would require the Treasury Department to issue "model" defined benefit and defined contribution plans for small employers to minimize regulatory costs and burdens.

Retirement Savings Opportunity Act

S. 649, cosponsored by Sens. William Roth Jr. (R-DE) and Max Baucus (D-MT), seeks to encourage greater retirement savings by increasing the contribution limits for qualified employment-based plans and individual retirement accounts (IRAs). The bill also would create so-called backloaded "Roth 401(k)" and "Roth 403(b)" plans (for education and nonprofit organizations) that would allow after-tax contributions and tax-free buildup and distributions. It also would include several provisions aimed at small employers.

The bill would provide a tax credit to small businesses with fewer than 100 employees for new plan start-up expenses of up to $500 per year for each of first three years. For small businesses with fewer than 50 employees that set up new plans, the bill would provide a deduction of up to 50 percent of employer contributions for nonhighly compensated employees (NHCEs), up to an annual maximum of 3 percent of total NHCE compensation, for the first five years of operation. This NHCE credit would be available only if the employer had no qualified plan for the three preceding years.

The bill also would raise the contribution limit for SIMPLE plans from $6,000 annually to $10,000 annually. It also includes the SAFE defined benefit plan for small employers (see H.R. 2190).

H.R. 352

H.R. 352, cosponsored by Reps. Roy Blunt (R-MO) and Ken Bentsen (D-TX), is designed to simplify the process of establishing and administering small-business retirement plans by simplifying administration, raising contribution limits, and establishing tax credits for new plans. In essence, it modifies the current SIMPLE plan.

The bill would allow small firms to claim a tax credit of up to $6,000 over five years to offset start-up and administrative costs of a retirement plan. The tax credit would provide $2,000 in the year the plan is established, and up to $1,000 per year for the subsequent four years. Administrative costs include the cost of establishing, administering, and maintaining the plan, as well as the cost of educating employees.

The bill also would relax pension administrative requirements, and would raise the contribution limits for small employer plans to $10,000 per year or 25 percent of compensation, to coincide with the limits for non-SIMPLE 401(k) plans.

Income Security Enhancement Act of 1999

S. 8, sponsored by Sen. Tom Daschle (D-SD), would create a tax credit for small employers that establish retirement plans. The credit would be available only to firms that did not maintain qualified plans during the previous year. Recipients would get a credit against income tax of 50 percent of the costs of establishing a qualified plan before 2002, with a maximum credit of $1,000 in the first year after the date the plan is established and $500 in the two subsequent years.

The bill also would allow small employers to adopt the Secure Money Annuity or Retirement Trust (SMART) plan, a simplified defined benefit plan similar to the SAFE proposal (see H.R. 2190). SMART would provide a minimum annual benefit equal to 1 percent or 2 percent of compensation (the employer could elect to provide a benefit of 3 percent of pay during first five years of the plan); prohibit employee contributions; and fully vest employees with two years of service and at least $5,000 in earnings in the current year.

SMART plans could be funded as an annuity or a trust invested in certain specified investment products, with excess investment returns, if any, credited to employees. SMART trust benefits would be guaranteed by PBGC at a reduced premium level.

The bill also would create a tax credit for small employers (100 or fewer employees) that establish pension plans. The credit would cover up to 50 percent of small employer pension plan start-up costs, with a limit of $1,000 for the first year and $500 for each of the second and third years.

Retirement Security Act of 1999

H.R. 1590, sponsored by Rep. Sam Gejdenson (D-CT), is another comprehensive package of retirement plan provisions, some of which are designed to encourage small employers to offer retirement plans. The bill would establish the Secure Money Annuity or Retirement Trust (SMART) plan, like S. 8 (see above).

The bill would create a tax credit for small employers (100 or fewer employees) that establish pension plans. The credit would cover up to 50 percent of small-employer pension plan start-up costs, with a limit of $1,000 for the first year and $500 for each of the second and third years.

In addition, the bill would require small employers that offer a SIMPLE 401(k) plan to contribute at least 1 percent of eligible employees' compensation to their accounts, whether or not the workers make an elective deferral.

Small Business Pension Start-Up Credit Act of 1999

H.R. 1021, cosponsored by Reps. Debbie Stabenow (D-MI) and Dave Camp (R-MI), would create a tax credit for small employers (100 or fewer employees) that establish pension plans. The credit would cover up to 50 percent of small employer pension plan start-up costs, with a limit of $1,000 for the first year and $500 for each of the second and third years.

Employee Pension Portability and Accountability Act of 1999

H.R. 1213, sponsored by Rep. Richard Neal (D-MA), would provide a tax credit to small businesses establishing new retirement plans and allow small businesses to offer simplified defined benefit plans. The provisions are substantially the same as those contained in H.R. 1021, H.R. 1590, and S. 8 (see above).

Policy Forum Attendees

Vineeta Anand
Pensions & Investments

Woody Anglade
Education and Workforce Committee, Democratic Staff

Angela Arnett
ACLI

William Arnone
Ernst & Young LLP

Laurel Beedon
AARP

Robert Birnbaum
Credit Suisse Asset Management

Dawn Bizzell
Pension Benefit Guaranty Corporation

Steve Blakely
Employee Benefit Research Institute

David Blitzstein
United Food & Commercial Workers Union

Kenneth Bombara
U.S. General Accounting Office

McKayla Braden
Deptment of the Treasury

Lynn Camire
Thompson Publishing

William Carroll
AT&T

Rachel Christensen
Employee Benefit Research Institute

Craig Copeland
Employee Benefit Research Institute

Anne Coveney
Putnam Investments

Robert Crane
Kaiser Permanente

James Delaplane, Jr.
APPWP–The Benefits Association

William Dennis
National Federation of Independent Business

John DeStefano
Fidelity Investments

Danny Devine
Employee Benefit Research Institute

John Doyle
T. Rowe Price Associates

Ann Dunbar
BEA

Lynn Etheredge
Health Insurance Reform Project

Gina Falconio
Senate Aging Committee

Holly Fechner
Senate Labor Committee

Edward Ferrigno
Profit Sharing 401(k) Council of America

Tom Fisher
J.P. Morgan

Howard Fluhr
The Segal Company

Celinda Franco
Congressional Research Service

David Frank
House Committee on Education & the Workforce

Robert Friedland
National Academy on an Aging Society

Edgar Friedman
William M. Mercer, Inc.

Russ Galer
Investment Company Institute

Ron Gebhardtsbauer
American Academy of Actuaries

Debra Golding
Pension and Welfare Benefits Administration

Christine Grady
Aetna Financial Services

Brian Graff
American Society of Pension Actuaries

Paul Graney
Congressional Research Service

Zack Granovetter
Metropolitan Life Insurance Company

Janice Gregory
The ERISA Industry Committee

David Gustafson
Pension Benefit Guaranty Corporation

Kathleen Havey
U.S. Chamber of Commerce

Sarah Holden
Investment Company Institute

Robert Hopson III
Fayez Sarofim & Co.

Thomas Hungerford
U.S. Social Security Administration

Richard Ippolito
George Mason University School of Law

Lynn Jacobs
CIGNA

Regina Jefferson
Catholic University

Keiji Kakinuma
Nikko Research Center, Ltd.

Jim Kearney
J.P. Morgan

Lana Keelty
NRECA

David Kemps
Investment Company Institute

Denise Kleis
Merrill Lynch

Louise Kuo
Putnam Investments

Jules Lichtenstein
AARP

Scott Lummer
401k Forum

John MacDonald
The Hartford Courant

Mike Mahoney
Milliman & Robertson

David Maslen
Aon Consulting

Judith Mazo
The Segal Company

Peter McCauley
Pharmacia and Upjohn, Inc.

Ken McDonnell
Employee Benefit Research Institute

Michael McKenzie
Morgan Stanley Dean Witter

Kim Millar
Investment Company Institute

James Mitchell
MassMutual

Samuel Murray
Profit Sharing 401(k) Council of America

Frances Nolan
TIAA-CREF

Jim Norris
The Vanguard Group

Shaun O'Brien
AFL-CIO

Lorie O'Malley
Scudder Kemper Investment

Byron Oliver
CIGNA Corporation

Kelly Olsen
U.S. Social Security Administration

Pamela Ostuw
Employee Benefit Research Institute

Michael Packard
Pension Benefit Guaranty Corporation

Bettye Page-Wilson
Pacific Maritime Association

Tom Pavey
American Express Company

Scott Peterson
Hewitt Associates

Bill Pierron
Employee Benefit Research Institute

Leon Piper
Delta Air Lines, Inc.

Carol Quick
Employee Benefit Research Institute

John Rea
Investment Company Institute

Robert Reynolds
Fidelity Investments

Robert Rosenblatt
Los Angeles Times

John Rother
AARP

Dallas Salisbury
Employee Benefit Research Institute

D.H. Sauvigné
IBM Corporation

Tom Schlossberg
Diversified Investment Advisors

Dala Scoblic
Principal Financial Group

John Scott
APPWP–The Benefits Association

Jason Scott
Financial Engines

Elizabeth Segers
Putnam Investments

John Seiter
Capital Guardian Trust Company

Larry Sher
PricewaterhouseCoopers

Kenneth Simonson
U.S. Small Business Administration

Robert Sollmann, Jr.
Metropolitan Life Insurance Company

Jack Stewart
Principal Financial Group

Ken Stockbridge
U.S. General Accounting Office

James Storey
Congressional Research Service

Nancy Tigner
TIAA-CREF

Mark Ugoretz
The ERISA Industry Committee

Julia Vander Els
Delaware Investments Retirement Financial Services

Jack VanDerhei
Temple University and EBRI Fellow

Michele Varnhagen
Education and Workforce Committee, Democratic Staff

Kurt Walten
ICMA Retirement Corporation

Christian Weller
Economy Policy Institute

Ray Werntz
Consumer Health Education Council

Sandy West
Investment Company Institute

Elizabeth White
Bureau of National Affairs

Alicia Willis
Employee Benefit Research Institute

Paul Yakoboski
Employee Benefit Research Institute